LETTERS I NEVER MAILED
CLUES TO A LIFE
BY ALEC WILDER

The publication of this volume was made possible,
in part, through generous support from the
HOWARD HANSON INSTITUTE FOR AMERICAN MUSIC
at the Eastman School of Music of the
University of Rochester.

LETTERS I NEVER MAILED

Eastman Studies in Music

Ralph P. Locke, Senior Editor
Eastman School of Music

(ISSN 1071–9989)

A complete list of titles in the Eastman Studies in Music Series, in order of publication, may be found at the end of this book.

LETTERS I NEVER MAILED
CLUES TO A LIFE

by
Alec Wilder

Annotated Edition

Introduction and Supplementary Material by
David Demsey

Foreword by Marian McPartland
Photographs by Louis Ouzer

 University of Rochester Press

Letters I Never Mailed: Clues to a Life © 1975 Alec Wilder
First published 1975 by Little, Brown and Company
Annotated edition published 2005 by the
University of Rochester Press

University of Rochester Press
668 Mt. Hope Avenue, Rochester, NY 14620, USA
www.urpress.com
and of Boydell & Brewer Limited
PO Box 9, Woodbridge, Suffolk IP12 3DF, UK
www.boydellandbrewer.com

ISBN: 1–58046–208–1

Library of Congress Cataloging-in-Publication Data
CIP applied for but not received at time of publication.

A catalogue record for this title is available from the British Library.

Typeset by Mizpah Publishing Services Private Limited
This publication is printed on acid-free paper.
Printed in the United States of America.

Contents

Illustrations

Photographs by Louis Ouzer and Others

Frontispiece: Photograph of Alec Wilder from the dust jacket of the 1975 edition of *Letters I Never Mailed*, photo by Louis Ouser

Foreword

Marian McPartland

Alec Wilder's music has been a part of my life for many years. As a teenager, long before I left England for the United States, I listened to his now legendary Octets—comprising harpsichord, clarinet, bass clarinet, bassoon, oboe, bass, drums, and flute—and was intrigued by the fascinating combination of classical melodies, graceful and light, that were played with a jazz beat. The pieces had style, elegance, and wit. Some of them were tender, some humorous; all had imaginative, sometimes puzzling titles: *Jack, This is My Husband*; *The House Detective Registers*; *The Children Met the Train*; *It's Silk, Feel It*; and so on. The melodies were so intricately woven among the various instruments that it was hard for me to pick out the main themes on the piano; I would just listen to records and let my imagination run riot.

Gradually I absorbed more Wilder music from the BBC. *I'll Be Around* was a song that became popular in England, and *While We're Young* was another. I never saw the sheet music. I just soaked up the melodies from hearing them. I've always gravitated toward harmonically intricate tunes with tender, romantic lyrics, and these songs had them. Later, after I came to the United States, I learned more Wilder compositions.

I first met Alec at the Hickory House in the 1950s, but it was just a brief meeting. Years later he came to hear my trio at the Rountowner in Rochester, Alec's birthplace. He evidently liked what he heard, for he kept coming back night after night. One night as he was leaving he said, "I'm going to write a piece for you—I'll bring it in this week." I was pleased, but I didn't really believe him. I forgot all about it until the next time he showed up at the Rountowner. He airily tossed me a sheet of music, on which was written, "*Jazz Waltz for a Friend*—a small present from Alec Wilder."

I was delighted, and I couldn't wait to play the piece. It had a haunting melody that had a way of turning back on itself that I found fascinating. It was deceptively simple to play, yet hard to memorize and improvise on. Many of Alec's pieces are that way, but they are rewarding, for as you delve into them and explore their intricacies, you find fresh ways to go. *Jazz Waltz for a Friend*—as well as many other songs Alec wrote for me—became a part of my trio repertoire, just as Alec became part of my audience from then on.

While sitting in a club listening to music he sometimes pulled out a pad of papers and wrote letters or material for one of his many projects. I think that much of the writing of the original edition of this book was done at the back table at The Cookery while I was working there. He sat night after night, puffing on his pipe, scribbling sheet after sheet from airmail letter pads, stopping only to applaud loudly at the end of each number. Once at the Carlyle, when I was playing for a particularly noisy crowd, Alec was at a table behind me scribbling away. I said waspishly over the mike, "I don't know which is worse, people talking or a guy writing letters while I'm playing." Alec leaned forward and said in a stage whisper, "Yes, but you can't hear me."

Emotionally, Alec was very complex. He made wild swings from an almost childlike gaiety to deep depression. The word "curmudgeon" might have been invented for him. When he was in one of those low moods, it was as if a mistral were blowing. Raging, swirling clouds of pessimistic observations were uttered in a doomsday voice. He spoke morosely of a "great toboggan slide" of "our darkened world." One tried to be cheerful, but to no avail. The only thing to do was to wait till the storm blew over.

Somehow, through all those changes of mood, which Alec seemed hell-bent on sharing with his friends, the friends all hung on, ready to sweat out the line squalls, sit through the slough of despond, and revel with him and share gales of laughter and witty remarks that usually followed one of his gloomy spells. His old friend George Simon, after waiting out one of those moods, once remarked, "I nominate his personality as the one most likely to split."

Alec's conversations, his comments on people and events, were spoken with a larger-than-life intensity, in a resonant baritone that cut through crowd noise in any room. He could have been arrested for noise pollution in the restaurants he patronized. He could have had a great career in radio. In fact, radio shows he and I did on WBAI in New York and TV shows in Rochester on Channel 21 (WXXI-TV) were always highlighted by the clear, strong quality of Alec's voice, his quick wit, great gusts of laughter punctuating eloquently phrased anecdotes and stories, his way of verbally underscoring points with his magic marker voice.

He constantly grumbled about being "forced" into the limelight by being on a television or radio show (see the letter to me on page 230 of the book). Yet he came across on both media with great charm and a strong personality, with vitality and humor. One had to know him to understand why he gave himself such a hard time about these things. In actual fact, he was a closet ham—once he was onstage, he was really on.

This book is an apt example of the conflict between Alec's passion for privacy and his need to explain himself. It is an autobiography—note the subtitle: *Clues to a Life*. He wanted to reveal himself, but not entirely. He didn't identify very many of those to whom the letters were written, so the clues were useful only to his close friends who could figure out whom he was addressing.

Thanks to the dogged detective work of David Demsey, those clues now give us a much better understanding of what Alec told us about himself. Now we can read the book with a greater insight into the enigma that was Alec Wilder.

Preface to the
Annotated Edition

Alec Wilder (1907–80) constructed his autobiographical book *Letters I Never Mailed* in 1975 as a set of "letters" to the friends, associates, and individuals who had been a part of his life. The letters appear to have been written over the span of Wilder's life, but in reality they were composed for the purpose of this book. He created an ingenious format that defies literary category. So ingenious, in fact, that the identity of many of the addressees was at times—purposely or not—lost on readers who were unfamiliar with the personal details of Wilder's truly unique life. That life traversed an amazing span of American culture, including literary society, the Algonquin Hotel, popular songwriting, opera, chamber music, jazz and cabaret, theater, and film. Some of Wilder's letters are hilarious, self-deprecating, and light-hearted; others contain his deepest, most heartfelt views on life, art, and music. Many are warm and affectionate, some are angry, and a few are embarrassingly private. Many letters are addressed simply to the person's first name.

In this annotated edition an Annotated Addressee List is provided which gives as many addressee identities as possible and "decodes" the letters, putting them into the context of Wilder's life. The Introduction draws upon Wilder's own words from his two unfinished autobiographical works, "The Search" (handwritten in two notebooks, 169 pages, 1970) and "Life Story" (typescript, 189 pages, 1971), both written just prior to this book. While Wilder's literary motivation for these two book-length pieces is not clear, the first work may have served as journal notes for the second, or both may have taken on that function as he worked on *Letters I Never Mailed* a few years later. Both are unpublished, and are still in their original form, housed in the Alec Wilder Archive at the Sibley Music Library of the Eastman School of Music.

Also included are a number of photographs taken by photographer Louis Ouzer (1913–2002), a lifelong Wilder friend, associate and collaborator. Ouzer and Wilder met as young men, and Ouzer's keen photographic eye and his equally clear perception of Wilder provide more clues to Wilder's life and complex personality. Complementing Ouzer's images are newly rediscovered school photos of Wilder that show him as a boy and young man.

Alec Wilder's original version of *Letters I Never Mailed* exists in this annotated edition unchanged, letter for letter. Readers who want to share the experience of the original edition and use Wilder's *Clues to a Life* to solve the biographical puzzle should avoid the Introduction and refer to the Addressee List as little as possible.

This edition could not have been completed without the help, advice, and work of Wilder estate executor, Rochester lawyer and jazz radio host Tom Hampson; Helen Ouzer; Wilder biographer and expert information detective, the late Desmond Stone, for past access to his notes and research, and his insights into Wilder's life and personality; Judy Bell at The Richmond Organization for her authoritative knowledge and assistance; Robert Levy, Glenn and Winifred Bowen, Margot and Anna Camp, Arlene Bouras, Karen and Laura Demsey, David Peter Coppen at the Sibley Music Library of the Eastman School of Music; The Rochester Public Library Historical Collection; Alan Guma, director of Alumni Affairs at the Collegiate School; Barbara Rockefeller at the Allendale-Columbia School; the alumni offices of the Lawrenceville School and Wells College; Karen Osburn of the Geneva Historical Society at the Prouty-Chew Museum, Geneva, NY, Ralph Locke at the Eastman School of Music, and Suzanne Guiod, Sue Smith, Louise Goldberg, and Timothy Madigan at University of Rochester Press.

David Demsey
January 2005

Introduction to the Annotated Edition

A Brief Wilder Biography

David Demsey

Alec Wilder was a man of many contradictions. One of the most prolific American composers, he created hundreds of songs, chamber pieces, and multi-movement solo works, but frequently gave the original manuscripts to friends, often losing track of their existence. In fact, he composed only for friends and angrily refused offers of commissions. He gave away the books he so loved that always hung from the pockets of his rumpled tweed jackets. Wilder was intensely private, yet so profoundly literate that his thoughts were as moving and evocative in conversation as they were in his writings. He detested the American media machine and seemed to derail intentionally several projects that would have brought wide recognition, yet he craved validation of his compositions and even his musicianship. Wilder claimed to be a coward in life, but he had enormously strong convictions about music, art, and society, and he did not hesitate to proclaim them loudly and vociferously. He was often lonely, yet he had a personality that, by many accounts, could fill a room. He possessed a charm that he claimed served as a smokescreen for what he termed his "terror." New York's legendary Algonquin Hotel was his home base for half a century while he traveled the country on the trains that he adored. He was a nomad and a loner, yet his warmth and dedication created a circle of friends, each of whom was made to feel as though he or she was Wilder's closest confidant. A group of his friends who remain committed to his memory now meet annually in New York City for a concert of his many-faceted music, now officially calling themselves The Friends of Alec Wilder.

Wilder's friends and associates formed the basis for *Letters I Never Mailed*. Rather than publish an autobiography in standard narrative form, Wilder created more than two hundred letters, literally addressing the story of his life to the people who lived it with him. Because most are identified only by their first name, it is a challenge to determine the addressees of Wilder's letters. For this reason, the book's subtitle, *Clues to A Life*, is particularly appropriate. Perhaps this phrase indicated Wilder's attempts at self-discovery, but his letters indeed create a biographical puzzle for the reader to solve.

In the earliest part of Wilder's life, people—rather than events—bind the fabric of memory together. His childhood recollections are not represented in a chronological way, but in a series of incidental snapshots, many funny and sad at the same time. "I've never chosen to view more than a small piece of my landscape at one time," he wrote. "I've never wanted to climb a hill so that I could look down on it all: the fields, copses, streams, ravines, houses, barns. . .that's how I've managed to keep my sanity: by never looking at my life as such."[1]

Wilder was born on February 16, 1907, and grew up in a privileged environment in Rochester, New York. His parents' families were prominent in banking and in society circles; indeed, the Wilder Building still stands in downtown Rochester. Wilder did not take this privilege for granted; rather, he saw it as a burden. He was an introverted, somewhat isolated boy who was the target of teasing and bullying for his personality, as well as for his given name: Alexander Lafayette Chew Wilder.

> There was a solemn presentation to me on some youthful occasion of a very fancy filigreed silver tea pot which I was told bore great significance. It had been presented to my grandfather upon his having become the godchild of [General Marquis de] Lafayette. And, splendid fellow though I'm sure he was, it's no simple feat to move about Western New York State in any era with such a name tacked on to your own. And even tougher to bear as well, your mother's strange maiden name of Chew. ("Search," 3)

Wilder's earliest memories and misadventures are reflected in his letters. He apologizes to mothers of his childhood friends for misdeeds and escapades, remembering the strange way that local druggist JOHN MCFARLIN* spoke, questioning the relationship between his mother and their pastor REVEREND [WILLIAM] GOODWIN, "kidnapping" his 3-year-old next-door neighbor ARTHUR POOLE with a cake as the ransom demand, and, later, setting his cousin THEODORA'S hair on fire as he demonstrated his St. Paul's School rifle drills with a dinner candle. One of his first trusted boyhood friends was WALTON COOK, with whom the young Wilder started to discuss relationships with parents, art, music, life, and his place in it. An early joy, and perhaps the beginning of Wilder's love for trains, was "riding around the block in my red cart (which had steel wheels and springs). . . . I loved my cart dearly and especially the 'thwack' sound of the steel wheels as they rolled across the cracks in the sidewalk" ("Search," 6). Until age eleven (sixth grade), Wilder was a student at Columbia School, today the co-ed Allendale Columbia School, but then a private school in Rochester that admitted boys only to its first two grade levels, allowing them to stay on in special situations. Such was the case with Wilder and several other boys in his classes, including Walton Cook.

Much of his interaction with relatives was with the large family of his mother, LILLIAN CHEW WILDER, in nearby Geneva, a town located in the Finger Lakes region of New York. Family members included his "Uncle Hilly," THOMAS HILLHOUSE CHEW; his cousin Bev, BEVERLY CHEW (a common Chew family name for males, as well as his mother's middle name); and Beverly's first wife Madelaine ("MRS. CHEW"), with whom he was quite taken and who died when Wilder was 20.

The family of his father, prominent Rochester businessman GEORGE WILDER, was smaller. Wilder frequently spent time with his two aunts, EMMA WILDER and his beloved CLARA WILDER HAUSHALTER. He had great affection for his sister, HELEN WILDER DEWITT, who died prematurely in the early 1930s when Wilder was a young man (her exact death date is unknown). He felt that Helen was the lone family member who understood him. Helen and their older brother GEORGE also attended Columbia

---

* Names of *Letters I Never Mailed* addressees appear in small caps.

School. Wilder had relatively little contact throughout his adult life with his brother.

After the untimely death of his father at age forty-six, when Wilder was only two, the family eventually left Rochester and moved to the New York City area in the fall of 1918, living first in Garden City, Long Island, then moving into Manhattan. Living in a number of locations in and around New York City further reduced Wilder's already minimal self-confidence. He bounced between three different private schools within a three-year period, and his experience at the first two was nothing short of disastrous. He was a student at St. Paul's School in Garden City from November 1918 until spring 1920. The atmosphere of the then newly established military school was as completely foreign to his personality as the concept of war itself. From there, he moved from bad to worse at Lawrenceville School in New Jersey. One of his widowed mother's suitors who had connections at Lawrenceville pulled strings to have a third-floor room made up for the 13-year-old Wilder in Cleve House, the most prestigious and in-demand dormitory on campus, typically reserved for upperclassmen. Consequently, from the day of his arrival, Wilder was the constant target of hazing, teasing, and abuse from the older boys. He stayed there for only the first semester of his freshman high school year, the fall of 1920.

> There's no point in describing these typical, dreadful, vicious scenes. It's obvious who was the perfect patsy for them. For even during this . . . persecution, I never fought back. Can you imagine these so-called normal little boys, decent enough amongst themselves (recognizing each other's similarity and instant self-defense if attacked)—can you imagine their reaction to the boneless coward, me? Why, it was like watching a cat's tail when an unsuspecting robin lands nearby. I suppose these years of being beaten up and made a fool of left a hefty scar. Had there been the least likelihood of future courage, these years killed it. ("Search," 18)

The summer of 1920 between the two years at St. Paul's and Lawrenceville failed to provide a respite from Alec's misery. At a summer camp on Lake Winnipesaukee in New Hampshire, his hopes of communing with nature in quiet privacy were shattered by more bullying and abuse. Other summer memories of the family's annual vacations in the town of Bay Head on the New Jersey shore were far more positive. It was here, staying with his family at The Bluffs, a seaside resort, that Wilder began to first express himself musically—as a banjo player, no less, using a tuning he was shown that allowed him to play using only three strings and simplified fingerings. Nonetheless, it was through this instrument that he first learned to strum pop tunes of the day and realized that he was truly attracted to music.

Two weeks before his fourteenth birthday, in 1921, Wilder was enrolled for the spring semester of his freshman year at the Collegiate School on the upper west side of Manhattan, where the family then lived. At Collegiate, Wilder found his first confidence as a young man, finishing that first semester and staying through three more years to earn his high school diploma in 1924 at age seventeen. Despite the fact that his letters to his apparently fictitious school friend MYRON suggest an unhappy school experience, Wilder grew to be a much-praised member of the debating team, served on the athletic association board, and in his senior class yearbook was voted Best Looking Fellow, Done Most for Outside Athletics—and, in what Wilder considered to be a great irony, Most Likely to Succeed. The cowering freshman was now a young man who had grown to be a respected leader in his class.

Another significant factor in his development was Wilder's friendship with two comrades, CARROLL DUNN (whom he had met in Bay Head) and LAVINIA FAXON (RUSS), relationships that further bolstered his confidence. Dunn heard Wilder's abilities as a composer and encouraged him to "write something more than pop songs."

> The hours we spent together endlessly talking, endlessly listening! We'd sit in Chinese restaurants drinking tea by the hour and eating almond cookies. Why didn't they ask us to leave? We'd never eat a meal. Oh, those dreamy, innocent, intense, searching days and nights! . . . [Lavinia] and Carroll and I had a marvelous time. It was the twenties and probably a lot of our behavior was pretty tacky. But, as I say, we had a beautiful time. ("Search," 26–27)

Dunn also encouraged Wilder to begin what would be a lifelong process of writing—to friends, to associates, and just for the sake of writing: "My recollection is that Carroll told me I should set the goal for a stack of paper three feet high and that by the time I had written that much, I'd know how to write. Now the memory becomes foggier. For I'm not sure that I accomplished this injunction. I only know that I wrote a great deal, typed it, I'm certain. I recall that there were stories, verses, biographical sketches, anything."[2]

Wilder's Aunt Clara also played a central role in his development at that time, inviting him to accompany her family to Italy in the summer after his graduation from Collegiate in 1924. It was Wilder's first major voyage, his first ongoing contact with family who treated him as something more than a little boy, and would be the setting for his first romance.

> Through long evenings in front of the fireplace, I found myself telling maybe for the first time, the whole story of my inability to adjust to an alien society.
>
> And Clara understood.
>
> Indeed, she understood so well that she persuaded my mother to let me accompany her, her husband and one of my cousins on a trip to Italy. Of all the people I met and things I saw, I remember only one of the former as opposed to hundreds of the latter.
>
> Her name was Luciana Aloisi. . . . Luciana aroused no sexual interest in me, but she was the first girl who listened to me seriously and who treated me as an adult. I would leave notes under her door and when our family group went to Venice, she wrote to me there, in Italian. How much more romantic a situation could I have asked for? . . . Oh yes, she was surely my first love. . . . Luciana, though arousing no desire, represented that mysterious, palpitating world of Woman. ("Search," 44)

When Wilder set out on the first solo journey of his young adulthood at age nineteen in 1926, the scenario was the reverse of many typical stories. He and his family had been in the New York City environment since the days of World War I. That metropolitan scene had been large and frightening for Wilder, save for his few close friends. Now he left the big city to return to his native Rochester, and he first visited Westminster Road where he had grown up. He found the atmosphere so warm and welcoming that he decided then and there to stay. In particular, he spent time with his neighbor ALLEN KELLY (whom he credits with introducing him to drinking) and first lived in a room over the apartment of his Aunt Emma.

His lack of confidence and self-described "cowardice" kept him from immediate study at the Eastman School of Music, already prestigious in reputation by the mid-1920s. Eventually, though, Wilder's urge for growth and his pursuit of what Carroll Dunn had called "something more than popular songs" brought him to the studios of Eastman faculty members EDWARD ROYCE and HERBERT INCH. Wilder took composition lessons with Royce and studied counterpoint with Inch, although he was never enrolled as a full-time student. Of the two, Inch had a greater impact on Wilder. Although he never details which specific works he studied, he was awestruck by the multi-layered contrapuntal genius of J. S. Bach. Counterpoint would be a hallmark of Wilder's compositions throughout his life.

Perhaps more important than the instruction he received at Eastman was the group of students he befriended there. These were musicians who were to form the foundation for many of Wilder's career collaborations. Although they were from different social backgrounds than he, they were immensely talented and energetic, passionate about music, and a source of creative joy and inspiration. The group consisted of such future luminaries as oboist MITCH MILLER, tenor Frank Baker, French hornists SAM RICHLIN, Jimmy Buffington, and JOHN BARROWS, clarinetist Jimmy Caruana (Carroll), composer Goddard Lieberson, conductor Emanuel Balaban, and others.

> It was a revelation for me to find boys from truly poor families coping with their poverty, laughing at it, doing extra jobs while studying music. These students opened up a giant slice of life for me and without them I probably would have remained a rabbity stick-in-the-mud. [They] turned me into a slightly less frightened person and also gave me a more realistic approach to the business of functioning in an alien world. ("Life Story," 47)

Wilder also met two individuals in Rochester during this time who would play central roles in his life. The first was DR. JAMES SIBLEY WATSON. Wilder biographer Desmond Stone[3] correctly characterizes Watson as Wilder's substitute father. Watson was a renaissance man, a major influence on 1920s American literature, and an inventor and pioneer in filmmaking and radiology. He was Wilder's mentor and, in numerous instances, his emotional and financial benefactor. Wilder's lifelong communication with Dr. Watson included thousands of letters, poems, and pieces of prose.[4] Many of Wilder's most probing letters in *Letters I Never Mailed* are addressed to Dr. Watson. These letters often function as biographical narrative (and, in the case of the book's first letter, as the preface) as Wilder comments on his life's accomplishments and his philosophy.

The other leading individual in Wilder's life was LOUIS OUZER. In contrast to the wealthy Watson, Ouzer was the son of poor European immigrants. At the time of their meeting, Louis was an apprentice in the photographic studio of his neighbor, Wilder's fellow Eastman student Joseph Schiff. Wilder and Ouzer quickly became inseparable, and continued to be lifelong friends as Ouzer eventually opened his own studio and his extraordinary talents led to his capacity as official Eastman School photographer for more than a half-century. Around this time Wilder changed his name from Alexander to "Alec" for his music career; Lou Ouzer was therefore one of the few people in Wilder's life who rightfully knew him as Alex, and called him that throughout their six-decade friendship. Wilder's highest praise was reserved for Ouzer:

> I sensed that he was as pure and good as eternal truth and that in his being there was the quality of what was once called "an old soul." . . . Ever since those days of forty years ago I have been in touch with Louis. When people ask me why I return to Rochester so often, I tell them it's for reaffirmation. For seeing Louis keeping his principles, coping with a life that, but for his courage and stubbornness, should have destroyed him years ago, gives me the courage to pick up the cudgels once more. He is a saint. ("Life Story," 100–101)

Wilder's compositional voice took shape at Eastman. Before coming back to Rochester, he had written some "tone poems" and other pieces that he had discarded, but now he wrote two large-scale works: *Eight Songs* for voice and orchestra premiered in Eastman's Kilbourn Hall in 1928; and *Symphonic Piece* for

Orchestra premiered a year later with composer Howard Hanson, director of the Eastman School, conducting. Wilder was displeased with the rehearsal of *Symphonic Piece*, got drunk at a speakeasy afterward, and missed the premiere performance, much to Hanson's displeasure.

Alec's self-described "oddness" was developing into a flair for the dramatic. He cut quite a figure in the Eastman hallways, with a rakish hat, a cape, and a cane that had originated as therapy for a broken leg. The strong artistic and musical beliefs he shared with his friends set him against the musical establishment at Eastman, sometimes in ways that threatened his existence there.

One of the fomenters, Sam Richlin, a glorious red-headed rebel, trusted me enough to let me see the broadside he'd written to be printed and distributed in every mail box. It was much too vilifying, too far out of control to achieve any result, in my opinion. I had money in those days and offered to pay for the printing if the horn players would permit me to rewrite the diatribe.

The permission was granted. I rewrote it; the sheet, it was decided, was to be called "The Bird," which in those days meant a nose-thumb, and caustic little remarks were invented to fill the opposite side of the printed sheet. . . .

The sheets were printed and placed in all the mail boxes. But before more than a few were picked up, the front office got wind of them and removed the remainder. This, however, worked for the project in that it made the ones which had been picked up by the box owners that much more valuable. And soon everyone who had any spark was making copies.

Well, I tell you! It was as if someone in Berlin had put on a screening of Chaplin's "Dictator." Hanson's gestapo . . . went steaming about town cross-examining every print shop, dozens of people were hauled into Hanson's office, speeches of treason were trumpeted and the peapatch was truly torn up. ("Life Story," 44)

Though his experience as a composer of larger-scale works was growing, the popular songs that had first attracted Wilder as a young boy were still at the core of his writing. Mitch Miller convinced him to write all the music and most of the lyrics for a fraternity show called *Haywire*. It was hilarious, from Wilder's tongue-in-cheek song titles and lyrics to his program notes, and met with an enthusiastic reception, particularly one song that included a marriage proposal entitled "How'd Ya Like My Name on Your Tombstone?" He had also been collaborating with New York lyricist EDDIE BRANDT, whom he had met before his return to Rochester, and the two managed to get a song accepted into the Broadway revue *Three's a Crowd*. Unfortunately, their song was called "All the King's Horses," and an English song became well known at that same time entitled "The King's Horses." Wilder and Brandt's chances for a hit evaporated.

This and other brushes with the reality of New York City's musical environment began to convince Wilder that he should return to that scene. Now, for the first time, he saw himself as a musician, not as the recent high school graduate who had left there six years earlier. Many of his friends and co-conspirators at Eastman had moved to New York after graduation. Rochester was losing its appeal. He needed musical independence, though later he was to realize what he might have gained by staying at Eastman.

> Speaking of disillusionment, the reason I stopped studying music at the Eastman School was because of my realization that . . . Howard Hanson was a megalomaniac and a man who would never help me resolve my composing problems unless I became a total sycophant.
>   Had I "adjusted" to Hanson's need for lick-spittles, he just might have taught me privately. I'm not that impressed with his music, but I'm certain that his highly professional approach to composition would have provided me with essential tools which I don't have to this day. ("Search," 77)

During Wilder's first years back in New York, the city that would serve as his home for the rest of his life, his earliest ongoing work came as an arranger. This important element is often overlooked in Wilder's music. His craftsmanship and imagination as an orchestrator and arranger won him immediate admirers in New York, despite the fact that he characteristically downplayed his ability: "To make a living I made a lot of arrangements for recording vocalists. I was never very good at this craft, and so was embarrassed when I was complimented for work I felt was inadequate." ("Search," 90)

It was Wilder's Eastman friends who opened doors for him in New York. Thanks to Mitch Miller, a tireless supporter, Wilder entered a highly visible collaboration with Jimmy Carroll as staff arranger for the well-known Ford Hour radio program where Miller was oboist. Wilder wrote witty, swinging arrangements (now all lost) of Bach pieces that he had so loved at Eastman, one on Ravel's *Pavane*, and another on Debussy's "Golliwog's Cakewalk," of which he was particularly proud. "That was a beauty," he would later reflect ("Search," 6). (Miller and Carroll themselves would later be involved in a well-known collaboration: Carroll wrote several of the arrangements and Miller played oboe on the legendary Charlie Parker "Bird With Strings" recordings.)

In the late thirties, it was precisely this skill and imaginative writing and arranging that launched Wilder's career. His legendary Octets created a cult following. The Octets first came about when harpsichordist Yella Pessl, another friend of Mitch Miller, came to Wilder having heard his arrangements for the Ford Hour radio show. Pessl asked him to write a "jazzy" version of a classical piece for a film project. Although the film was never made, in the process Wilder fell in love with the sound of the harpsichord. Producer and friend MORTY PALITZ set up an audition for Wilder at Brunswick Records, and as a result he was asked to write some instrumental arrangements. Wilder used the instruments played by his friends and associates to create the instrumentation. "When asked what instruments I would use, naturally I thought first of the oboe, Mitch's instrument. Then I added flute, bassoon, clarinet, bass clarinet—all woodwinds—and suddenly I recalled the marvelous sounds the harpsichord made. So I added that. Later I added bass and drums for rhythm. Thus, haphazardly, I arrived at an octet."[5]

The now famed Octets are short, whimsical pieces that swing in an indescribably unique way. There are thirty-one in all, and include the original group recorded in 1939, followed by two more subsequently composed collections recorded in 1942 and 1947. There are 28 originals (three never recorded) and three more that were arrangements of pop standards. They each ingeniously combine the "classical" chamber music sound of the woodwinds and harpsichord with a swinging rhythm section, interweaving Bach-style counterpoint with jazz arranging. Gunther Schuller points out in his book *The Swing Era* (Oxford University Press) that the Octets preceded by years the much-studied Third

Stream movement of the 1950s that combined jazz and classical concert music.

The octets were assigned titles Wilder called "eccentric, sometimes witty," such as *The Children Met the Train*, *Neurotic Goldfish*, *The Amorous Poltergeist*, *It's Silk*, *Feel It* (this title suggested by Sam Richlin), and the thought-provoking *Jack, This Is My Husband*.

Wilder's career and reputation continued to grow. In the early forties, now something of a New York commodity as a result of the Octets, he wrote his first hit songs. The first of these was "It's So Peaceful in the Country" with music and lyrics written by Wilder in 1941. The song was introduced by singer MILDRED BAILEY after it was refused by three different publishers who couldn't understand why there was no woman involved in the lyrics. This song is now standard repertoire and has re-emerged as a favorite of jazz musicians within the last decade.

A year later, in 1942, Wilder wrote the lyrics and music for the song that has become his signature: "I'll Be Around." The late musicologist Mark Tucker praised this song, making note of a quality that Wilder himself thought was important: the melody can stand on its own without accompanying chords. Tucker wrote, "First, there is the tune, forthright and strong, needing no harmony for support, flowing smoothly and without effort. Second, there is the intervallic expansion that takes place over the course of the thirty-two-bar, AABA form . . . In the last eight bars, instead of repeating the pattern of the first two A sections, Wilder widens the intervals further, stretching up with two major sixths that give the lyrics added urgency."[6]

In the manner of many instances of great artistic inspiration, the act of composing the tune itself came almost as a surprise to Wilder.

As I recall, I was crossing Baltimore in a cab to take an interurban trolley to Annapolis when the title of [this] song popped (literally popped out of nowhere) into my head. I scribbled it on the back of an envelope. Quite by accident I spotted it as I was crumpling the envelope some days later. Since I was near a piano, I wrote a tune, using the title as the first phrase of the melody. I remember it only took about twenty minutes. God bless Frank Sinatra for singing the definitive version of this song.[7]

A year later, in 1943, another songwriting success came from Wilder's collaboration with WILLIAM ENGVICK and with songwriter and producer Morty Palitz, resulting in "While We're Young." Wilder was to develop a long partnership with the brilliant lyricist Engvick, who is known for his lyrics to the song "Moulin Rouge." They worked together for decades on songs, shows, and operas. "While We're Young" has become a commonly known standard in the popular song repertoire and has been recorded and featured by numerous singers, most notably the first soloist to introduce it, Wilder friend and admirer MABEL MERCER. Its long, sustained notes and arching melody again baffled the song producers Wilder first approached, but these qualities eventually became the selling points of the song. "I could never write a simple hit," Wilder wrote. Engvick's lyric is also exceptional; Wilder quotes James Thurber as telling him it was "the single best piece of English he'd ever heard." ("Search," 92) Wilder had also collaborated with Engvick and Palitz on the earlier "Moon and Sand," an evocative Latin tune originally recorded by Xavier Cugat that has become something of a jazz standard. It has been recorded by a number of notable jazz musicians, including an arrangement by Gil Evans on Kenny Burrell's legendary *Guitar Forms* recording and other well-known recordings by Marian McPartland, Chet Baker, and Keith Jarrett.

When Wilder first began writing songs in Rochester, he recalled, "In those days, my idols were Ethel Waters, Bing Crosby, and Mildred Bailey. So all my songs were written with them in mind even though I knew no one who knew them, or who knew anyone who knew them." Once in New York, however, Wilder's reputation grew; a who's-who of great American singers introduced songs he wrote specifically for them. PEGGY LEE introduced several tunes, including "Goodbye John" and "Crazy in the Heart." Maxine Sullivan recorded with a studio pickup group that took the name of the Alec Wilder Octet. Teddi King, Bing Crosby, TONY BENNETT, Billie Holiday, Cleo Laine, and many others were attracted to the challenges and rewards of Wilder's melodies. Later, Wilder friends and collaborators Jackie Cain and Roy Kral championed Wilder's music on record and in their live concerts and club sets. Marlene VerPlanck, a successful studio singer, showed that she was equally evocative as an interpreter of popular song as she recorded an all-Wilder album and featured his music in her shows. Barbara Lea recorded a number of Wilder songs as well. Opera star Eileen Farrell used Wilder's songs as her inspiration as she branched out so successfully into the realm of popular song, recording an all-Wilder album in the process. She was also the inspiration for a number of Wilder's art songs, compositions that arise from the popular song mode to become concert works. The best known of these art songs is a true masterpiece, "Did You Ever Cross Over to Sneden's?" introduced by Mabel Mercer and referring to Sneden's Landing on the Hudson River north of New York City.

Wilder's ongoing friendship during this time with the most sensationally popular of these singers, FRANK SINATRA, would be crucial to a successful 1945 recording project. Sinatra, who already was a major pop sensation by that time, had become aware of Wilder's music when Wilder had done some all-vocal arrangements for him, made necessary by an early-forties musicians' strike that prevented the use of instrumentalists in recording sessions. Wilder had written some small pieces for orchestra and soloist for some of his friends, to be sent to the BBC in England as part of a wartime music exchange program. They included *Air for Flute* for Julius Baker, *Air for Oboe* and *Air for English Horn* for Miller, and others. When Sinatra heard two of them in his backstage dressing room at the Paramount Theater, he placed an urgent call to Wilder and excitedly told him they should be recorded. Sinatra approached Columbia records on Wilder's behalf, but Columbia agreed to record the pieces only when Sinatra made the incredible offer to conduct the recording session himself—one of only a handful of occasions in his storied career in which he took the podium. At the session, he disarmed the orchestra of hard-nosed New York studio musicians by telling them he knew nothing about conducting, but that he desperately wanted this music to sound its best, and appealed to their leadership. The result was a success, musically and commercially. The recording *Frank Sinatra Conducts the Music of Alec Wilder* (with Sinatra insisting on Wilder's name appearing in the same type size as his own on the album cover) brought Wilder's name and reputation to a larger market. Wilder was featured in portrait articles in such diverse national publications as *Downbeat*,

Metronome, *Variety*, *Newsweek*, and *Seventeen*. His career was under way.

As Wilder's career moved into the late forties and fifties, his musical life took a less linear path. His collaborations resulted in larger-scale works, expanding his song concept into short operas and musicals. Wilder's first operatic efforts were two works for children, written in 1946 with lyricist Ben Ross Berenberg: *The Churkendoose*, which was recorded by Ray Bolger, and *Hermine Ermine in Rabbit Town*.

Wilder teamed with his songwriting partner Bill Engvick on *Miss Chicken Little* (1953), based on the familiar children's story and considered an opera although it was broadcast as an Omnibus television program, produced by ROGERS BRACKETT. Wilder had known Brackett through earlier West coast projects; he became important in Wilder's life and provided the connection to his association with the young actor James Dean. Wilder was unusually proud of another production with Engvick called *The Long Way* (1955, later retitled *Ellen*). To Wilder's dismay, this show was produced only during its premiere at a school in Nyack, New York, a location that did not attract the New York theater insiders, and it was never heard again. Other Wilder-Engvick collaborations included two NBC-TV productions, *Pinocchio* (1957), with a cast recording featuring Mickey Rooney and Fran Allison, and *Hansel and Gretel* (1958). Perhaps the most endearing of the Wilder/Engvick works is the songbook *Lullabies and Nightsongs*, based on forty-eight children's songs and nursery rhymes composed, harmonized, or arranged by Wilder, edited by William Engvick, and beautifully illustrated by Maurice Sendak.

The Impossible Forest, produced in Westport, Connecticut, in 1958, with libretto by Marshall Barer, was also produced by Brackett. Rather than utilizing a rehearsal hall, auditions for *The Impossible Forest* were held in the unusual locale of a suite in the Algonquin. These sessions gained an audience that included such names as Leonard Bernstein, Mark Blitzstein, Mary Martin, and Nancy Walker.

Wilder also had ongoing collaboration with lyricist ARNOLD SUNDGAARD, known for his work with Kurt Weill, the short folksong opera *Down in the Valley*, and for his Pulitzer Prize-winning

1951 opera *Giants in the Earth* with Douglas Moore. Wilder and Sundgaard collaborated on three short, one-act operas written for schools: *The Lowland Sea* (1952), *Cumberland Fair* (1953), and *Sunday Excursion* (1953), and another children's work, *An Axe, An Apple, and a Buckskin Jacket* (1957), which was recorded featuring Bing Crosby. The two also completed a larger-scale musical comedy, *Kittiwake Island* (1953), which eventually did an off-Broadway run, and a less successful show, *Western Star* (originally titled *The Wind Blows Free*), the latter yielding two songs that gained reputations on their own: "Where Do You Go?" and "Douglas Mountain." Their association continued into the 1970s, as they produced three short works: the one-act *The Opening* (1972), *The Truth about Windmills* (1975), and the musical comedy *Nobody's Earnest* (1978), which was produced in Williamstown, Massachusetts. Sundgaard's lyrics were a source of inspiration for Wilder that led to some memorable songwriting, including "Baggage Room Blues" and a song from *An Axe, An Apple* . . . that should be a holiday standard: "How Lovely Is Christmas."

Wilder used material from other sources for some remarkable large works. The Civil War-themed writing of historian BRUCE CATTON provided the impetus for Wilder's 1960 work *Names from the War* for narrator, chorus, and chamber orchestra. His *A Child's Introduction to the Orchestra*, with text by Marshall Barer, has eighteen movements, each illustrating an instrument in the orchestra, such as Bobo the Oboe, Muldoon the Bassoon, Max the Saxophone, Poobah the Tuba, and Mr. Forlorn the French Horn. It is on a level with any of the better-known pieces of this nature by Britten and others.

The last of Wilder's long associations with lyricists was with composer/lyricist Loonis McGlohon, known for his composition "Songbird" and his many collaborations with fellow North Carolinian Charles Kuralt. Wilder and McGlohon collaborated on a number of songs, most notably the now-standard "Blackberry Winter," as well as two productions: the church cantata *Mountain Boy* (1980), based loosely on Biblical themes, and an outdoor production called *Land of Oz*, which had ongoing presentations that most resembled a modern-day theme park in the North Carolina mountains each summer.

Closely related to his large-scale opera writing was Wilder's work on film scores. Filmmaker JEROME HILL asked Wilder to do three film scores during the fifties: *Albert Schweitzer* (1957), based on the scientist's life story, *The Sand Castle* (1959), and *Open the Door, See All the People* (1963).

Wilder's continuing relationship with Eastman friends led to associations with other world-class musicians. These were the versatile, virtuoso instrumentalists who populated New York's busy recording studios, Broadway theaters, and its legendary orchestras. Through Eastman friend John Barrows, as well as Mitch Miller and Jimmy Carroll, Wilder met trombonist John Swallow, flutist/woodwind doubler Don Hammond, tubists HARVEY PHILLIPS and Roger Bobo, bassoonists BERNARD GARFIELD and Harold Goltzer, bassist Gary Karr, and the renowned ensembles of the New York Woodwind Quintet and New York Brass Quintet, which included some of the above individuals as members, as well as flutists SAMUEL BARON and Julius Baker. Baron not only performed Wilder's music throughout his long career, but also conducted many Wilder projects and film scores.

These individuals and ensembles each came to have Wilder solo or chamber music compositions dedicated to them. Expanding from his focus mainly on songwriting, Wilder derived great joy and inspiration from associating with such strong instrumentalists.

> Without nearly the knowledge or technique necessary, I undertook the task of writing sonatas for every instrument, though the plethora of violin music caused me to omit a violin sonata. [Wilder later did write a violin sonatina for his physician, Dr. Max Presberg.] I found myself tripling the amount of chamber music I'd ever written in any given time theretofore and was happier than I had been in years.
>
> Gone were the rough and tumble pop music people, gone were the dreary assignments for vocal recordings and the hollow exchanges with all the hollow people.
>
> For I was now concerned with only those great musicians whom I had met mostly through the kindness of John Barrows. Granted, there was no financial reward in it but, God knows, limitless nourishment from the very act of writing and from the respect of these great musicians. ("Search," 93–94)

Eventually, there would be dozens of pieces for every imaginable combination of duos and trios: separate duos for flute, horn, and other instruments, each paired with improvised percussion; other duos for alto and bass flute, for oboe and English horn, and for many other combinations. There were numerous small ensemble works, including a saxophone quartet, nearly twenty woodwind quintets written for the New York Woodwind Quintet, and ten brass quintets composed for the New York Brass Quintet. Some of these chamber works reached back into the realm of theater. Wilder wrote incidental music for Lewis Carroll's *Alice in Wonderland* for the New York Woodwind Quintet, and this was later released as a suite.

These pieces consistently display the qualities of Wilder's unique compositional voice. He was a melodist; the movements of his suites, sonatas, and concertos feature beautiful, soaring melody lines that leap into the same wonderfully unexpected large intervals that are in his popular songs. The harmony darts from phrase to phrase between the worlds of classical music and jazz, one moment sounding like Hindemith with angular fourth intervals and counterpoint, the next moment landing on a lush jazz harmony reminiscent of Billy Strayhorn. If all of this is not difficult enough for the instrumentalist, the stylistic element provides the biggest challenge. As Harvey Phillips has commented, "If you try to play a whole sonata in a classical form, some movements are going to sound terrible. If you try to play the whole sonata in a jazz form, other movements are going to sound terrible . . . take it a step further, within any given movement, he may have eight or sixteen bars of straight classical interpretation and then suddenly you've got to swing for four bars."[8] Indeed, one of the reasons Wilder's instrumental music, even his songs, are not more frequently performed is very clear: they are difficult. In terms of their communicative power and uniqueness, they are certainly worth the effort.

Although he never discussed or wrote about the title designations of his solo works, Wilder seemed to categorize them into three levels of "seriousness." His concertos are virtuoso vehicles, the most technically demanding and "classical" of his forms, with accompaniment by a large group such as orchestra or wind ensemble. Sonatas still contain many classical elements, but are infused with a more lyrical quality and often mix styles, with movements in the style of a jazz waltz or a popular ballad. Wilder's suites are the "lightest" and most melodic of his multi-movement writing, giving the feeling of groups of songs without words. These maintain the closest connection with his popular songwriting style, with large interval leaps and cadences that are deceptively difficult for the performer.

Not all of Wilder's music is technically demanding. The Small Suite for Flute and Piano was written for Wilder friend, actress JUDY HOLLIDAY, who had taken up the recorder. Robert Levy's daughter Randi, a young French horn player, was given as a gift the three *Little Detective Suites*. *Pieces for Young Pianists* (edited by Sam Baron's wife Carol), and the *Small Fry Suite* provide piano students with richly melodic study material.

Reading concert listings and reviews from the late fifties and sixties, it would appear that hardly a month passed in New York or surrounding areas without a premiere of a newly finished Alec Wilder chamber or solo piece. Wilder and his contemporaries in the community of New York artists drew from each other mutual inspiration, energy, praise, and admiration.

Two individuals did much to make Wilder's music available to the rest of the world. One was CLARK GALEHOUSE, owner of Golden Crest Records. Galehouse recorded and released numerous Wilder solo and chamber pieces, often performed by the musicians for whom they were written. Several dozen Golden Crest releases during the fifties and sixties feature Wilder's music either exclusively or in combination with other composers. There were all-Wilder or Wilder-oriented albums by the New York Woodwind Quintet, Gary Karr, Harvey Phillips, Don Hammond, John Barrows with his second wife, Tait Sanford Barrows, Joe Wilder, and later Robert Levy, Virginia Nanzetta, marimbist Gordon Stout, the Clarion Wind Quintet, the Tidewater Brass Quintet, and David Demsey. Legendary pianist Milton Kaye, formerly accompanist to Jascha Heifetz, served as accompanist for the recordings by Phillips, Joe Wilder, and Nanzetta. Galehouse and Wilder were often present at the recording sessions, Wilder listening intently and appreciatively, giving the musicians the choice to interpret the music in the way they wanted, Galehouse lovingly guiding the technical aspects. It is doubtful that Galehouse made money on any of these recordings, particularly since he often personally sent free copies to Wilder's friends.

Another Wilder ally who would have a profound effect on the availability of his music, as well as being a steadfast Wilder friend and musical inspiration, is tubist HARVEY PHILLIPS.

> The fact that the quintet he played in, the New York Brass Quintet, played and recorded my piece was of course a great delight, but much more valuable to me was that because of the piece I came to know this stalwart rock of a man. I know of no one in the world who loves as he does and who gives such daily proof of it. He is a switchboard of vitality, has endless ideas for helping out the sick state of music, [and] is the most concerned husband and father and a man of exquisite musical taste and talent. ("Life Story," 146)

It is safe to say that a large percentage of the existing solo music for tuba was written by Wilder, dedicated to Phillips and to the members of his family with whom Wilder grew so close. There are pieces for tuba alone, concertos, sonatas, and solo suites (including the famed Effie Suite, for the typically Wilderian jazz/classical instrumentation of tuba, vibraphone, piano, and drums), all premiered, recorded, and promoted with unflagging energy by Phillips. There is an entire series of tuba works written for the members of the Harvey Phillips family: Suite No. 2 (*Jesse Suite*), Suite No. 3 (*Suite for Little Harvey*), and Suite No. 4 (*Thomas Suite*) were all written for Phillips' sons. *Song for Carol* is dedicated to Mrs. Harvey Phillips, and Sonata No. 2 is for Phillips' mother Lottie. Perhaps the smallest Wilder work done for Phillips may be the best known: at Phillips' request, Wilder responded literally overnight with a set of more than twenty imaginatively arranged Christmas carols, in four part harmony, for tubas. This repertoire is today played internationally, and is the music used annually by Phillips in his cross-country tours known as TubaChristmas, often involving hundreds of tubas in each city's holiday concert.

In 1964, Phillips created Wilder Music, the first concerted attempt to track down, publish, and promote the numerous works that had been given away by Wilder to friends, associates, and students across the country. It would take a man and musician of Phillips' energy to accomplish this, and accomplish it he did. All the while, however, Wilder was a creative whirlwind, adding pieces to the catalog faster than even Phillips could keep up. In 1976, Phillips worked with contemporary composer, author, and conductor Gunther Schuller to transfer all of Wilder's works to Schuller's Margun Music publishing company, which already had a staff and a catalog in place. Upon his retirement from publishing, Schuller sold the music sales rights to the large G. Schirmer Publishing and Shawnee Press, both divisions of Music Sales Corporation.

In the last two decades of Wilder's life, he came into contact with a new, younger generation of musicians who were equally taken with him and his music. Like Wilder's earlier New York circle, they tirelessly promoted his music, put their energy behind premieres and recordings of sonatas, suites, trios, and quintets. He met these younger players primarily through several summer residencies in which he was involved. Two were on the campuses of the University of Wisconsin, one being the main campus in Madison, where John Barrows eventually taught and Harvey Phillips joined him on the summer faculty. Another residency program on the University of Wisconsin Milwaukee campus had been developed by the New York Woodwind Quintet. Through these, Wilder met clarinetist Glenn Bowen, to whom Wilder dedicated a number of works. Bowen premiered several of the later woodwind quintets, and later wrote his Eastman doctoral dissertation on Wilder's clarinet solo and chamber music. Another important Wilder association was at the Tidewater Music Festival in Maryland. It was there that he became close to trumpeter Robert Levy and flutist Virginia Nanzetta. As a member of the Tidewater Brass, Levy premiered several solo trumpet works as well as Wilder Brass Quintets Nos. 4 through 8 (although No. 4 was written for Harvey Phillips), and recorded an all-Wilder CD in 1994. Nanzetta also premiered a number of his flute works that were dedicated to her.

Because Wilder's solo and chamber works are so often marked by classical and jazz influences, his music attracted the attention of a number of major jazz figures. Wilder wrote major multi-movement works for several musicians who have played a large part in jazz history. Saxophonists Stan Getz and Zoot Sims, both of whom had made their reputations as soloists in Woody Herman's bands, separately collaborated with Wilder. The emotional *Three Ballads for Stan* for tenor saxophone and strings (also known as Suite No. 1 for Tenor Saxophone in a later piano version by Wilder) was recorded by Getz with Arthur Fiedler and the Boston Pops, along with a gorgeous arrangement Wilder did of his own song "Where Do You Go." Another piece for tenor saxophone and strings was written for and premiered by Zoot Sims, although it has only recently been recorded after Sims' death by the Manhattan Chamber Orchestra led by Richard Auldon Clark. Baritone saxophonist Gerry Mulligan was featured in two Wilder pieces for baritone sax and woodwind quintet, both of which called for saxophone improvisation during the course of the piece. Jazz trumpeters Clark Terry, Joe Wilder, and Doc Severinsen all collaborated. Wilder dedicated concertos to both Terry and Severinsen (Terry's featuring both trumpet and flugelhorn) and the versatile Joe Wilder, a consummate classical as well as jazz trumpeter, did an entire album of Wilder's solo trumpet works. In 1957, Wilder wrote an album's worth of arrangements for guitarist Mundell Lowe, called *New Music of Alec Wilder* and featuring a studio band made up almost entirely of the individuals for whom Wilder had been writing solo and chamber music. Wilder also had close associations with Jackie Cain and Roy Kral, Jimmy Rowles, and Red Norvo, and with pianist Ellis Larkins, about whom Wilder wrote a touching *Down Beat* tribute article in 1972. In addition, he is well known for his lyric for Thad Jones's originally instrumental tune "A Child Is Born," added by Wilder after hearing the Thad Jones–Mel Lewis Orchestra perform the simple masterpiece.

As Wilder expressed his amazement at the ability of jazz musicians to create melodies spontaneously, he also demanded that that they first give his original melody its due.

> Jazz musicians are a phenomenon. I don't believe the layman has any notion of the miraculous chain of events which occurs when a jazz musician plays. . . . But it is a perverse fact that jazz musicians presume (and it is a presumption!) that it is their inalienable right to change whatever notes of the "theme" they choose even before they arrive at the variations (or jazz). To me this is the sheerest arrogance. If they are so fond of the tune they plan to improvise upon, why don't they state it as written? . . . Mind your manners, ladies and gentlemen![9]

One of the jazz musicians whose playing Wilder most appreciated, and with whom he was closest personally, is pianist MARIAN

MCPARTLAND. Her 1954 arrangement of "I'll Be Around" was widely heard and appreciated, and Wilder could be seen regularly at her club engagements in New York and in Rochester from the time they met in 1963. He greatly admired McPartland's musicianship and her inventive abilities as an improviser. He wrote of her, "In three unplanned minutes, she can, and consistently does, invent rhythms, harmonic sequences and melodic flights which would take me three weeks to achieve as a composer. And even then, not half as well.[10] Wilder composed *Fantasy for Piano and Wind Ensemble* as a concerto for McPartland, and also wrote smaller pieces for McPartland that were unique in Wilder's repertoire: songs without words that were made to be improvised upon, including "Jazz Waltz for a Friend" and "Homework." He liked to kid McPartland about her improvisational excursions. On the manuscript of "Jazz Waltz for a Friend" he gave to McPartland, he wrote "Kindly McPartlandize!" At the finish of another page, when he knew McPartland would return to the beginning of the form and begin to improvise, he wrote, "Okay, school's out!"

Indeed, Wilder's affinity for beautiful song melody still remained at the core of his music, even as he produced prolific amounts of solo and chamber music. This kinship, along with his continuing love for books and writing, culminated in what could be called the crowning achievement of his career, the book *American Popular Song* (Oxford University Press, 1972), edited and with an introduction by James T. Maher. The book was initiated with a grant from the Avon Foundation, an entity of the wealthy family of Jerome Hill. The book received great praise at the time it was published, and is still considered a seminal work on the analysis of popular song. The project was massive by any scale, with original impetus and advocacy from Oxford editor SHELDON MEYER. There were over four years of work in the offices of publisher HOWARD RICHMOND, owner of The Richmond Organization/ TRO, the company that today publishes Wilder's popular songs and octets through the efforts of Judy Bell. Over 17,000 popular songs were surveyed. James Maher, a veteran writer who was deeply committed to this project, served as Wilder's virtual co-author. Although Maher receives only a parenthetical mention in *Letters*, Wilder praised him at length in *Life Story*.

I made one sensible move—I obtained the editorial and advisory assistance of one of the most astonishing men I have ever known, James Maher. . . . Usually very informed men have the tendency to be pompous or humorless or both. James Maher is a truly modest and humble man.

   I'm sure I was a very difficult personality for him to adjust to, though he gave no signs of impatience. He advised, he suggested, he relinquished his own inclinations graciously, he put up with my unpredictable intuitive methodless ways of work. Without him there would have been no book. ("Life Story," 176)

Maher and Wilder met in Richmond's offices for days at a time, surrounded by stacks of sheet music. Wilder sat at the piano provided by Richmond, Maher took notes, spurring Wilder on, questioning him, guiding the proceedings. Maher saved the entire project numerous times when Wilder would quit in disgust, luring Wilder back into work through a newly edited chapter he had finished, or by a well-timed compliment that would help Wilder regain his momentum. A notable, although not surprising, omission from the book: Wilder does not mention a single one of his own songs.

   The book had such an effect that it spiraled into another song celebration, the *American Popular Song with Alec Wilder and Friends* series on National Public Radio which was broadcast from late 1976 until early 1980. Although it seems unbelievable that such a private person as Wilder could be made to sit in front of a microphone, his friend and collaborator LOONIS MCGLOHON made it happen. Done in the comfortable surroundings of the living room of series producer Dick Phipps's South Carolina home, microphones were deftly hidden in large houseplants and the sessions were made to feel as relaxed as possible. Recorded in a total of forty-two hours, the thirty-eight programs featured an incredible array of singers talking with Wilder and singing the best of American popular song, often accompanied at the piano by McGlohon. Such legends as Tony Bennett, Johnny Hartman, Mabel Mercer, Dick Haymes, Bobby Short, Margaret Whiting, George Shearing, Woody Herman, and younger artists such as Barbara Lea, Marlene VerPlanck, Mary Mayo, and Mark Murphy all came to South Carolina to take part. This time, Wilder songs were featured regularly in the repertoire. These programs now exist only on archival tape, yet they represent one of the best-recorded showcases of popular song, and of Wilder's personality.

Wilder had just completed *Letters I Never Mailed* around this time, working with veteran literary editor HARRY SIONS at Little, Brown and Company publishers. The unique format for the book likely arose from the fact that Wilder was a prodigious letter writer. Composer and fellow Rochesterian David Diamond shared a friendship with Wilder for fifty years, and recently donated a collection of eighty Wilder letters and postcards to the Wilder Archive at Eastman. That archive also holds hundreds of letters from Wilder's lifelong correspondence with Dr. Sibley Watson. Wilder's opening letter in *Letters I Never Mailed* tells Dr. Watson about "letters, my letters, letters I've written since I was a child but letters I have never mailed. Two distinct puzzlements: why didn't I mail them and why did I keep them? They go all the way back to Westminster Road when I went to Columbia School and they have piled right up to this week." The real answer to Wilder's questions, except for a few letters he told Lou Ouzer that he found in one of the suitcases he kept behind the Algonquin switchboard, lies in the fact that nearly all of the letters were actually written for the purpose of this publication. Ouzer remembered several of their long car rides together, when Widler would be writing in a notebook, look over at him and say, "Now, how would a seven-year-old boy say this?"[11] Rather than being an act of dishonesty, this is a standard literary device carried to a new place by Wilder. Some of the letters are thank-you missives, such as the one to author WHITNEY BALLIETT, whose *New Yorker* feature article "Alec Wilder: President of the Derriere-Garde" is still considered to be the best written portrait of Wilder that exists, and became a chapter of Balliett's book *Alec Wilder and Friends* (Houghton Mifflin). Many of the most telling letters, expressing Wilder's innermost thoughts about his life, art, music, and culture, are written to his mentor, Dr. Watson, and to artist and critic HARRY BOURAS, who, with his wife and former Eastman piano student Arlene, were among Wilder's closest friends. The Bourases frequently hosted Wilder at their home in Chicago and took many memorable train rides with him. Wilder wrote several piano works for Arlene. One particular letter to "Dear Harry" (found on pp. 202–5 of original edition), which uses material taken from Wilder's own 1974 *Allegro* article, is perhaps Wilder's most succinct statement of his artistic beliefs, of his indictment of modernness and newness for their own sake, and of "contemporary music" in particular. *Letters I Never Mailed* received very positive reviews at the time, including praise from the noted writer Gene Lees and a heartfelt article in *Music Journal* from Ouzer himself.

Wilder also wrote a third book, "The Elegant Refuge: Memoir of a Life at the Algonquin Hotel." The manuscript was never published, presumably because the publisher had wanted a history of the Algonquin and all of its legends to include tell-all stories about the famed Round Table crowd and the countless other literary and entertainment legends who could be seen there over the preceding decades. This was just the type of name-dropping that Wilder most detested. Instead of gossip-laden stories, he wrote a tribute to his life at the hotel. Equal time is given to the front desk staff, waiters, and busboys as to the numerous famous names who were Wilder's friends or acquaintances from chance encounters in the lobby, hallways, and elevators. HENRY BROWN ("Brownie"), a front office employee who often helped Wilder plan his constant train trips, is a perfect example of these not-famous people whom Wilder treated like royalty, both in person and in the book.

With the Algonquin, rich in New York literary and cultural history serving as his home base, Wilder maintained the existence of a nomad through his adult life.

> I had no desire to keep a record of my life. I hated to be photographed, I very early on shied from possessions, I bought nothing bigger or heavier than could be carried in a suitcase.
>
> I've denied myself all possessions, whether they be books, clothes, photographs, houses, cars, news clippings, recordings, jewelry. . . . I never unpack. I must know that I can leave wherever I am in no more than ten minutes. ("Search," 37, 60)

Wilder's life often revolved around long-distance train schedules, which he had memorized in great detail. He could create and follow complicated itineraries that would take him zigzagging across the country as he worked, visited friends, and was alone with his thoughts. He often composed on trains, remaining on board until the piece was finished, transferring to whichever train was leaving a station next if he were confronted with the end of a line.

> Trains, since I can remember, have been miracles. They have always given me a sense of peace, security and fulfillment, that very, very few people have. To a coward safety is of paramount importance, or even the illusion of it. . . .
> I still prefer to spend most of my time alone and I was happier in towns where I knew nobody, had no fears of the phone ringing, no threat of appointments or dinner dates.
> So I went to Abington, Virginia, Charleston, New Orleans, Chicago, Saint Petersburg, and countless villages whose names I've forgotten. But they had one trait in common: they all must be reachable by railroad. I disliked entering a town by automobile. Railroads to this day make a romantic mystery of travel. ("Search," 73)

There were some locations that were havens for the nomadic Wilder. He returned to these places again and again. The earliest had been the aforementioned family vacation spot of Bay Head, New Jersey, about which Wilder would daydream the rest of the year, waiting to return. The hometown atmosphere of Rochester was another, where he would hold court for hours in the Eastman main hall or across the street at the Manhattan Restaurant, waited on by GRACE WILLIAMS. In the fifties, the house of Mitch Miller, his wife Frances, and their son MIKE MILLER in Stony Point, New York, became such a haven. Wilder, who rented a nearby carriage barn also grew close to the Millers' housekeeper MAGDALEN DAEDE. For a long period, there were Sunday musicales at the Miller home, with Bill Engvick, John Barrows, Frank Baker, and others all in attendance.

> Other musicians heard about our Sundays and asked to be included . . . before it was over, the group consisted of three French horns (two turtle doves?) bassoon, violin, cello, piano, voice (vocalise) and an occasional trumpet. . . . I suppose overall I must have written sixty short pieces. And though I did rewrite and reuse four or five of them for other groups, all the others have never been heard since. As far as I'm concerned they needn't be. They served their purpose: fun, friends meeting, laughter, drinking, eating, relaxing, playing, writing. To the contemporary mind

this would be incomprehensible. Thank God it wasn't to those who par-
ticipated. ("Search," 155)

Other locations were constants in Wilder's travels. One was
Key West, Florida. From time to time later in his life, he could
be found as a guest at the home of his friend, architect DAN
STIRRUP, where he found solace in Stirrup's sense of joy and love
of laughter amid his own bouts of depression. His trusted physi-
cian, DR. WILLIAM PLOSS, was in Gainesville, and Wilder made
many trips there to see him, including his last journey, for surgery
when he was fighting lung cancer. He often stayed at the Atlantic
Shores Motel in Key West, which he loved.

> The motion of the curtains calms me. The unlikelihood of the telephone
> ringing lessens my normal tenseness. The occasional burst of a mocking-
> bird's song makes me forget that I'm old. The consciousness that I exist,
> even though only temporarily, on the last of a string of small coral islands
> makes me feels as if I escaped from a horde of slavering barbarians.
> ("Search," 166–67)

The sublime peace of the country was not only the subject of
one of Wilder's most widely known songs; it was also truly an
attraction for him. In his early New York days, he spent what he
described as some of his most pleasurable moments working in
the garden of his Eastman friends EDDIE FINCKEL and his wife
Helen at their country home in Pennsylvania. "I remember one
afternoon, during the second summer [there], lying flat on my
stomach on one of the crushed limestone paths. The Finckels had
gone into Kutztown, the nearest community, the garden had
responded miraculously to my obsessive care and I was, as probably never before or since, content" ("Search," 113–14).

In the late sixties, Wilder met FATHER HENRY ATWELL, who
was a close friend of Lou Ouzer in Rochester. Wilder, who was at
first hesitant about meeting a Catholic priest, quickly grew to
love Atwell's character and honesty. Atwell's blunt writings on war
and peace and his views on birth control (he had been on the
board of Rochester Planned Parenthood!) resulted in his transfer
to a parish in the farming community of Avon, thirty minutes
south of Rochester. Wilder fell in love with that rural setting, and

often stayed at the rectory of St. Agnes Church, Father Atwell's parish. The friendship of Wilder, Ouzer, and Atwell resulted in one of Wilder's most powerful compositions, a 1968 work for children's chorus, narrator, and wind ensemble called *Children's Plea for Peace*. Wilder had been deeply affected by the sound of a children's choir rehearsing at Eastman, and it was decided that the sentiments of peace during that Vietnam era could best be expressed by the words of children. Seizing on that, Atwell set about gathering a set of letters from young students at his parish school on the subject of peace. "In a short time, I received three hundred [children's letters]. They were, for the most part, absolutely wonderful. They were also heart breaking. They made very angry and discerning comments and attestations. It was an embarrassment of riches. In fact, it took me as long to choose and juxtapose the statements as it did to write the music" ("Search," 111). Those letters became the narrator's text in Wilder's composition. The work received widespread praise, and its meaning has only deepened in the ensuing decades. It is still performed today.

Avon was not only a spot Wilder loved in life, it was also where he wished to be buried when he learned how ill he was a year before his death on Christmas Eve in 1980. Ironically, as Wilder had avoided publicity in life, such was the case upon his death. The news of his passing came over the wires on Christmas Day the one day in the year when people are least likely to read a newspaper or hear a news broadcast. It is in the St. Agnes Cemetery that Wilder is buried, only a few feet from the grave of Father Atwell. Despite his wishes for no marker in his will ("I wish none, no name, dates, and certainly no maudlin phrases in the style of Rod McKuen"), his friends, led by his executor, Rochester lawyer, author, and jazz radio host Tom Hampson, saw a deep need for at least a plain gravestone. Many of the wishes in Wilder's will reflect his commitment to nature and conservancy. To this day, portions of Wilder's estate contribute to the Audubon Society, the Save the Redwoods Society in California, the Jersey Wildlife Preservation Trust in the Channel Islands run by naturalist GERALD DURRELL, and others.

Since Wilder's death, his stature has continued to grow, with new legions discovering his music and efforts expanding to make Wilder's music more available. Yet another generation of musicians, too young to have known Wilder during his lifetime, now champions his music. These include hornists David Jolley and Thomas Bacon, jazz guitarist Vic Juris, flutist Laurel Zucker, soprano Valerie Errante, and pianist Robert Wason, saxophonists David Demsey and Bob Rockwell, conductor Richard Auldon Clark and the Manhattan Chamber Orchestra, all of whom have recorded all-Wilder CDs. The Alec Wilder Archive and Wilder Reading Room have been established in the Sibley Music Library of the Eastman School of Music in Rochester. Wilder was posthumously elected to the Songwriter's Hall of Fame in 1983. Rochester newspaper editor Desmond Stone completed the definitive biography *Alec Wilder In Spite of Himself*, published in 1996 by Oxford University Press, the same publisher that worked so tirelessly with Wilder on his popular song text nearly a quarter century earlier.

If Wilder could somehow write this new edition of *Letters I Never Mailed* today, it would undoubtedly be much more extensive than the original. The numbers of friends and admirers continued to grow after the writing of this book, even more so after his death. Those who knew him as a friend loved him fiercely, yet few had chances to demonstrate that admiration in his lifetime. Ironically, he and his music have become more widely known after his death than while he was alive, as new generations of musicians and readers are attracted to his uniqueness.

Notes

1   Wilder, Alec, "The Search" (unpublished, 1970, Alec Wilder Archive, Sibley Music Library, Eastman School of Music, 4). Further citations for this work appear in the text.

2   Wilder, "Life Story" (unpublished, ca. 1971, Alec Wilder Archive, 17). Further citations for this work appear in the text.

3   Desmond Stone, *Alec Wilder In Spite of Himself: A Life of the Composer* (New York: Oxford University Press, 1996).

4   This material is housed in the Alec Wilder Archive, gift of Nancy Watson Dean.

5   Wilder, "The Elegant Refuge: Memoir of a Life at the Algonquin Hotel" (unpublished, 1976, Alec Wilder Archive, 74–75).

6   *Newsletter of the Institute for Studies in American Music* 17, no. 1 (November 1987): 8–9.

7 Wilder, *Songs by Alec Wilder Were Made to Sing* (New York: TRO Publishing; Ludlow Music, 1976), 86.
8 Harvey Phillips, interview with David Demsey, February 1995.
9 Wilder, unpublished manuscript page, looseleaf, Alec Wilder Archive.
10 Wilder, liner notes for McPartland's 1973 recording *A Delicate Balance* (Halcyon 105).
11 Conversation with the author.

Key to Original Edition

Original	Annotated	Original	Annotated	Original	Annotated	Original	Annotated	Original	Annotated
3	51	51	94	100	137	148	180	199	223
4	52	52	95	101	138	149	181	200	224
5	53	53	96	102	139	150	182	201	225
6	54	54	97	103	140	151	183	202	226
7	55	55	98	104	141	152	184	203	227
8	56	59	99	105	142	153	185	204	228
9	57	60	100	106	143	154	186	205	229
10	58	61	101	107	144	155	187	206	230
11	59	62	102	108	145	156	188	207	231
12	60	63	103	109	146	159	189	208	232
13	61	64	104	113	147	160	190	209	233
14	62	65	105	114	148	161	191	210	234
15	63	66	106	115	149	162	192	213	235
16	64	67	107	116	150	163	193	214	236
17	65	68	108	117	151	164	194	215	237
18	66	69	109	118	152	165	195	216	238
19	67	70	110	119	153	166	196	217	239
20	68	71	111	120	154	167	197	218	240
23	69	72	112	121	155	168	198	219	241
24	70	73	113	122	156	169	199	220	242
25	71	74	114	123	157	170	200	221	243
26	72	75	115	124	158	171	201	222	244
27	73	76	116	125	159	172	202	223	245
28	74	77	117	126	160	173	203	224	246
29	75	81	118	127	161	174	204	225	247
30	76	82	119	128	162	175	205	226	248
31	77	83	120	129	163	176	206	227	249
32	78	84	121	130	164	177	207	228	250
33	79	85	122	131	165	178	208	229	251
34	80	86	123	132	166	179	209	230	252
35	81	87	124	133	167	183	210	231	253
39	82	88	125	134	168	184	211	232	254
40	83	89	126	135	169	185	212	233	255
41	84	90	127	136	170	186	213	234	256
42	85	91	128	137	171	187	214	235	257
43	86	92	129	138	172	188	215	236	258
44	87	93	130	141	173	189	216	237	259
45	88	94	131	142	174	190	217	238	260
46	89	95	132	143	175	191	218	239	261
47	90	96	133	144	176	195	219	240	262
48	91	97	134	145	177	196	220	241	263
49	92	98	135	146	178	197	221	242	264
50	93	99	136	147	179	198	222	243	265

Figure 1. Wilder home on Westminster Road, Rochester, New York. Photo by Louis Ouzer.

Figure 2. Young Wilder in 4th class at Columbia School (now Allendale-Columbia School), Rochester, NY. April 1916. Wilder is second from left in front row; Walton Cook is on his right, neighbor Elizabeth Poole is second from left in back. Courtesy of Allendale-Columbia School.

ALEXANDER LAFAYETTE CHEW WILDER
"Alex"

"All great men are dying. I feel bad myself."
—Rogers.

40 East 62nd St., N. Y. C.

Born, February 16, 1907. Entered Collegiate 1921.
Class Secretary, 1922-'23.
Vice-President of Class, 1921-'22, '23-'24.
Debating Team, 1922-'23, '23-'24.
Treasurer of Athletic Association, 1923-'24.
Glee Club, 1922-'23, '23-'24.
"Dutchman" Board, 1923-'24.

ENTERS PRINCETON

Al who habben had the plesaunce of spekyng with Wilder knowen the gret scope of hes wisdom, the keneness of hes witte, and the sounness of hes resounyng, althagh, nou and thanne, hes conversacioun rescend too fer, outher ascend too hegh. Feyne wulde we speken abouten hes musical accomplishments; buten 'twere useless. Al habben had ample proeve. In the Gle Club he ben verray bisi trienyng, at oon tyme, to refreinen from laghyng at Seib's grotesque attempts to kepen a streht face and trienyng to discovern which membes of the organizacioun ben singyng the sourest, that he may after-ward balle them ute. Of "Alex's" character we cannot speken lightly, for it ben eek verray dep. Certayne it can be sayn that he ben a gret philosophre; buten the subject of women; oon of hes studies, baffleth hem alwys. Hes intellectual pouers may best be conceyved when we tellen you that for nought less then seofenteen Monendeis in successioun he hath ben able to invent a good excuse for nought havyng done hes Latin composicioun

30

Figure 3. Wilder at the Collegiate School during his senior year, 1923–24. Collegiate School senior yearbook, 1924. Courtesy of the Collegiate School.

Figure 4. Wilder in the Glee Club in his senior year at the Collegiate School, 1923–24. Wilder is in the middle of the front row. Collegiate School senior yearbook, 1924. Courtesy of the Collegiate School.

Figure 5. Wilder as a member of the Athletic Association in his senior year at the Collegiate School, 1923–24. Wilder is on the far right. Collegiate School senior yearbook, 1924. Courtesy of Collegiate School.

Figure 6. Dr. James Sibley Watson, *c.* 1940. Photo by Louis Ouzer.

Figure 7. Magdalen Daede ("Madelaine" in Wilder's letters to her) with Mike Miller, son of Mitch Miller at Stony Point, 1951. Courtesy of Mitch Miller and David Diamond.

Figure 8. French Horn virtuoso, educator, longtime collaborator, and fellow Eastman student, John Barrows, 1960s. Photo by Louis Ouzer.

Figure 9. Alec Wilder, Jackie Cain, and Roy Kral, early 1970s. Photo by Louis Ouzer.

Figure 10. Harold Arlen and Alec Wilder, April 17, 1972. Photo by Louis Ouzer.

Figure 11. Marian McPartland and Alec Wilder, April 10, 1974. Photo by Louis Ouzer.

Figure 12. Mitch Miller and Alec Wilder, 1974. Photo courtesy of the Friends of the Rochester Public Library.

Figure 13. Mary Mayo, Alec Wilder, and Mabel Mercer, September 14, 1976. Photo by Louis Ouzer.

Figure 14. Trumpeter Joe Wilder and Alec Wilder, September 14, 1976. Photo by Louis Ouzer.

Figure 15. Louis Ouzer and Alec Wilder, April 1974. Photo courtesy of Louis Ouzer.

Letters

I Never

Mailed

Alec
Wilder

To James Sibley Watson

Dear Dr. Watson:

Certainly by now you're familiar with my perhaps abnormal attitude toward possessions. But in case you don't realize how profound my obsession has become, I've brought myself down to three suitcases. I admit to a couple more behind the Algonquin switchboard in a chaotic cubbyhole they let me use.

I've furnished about fifteen homes with the books I've read. Indeed I have a special list which I consult after finishing each book to see which person would like it most.

But all this is primarily to tell you about the only objects I *have* saved and my puzzlement over having done so.

They're letters, my letters, letters I've written since I was a child but letters I have never mailed. Two distinct puzzlements: why didn't I mail them and why did I keep them? They go all the way back to the early years on Westminster Road when I went to Columbia School and they have piled up right to this week.

I'm never anyplace for more than a few weeks; and though I never unpack a bag I do have to shift everything when a bag wears out. Then is when I come across these strange space consumers, these batches of letters. Since I admit to being obsessed about not adding anything to what I absolutely need, what is it that impels me to adjust to and put up with these packets of letters?

It's not that I make a practice of rereading them. I've never reread them; I don't dare to. The other puzzlement as to why I never mailed them will never be resolved until I read them.

So I've decided to send the whole bunch to a marvelous girl I know who types like an angel and never has a problem deciphering my handwriting. It will be worth whatever it costs. For once they're typed they will no longer have that "lost and by the wind grieved" quality of yellowing paper and faded ink. I'll be able to read them as might an editor read a manuscript. I won't be so deeply drawn back to the past which I've always loathed. And perhaps by so doing I may find out why I never mailed them and why I've kept them so troublesomely for, heaven help me, almost sixty years!

Since I send you almost everything I put to paper, I'll send you carbons of the letters. Please don't feel obligated to read them all! However, you might be entertained by those I never mailed to you!

ALEC

Dear Walton:

It's very nice to know you and I'm glad you like me. I don't like any of the other boys at school. All they want to do is fight and play games where you get knocked down and laughed at.

I like the detective game we play where I come in the room every time with a different hat on. And I like hearing you speak French to your mother. She's a very nice lady and she's nice to me.

I should not have left that note at the grocery store about that kid that stole the marble and threw it at the big window and cracked it. But he made me so mad kicking all our marbles around and stealing that blue agate.

I guess no one likes us at school but I don't care as long as you go on playing those indoor games with me and talking French to your mother. I don't understand it, but I like the sound of it.

ALEXANDER

Dear Walton:

The last time I saw you was on the corner of Vick Park B. We sat under a flowering cherry tree. We talked fast because I had to catch a trolley to Geneva and you had to go away to York Harbor in Maine.

I had a terrible feeling I was never going to see you again. I wanted to tell you lots of things and instead I just picked at blades of grass and laughed at nothing.

My mother told me we are going to move away from Rochester late this summer. If we are gone by the time you get back from Maine, could I come up to visit you later on?

I don't like other boys. Girls scream and tease and won't listen when you or I talk. I hope I can see you before long. I'll send this to York Harbor.

I miss our smoking cubebs behind the Wards' barn and trying to see who could pee the highest on the wall.

There's a nice girl who works at Elizabeth Poole's house and sometimes when she's making up the beds in the front bedrooms I stop my cart and sing songs I learned from my sister. She waves her duster at me and tells me not to be silly.

Then sometimes I ride down to Mr. McFarlin's drugstore on my new bicycle. I have to watch out more and more at corners because there are more automobiles around and they go pretty fast and the drivers don't look both ways when they come to a corner.

Mr. McFarlin still talks with a funny lisp and his voice sounds as if he had something stuck in his throat. Mrs. McFarlin comes out from that room in back once in a while looking like the sheep in *Alice*. They are both very cheerful but I have never heard them laugh.

The store smells good but not as nice as the grocery store up near where you live — Gribbrook's.

I always buy those Regina cubebs at McFarlin's and every month I buy copies of those funny magazines, *Life* and *Judge*.

I hope you're having a good summer.

ALEXANDER

Dear Reverend Goodwin:

I'm writing to ask you why you were sitting on my mother's bed when I came in before supper last night.

You were eating lamb chops and peas from a plate on a tray. My mother was on the other side of the bed under the covers in her nightgown.

Why were you eating those chops sitting on my mother's bed? You wore the same clothes you wear when you give the sermon every Sunday at Saint Paul's. It looked funny to me seeing the family clergyman sitting on the bed of anybody's mother.

And why were you eating your dinner in our house instead of your own house? Your house is right behind our house and wasn't your wife and your son and your daughter waiting for you over there?

If you wanted to eat dinner in our house why didn't you come downstairs and eat it in our dining room?

I don't see why you were sitting on my mother's bed eating chops and peas.

ALEXANDER WILDER

Dear Katherine:

I'm leaving this note with this bunch of flowers which cost me my week's allowance (25¢).

You don't know me very well, but I like you very much. It would be very nice if you liked me back. Last week my mother told me there was no Santa Claus. It makes me sad so I hope you like the flowers.

Anyway, they are pretty and the man in the flower store said they should last at least four days if you put an aspirin tablet in the water.

See you in school and you don't have to thank me unless you want to.

ALEXANDER WILDER

Dear Mrs. Poole:

If your cook doesn't bake me a cake you'll never see Arthur again. I have him in my red cart and he's having a good time. But no one can ever find us so don't start looking.

I want a chocolate cake and your daughter Elizabeth can leave it back of the Wards' barn at five o'clock. Tell her she can wait until dark but I won't pick it up until she's out of sight. Arthur will be home ten minutes after I get the cake.

ALEXANDER WILDER

Dear Miss Milme:

The story I wrote about the man on the horse and the woman waving goodbye was not my story. My sister wrote it for me and when you gave me second prize for it I didn't say anything.

This was a bad thing to do. No one knows about it but you and my sister and me. Do you have to tell the principal of the school? If you do will you tell him that I have an idea for another story about a mouse who makes friends with a cat. Something happens at the end which I won't tell about now. I think you and Mr. Harris will like it very much.

ALEXANDER WILDER

P.S. I'll hand-print it like this: ONCE UPON A TIME.

Dear Mrs. Gumm:

My mother told me to write to you. She doesn't know what happened. Your daughter told you I did something bad.

It wasn't really bad at all. We were playing down in the place where they're digging out a cellar and I told her every person had twenty parts to their body. I told her I had seen nineteen of them but I had never seen the twentieth part. So I asked her to show it to me. That's all that happened except she never showed me her twentieth part.

Do I have to apologize for this?

ALEXANDER WILDER

Dear Mrs. Rogers:

My mother says you called up and said I was bad. She also said I should write you a letter.

Here's what happened. Your two sons and I were sitting in a tent and we got to talking about our things. I asked Bobbie to let me see his and just when he did some grown-up pushed the flap of the tent and I wriggled out underneath.

I don't know what would have happened if I had stayed. Bobbie must have told and now everybody's mad because I ran away.

I'm sorry I ran away but that's all.

ALEXANDER WILDER

Dear Mother:

You all treat me like a fool. Only Helen is nice to me. She washes my hair and dries it in front of the gas log. You and George act as if I were crazy. Last night I said that lambs eat grass and cows eat grass but they both taste different. You laughed and George frowned.

When I kissed Sarah the other day you dragged me out of the kitchen and you said, "We don't kiss those people." I love Sarah better than anyone and you tell me not to kiss her. Helen says it's because she has brown skin. I'm not crazy. I think you're all crazy.

You walked into the bathroom the other day when I was doing Number One and you said, "Be careful of that! Don't touch it too much and don't bang it against anything!"

I don't understand you. You tell me to stop reading and go out and play. I go out and play and I ask you to look at me hop and you're sitting right in your window and you say, "I'm threading a needle."

I say maybe the moon is only ten miles away and you laugh and George frowns.

I say I hear tapping in the cellar and you and George say I'm wrong. And then you find old Joe lying down there tapping with his shovel. He can't get up. He's sick.

I wasn't wrong. And what's so funny about lambs and cows?

And what's so funny about my hand-printing that Grimm fairy tale for the teacher? I thought it was pretty.

And I like to take dough from Sarah and bake it in Helen's little tiny stove. What's the matter with that?

I guess I better go away. If I could get some money I would take Helen and Sarah and go someplace else.

Maybe I'll go alone. I hope you're sorry. Goodbye.

ALEXANDER

Dear Walton:

You love your mother enormously. Well, I'm afraid I don't feel the same way about mine. Every time I use words like "enormously" she tells me I ought to go out and play. "I don't think it's healthy for you to sit in your room all day Sunday" — (not quite, because I have to go to Sunday School *and* church) — "reading those grown-up novels. I don't think the library should let a boy as young as you are take out those two-volume novels! Why don't you read more books like Frank Merriwell and The Rover Boys? It isn't right for a boy as young as you . . ." And on and on and on.

You're the only friend I have. So how can I go out and play? Lee Wood and Al Kelly and all those boys are older, anyhow. And they know I'm no good throwing or catching. And they know I get sick when a fight starts. Sure, I run every time they catch sight of me!

I suppose they think you and I are sissies. I don't care if they do. I want to be left alone. I hate to say it, but my mother doesn't understand. You're lucky, Walton. Your mother acts as if she understands just about everything. My sister understands, but she's busy with her friends and I never see her when I need her.

I sure hope we don't move away from Rochester this winter! I wouldn't be able to see you anymore.

ALEXANDER

Dear Helen:

Why did I get sent to Geneva? It's not even vacation time. And I'm not sick. Is Mother sick again? Are the green shades down in her bedroom in the afternoon?

It's all right over here but I can't make Aunt Hattie hear a thing. There's nothing to do but look at old *Geographics* and smell the boxwood. When I go down to the barn to see the bantam chickens, the Truslow kids hoot and holler at me from the top of their fence. I don't answer them. I pretend I don't hear them.

Yesterday I picked out "Alice Blue Gown" on the piano with one finger. It took a long time before I got it right. Sometimes I put on those old piano rolls like "The Prince of Pilsen" and "Marche Militaire." "Marche Militaire" makes the chandelier jingle and Uncle Hilly doesn't like that. He says the chandelier is very old and valuable.

Sometimes after dinner he and I sit out on the front porch and I try to count all the Dutchman's pipes I can see in the vine and all the time he rumbles on about Mother being all alone now that Father's dead and how I should be very good to her.

How can I be good to her in Geneva when she's in bed in Rochester?

Is that funny sweet smell in her room again? And what's that funny smell in the bathroom? It's not you-know-what, but it smells like tobacco?

She told me before I got on the Geneva trolley that there wasn't any Santa Claus. But I've seen him through the keyhole in the linen room, all dressed up in red. I didn't see his face, but I saw that Christmas red color moving around. And now she says he's just a story. I'm sad about that and I'm not sure I believe her. I did get an answer from him when I left that letter in the empty fireplace, and that Christmas I got all the things he promised in the letter!

Miss Smith keeps giving orders around here and she doesn't even live here. She tells Henry when she wants him to drive her downtown and I don't see why Uncle Hilly lets her do it. She says she's the niece of some poet by the name of Dickinson. I don't believe anyone as dull as Miss Smith could be related to a poet. But maybe the poet's no good.

The next time you come over to Geneva with me don't ask me to do those things you did the last time!

ALEXANDER

Dear Uncle Hilly:

Why didn't I think or dare to write you while you were still alive? Probably because I was afraid of your reaction to a personal, introverted letter from a young nephew or else because I assumed you'd be irritated, downright angry or bewildered by such a document.

I knew you as a short, overweight, somewhat truculent elder whose eyes always telegraphed every cement-heavy funny line by "twinkling." I knew you were president of a bank, a highly respected citizen of Geneva, a Republican (yes, I even knew that at the age of ten!), a public-be-damned autocrat, and probably lonely.

The Mayor of South Main Street, the witty Negro bootblack next to your bank, who knew more about what was happening to the bigwigs uptown than they knew about themselves, knew that Elizabeth Smith had some kind of hold over you. Either she was your mistress or had been; he said that one of your nephews married the second time just soon enough to make the baby seem legitimate.

I knew you as a "Harrumpher," a man who ate steak for breakfast, a man given to a considerable allotment of whiskey and, strangely to me, a great collector of old glass.

I knew your presidency at the bank was inherited from my grandfather and I knew you kept candy in your bank desk drawer and that it was not to please us kiddies but simply to be another outlet for your gluttony.

I stayed in your beautiful inherited Colonial home many times, and even spent the night alone with your corpse. The circumstances which brought about that strange vigil I for the life of me can't recall.

You approved of my having taken up music as a profession only when you assumed that a song which had become a great hit, known even to *you*, had been written by me. I never told you of your mistake. I much preferred you to think I was making money from music. You believed in money. By now you may have had time to consider how easily a composer can be damned by a banker. My song was called "All the King's Horses." The hit was called "The King's Horses." Happy autocratic Paradise to you!

Alexander Wilder

Dear Allen:

I was just now writing to a friend I have known for less than half the years I've known you. We see each other seldom simply because the elements that held us together have themselves separated, virtually vanished.

But you, who have known me since I was being pushed down Westminster Road in a baby carriage or, if not quite that early, at least toddling about, I have seen only once in the past twenty-five years!

Okay, so you live in San Francisco and I live in the East, never anyplace for very long, but I do come to San Francisco every few years. Why don't I call you? You are my friend. We have lived through all kinds of thinnesses and thicknesses together, we've laughed at the same things, we have many happy memories, yet I never call and very seldom write.

This is dreadful!

Perhaps I'm being maudlin to say this, but I feel that I owe a measure of reverence to the memory of watching you, my brother George, and Lee Ward tossing a football around that flowerless front yard of ours and, when the ball got lost in some bushes, hearing you call out "Où est la pill?"

I won't vivisect it to define the small-boy humor of that question, but simply say that after nearly sixty years I remember your calling that out in that raunchy, inanely grinning way kids do.

So doesn't that alone demand my hanging onto my end of the rope?

Or those nutty evenings we spent in your house years later after I came back to Rochester to study at the Eastman School when I'd play some current song badly on the piano and you would astound me by playing what to me at that time seemed incredibly accurate chord changes on the ukulele?

Or the rides down those high-crowned narrow blacktop roads on spring evenings *all the way* to Krebs in Skineatalis!

You and Jane, that beautiful black-haired sister of yours, and me. Even back in those dreamy days you thought I was a nut! All these years later I'm considered eccentric for carrying boxes with bobble birds in them which I set up on the rims of tumblers in hotel rooms — and I even open bottles of soap-bubble liquid and send bubbles floating over the tables and chairs, and out the window.

We drank spiked beer together in speakeasies. I threw up in your father's Cadillac and we spent hours getting the smell out.

Your daft but endearing brother John used to like to pursue me from the living room through the dining room, the kitchen, the pantry, back into the living room as many times as I'd oblige.

When you married I drank with Kitty and you, played foolish games with your daughters, even joined Kitty in her hometown of Augusta, Georgia, and hung around for a week drinking and laughing with her and her sister, waiting for you to show up from Rochester.

I left, I remember, before you got there, too embarrassed to tell anyone I was too nervous to wait any longer, stole out of Kitty's family's house at dawn, took a marvelous straight-as-an-arrow train ride to Yamassee, changed to an Atlantic Coastline train, got off at Savannah, sent Kitty a telegram, and continued on down to West Palm Beach where I'll be damned if you and Kitty didn't show up a week later and she won a large doll in a raffle.

How's that for someone who can't remember the piece of music he wrote last week?

I'm beginning to figure out why I don't stay in touch: the past isn't enough to keep the relationship glued together. All we have in common is memories and our loathing of the current crop of corrupt political leaders, our intolerance of intolerance and the memory of "Où est la pill?"

ALEC

Dear General Saunders:

I am ten years old. I live in a house right in back of that platform where all the troops unload on their way to Camp Mills. The trains keep coming in all day and all night and the troops keep counting off one, two, three, four, over and over again until I get real dizzy and can't sleep.

My school has become military because of the war so I feel I am doing my bit for the war effort. And I can't do it very well if I can't get any sleep.

Do you think it would be possible to ask if the men could count off without barking out the words. I don't mind the marching but the counting is driving me crazy and my dog, Prince, whimpers in his sleep.

ALEXANDER WILDER

P.S. Why are you all fighting?

Dear Mix Up:

When you get back to New York this will be waiting for you.

Just so you won't forget or say to yourself that nothing happened, I want to put it on paper that you did get into Herbie Slawson's bed and you did let him rub his fingers up and down your thing (I hate the word "penis"). And when you began to feel dizzy you told him to stop because you thought you were going to throw up. But it felt very good while he was doing it and you *don't even like Herbie* or his pimples or his eyes that never look at you. So what's happening to you?

Dear Mrs. Chew:

I'm not old enough to call you by your first name but I think of you that way.

I've only met you twice and all I know is that you make me feel safe and happy.

I don't feel safe or happy very often so I am very grateful to you for making me feel good. It's like vacations you read about.

I didn't have to explain anything to you. I didn't have to pretend or keep saying to myself, "Remember, you're only twelve years old and older people think twelve-year-olds act a certain way." I could behave my true way, which isn't twelve years old; it's just being alive and hoping you'll find someone who says to himself "I like him" and doesn't say "I like that twelve-year-old boy."

I don't know how old you are and I don't care. I know you are older than I am and I know you know much more than I do and I know you're married to my cousin and I don't understand that at all. You're not like him one bit. You seem so free and Bev seems so formal and stuffy.

Now I'll act like a grown person's opinion of twelve-year-olds and say you have to forgive me because I'm too young to know what I'm saying.

I certainly do love you. But I don't mean I wish you were my mother or my sister. I don't know. I guess I wish we were acting in a movie together and in the plot I turned out to be eighteen instead of twelve. Anyway, I love you a lot.

ALEXANDER WILDER

Dear Theodora:

My mother wishes me to write a letter to you and your mother about what happened last night.

You or your mother sent me an invitation to come to dinner. To tell the truth I told a lie when I said I had to wear my uniform even during Christmas vacation. I feel very ashamed about this because I don't believe in war or fighting of any kind. But when I wear that uniform it makes me not as scared as I usually am. I hate putting on the puttees but I like the brass buttons.

It was on account of the uniform that I got so excited at the dinner table. When I picked up the candlestick it was to show how they make us do bayonet practice on dummies every day. It was a crazy thing to do because I could have picked up a knife just as well.

If I hadn't waved the candlestick around, your hair wouldn't have caught fire.

I'm very glad I thought of throwing my napkin over your head because you might have been badly burned if I hadn't.

My mother says that your mother is very mad and says it will take months for your hair to grow out on the lefthand side of your head. But she said your face and the skin on your head weren't burned.

I'm very glad about that but I don't see why no one says anything about my putting the fire out. Is it just because I started it?

Anyway, I'm very sorry and all I can say is that if St. Paul's School hadn't gone military on account of the war all this would never have happened. I blame it on the Kaiser and the war profiteers.

So if I find that your father is in the steel business I will refuse to mail this apology.

ALEXANDER WILDER

P.S. He is so I won't.

Dear Walton:

This place is all wrong. I envy you in York Harbor. No counselors, no waiting on table, no one ganging up on you. Or are there bullies in York Harbor like here?

In the leaflet I saw pictures of woods and little coves, peaceful scenes with only a few people in them. I don't know why I thought a summer camp would be like those pictures. I guess I don't think about possibilities. I have emotions and they close up my mind. Mind? I can't learn Latin or mathematics and I can't remember the capital of South Dakota. If you have a mind, at least you should have a memory, shouldn't you? Not me.

This place is horrible. I don't like the counselors, I don't trust them, and as for the boys, I can't stand them! They're all loud and brassy and they shove and jeer and you can imagine how they love me! I don't play games well and I hate yelling and being dared and yet they make you play games here and if you don't yell they look at you as if they were going to wring your neck!

They have no use for me except one and that is to bully me. But I won't fight so they get madder and beat me up even worse. The only time they ever liked me was when I swam under water for a hundred feet. But then they hated me again because another boy swam a hundred and ten feet.

That gun you sent me was used in a play and it didn't shoot the blank in the performance. So they hate me for that! ! Where did you ever get a gun and why did you send it to me? To shoot myself?

ALEXANDER

Mr. Olds:

When those catalogues of your camp were put in every boy's desk at school last year, I saw pretty photographs of woods and brooks, waterfalls and hills, all quiet things.

There was nothing in there about giving new boys nicknames and beating their bottoms afterwards with wet canoe paddles.

There was nothing about having to wash dishes and play games you hated.

There was nothing about not ever being allowed to take walks alone or swim alone or paddle a canoe alone.

There was nothing about scary nighttime games and not getting a meal if you were one minute late.

I hate you, Mr. Olds, and I hate all but one counselor. I think you love to make all that extra money besides your salary teaching gym at school and I think you really like to see small boys punished. I saw your eyes get funny that day you tried to scare me by snapping that whip when you were telling me I was a coward.

But soon you are going to get very tired and very old, Mr. Olds.

ALEXANDER WILDER

Dear Mrs. McDermott:

I'm sure you know my mother, Mrs. Wilder, and I've been with her when you have met in Johnson Street. I know your son Jack but am not a close friend.

You may think it is none of my business to write you this letter. But I have to do it because every time I see you I think about how I feel about you.

I am only twelve years old but I am very reliable and don't talk to the wrong people about things I believe should be kept quiet.

So I promise you I won't tell anyone about this letter.

'I often walk down Johnson Street on my way to the creek where I moor my rowboat. So I pass your house. I often see you out playing the hose on your small lawn. You wave, I guess, because I do. I don't think you remember I'm the son of Mrs. Wilder.

But then I think about what my mother told me about you. I hope you don't mind her doing this. She knows I wouldn't tell anyone. She told me that when your husband died he didn't leave any money. So my mother said you moved down to Bay Head and rented the little house you live in now. She says this all happened many years ago and that your son grew up with the local boys because the summer boys left in early September. She says he "went native."

It's hard to understand this because Bay Head is only seventy miles from New York City. But in another way I see what happened. All the "natives," as we summer boys call the boys who live all year round in Bay Head — well, they don't like us, they think we think we're better than they are.

So maybe your son has gotten to feel the same way. I don't understand this, because you don't act as if you minded living in a small house with a small front yard. You are cheerful and you walk down the street as if everything was hunky-dory.

So my letter really is all about my respect for you and the hope I have that your life here in Bay Head in the winter isn't very lonely. The reason I say this is because I know your best friends are all ladies who only spend the summer here.

I'll bet you read lots of books in the winter and knit sweaters and write letters to your old summer friends.

Do you go to church suppers? Do you get along with the native ladies all right?

I suppose it's lonely when the northeasters blow and when there are no flowers and the trees are bare.

But I hope things aren't too bad. I want to give you my best wishes and I won't even tell my mother about writing this letter.

ALEXANDER WILDER

Dear Laura Perkins:

I have become very religious this summer. My Bible teacher in St. Paul's School was the only person who treated me like a human being the whole two years I was there, and that includes all the students except one, Paul Turner. Reverend Barton laughed a lot but he got serious when he talked about Jesus. So I'm trying to tell my friends what he taught me.

I tell you this because last week I saw you on the beach and you had on a bathing suit which was what Reverend Barton would have called evil. It showed your large chest very clearly.

But I don't want you to think that I walked up and down in front of your house whistling "Oh by Gee by Gosh by Jingo" just to attract your attention.

I was trying to get the courage to come up on your porch and tell you not to wear that bathing suit anymore.

Yesterday, as you know, I rang your bell and when you came to the door I had a very strange sensation. I almost fainted, and then I had a sudden peculiar spasm as if I had been struck by lightning.

I think this must have been a true religious experience like Paul on the road to Damascus when he saw a vision of Jesus.

Now I don't think you are like someone in the Bible, unless it is Jezebel, but I'm sure what happened to me means something very important.

Maybe you are very religious like me and maybe we should discuss religion. Not at your house but down on the beach.

ALEXANDER WILDER

Dear Carroll:

You made me feel very good by telling me you thought I could be a writer. Surely you didn't decide that from reading those "what-if-all-mankind-were-made-of-good-people?" notebooks of mine?!

But I don't know very much — I haven't read very much and I haven't seen very much. What would I write about? You say it doesn't matter at first what you write about as long as you put the words down. Supposing I wrote about that time in the train when the football players stripped me down to my shorts and threw my clothes the length of the train and I had to go to each car begging for a sock, a shoe or a shirt?

Oh, I forgot, you said "write whatever comes into your head." And then you said "after you've written a stack of paper three feet thick, I'll pick up the top sheet and if it reads well, then you'll know you're a writer." Or something like that.

Well, I'll try. But how can I possibly write up in that East Side apartment of my mother's? Do you suppose I could come down to that room you have in that tenement house on Fourth Street and write after school? That is, would you let me have a key? I'd be very careful about locking up when I left. Or is someone else using the room? Please let me know.

Here's an unrhyming poem I just wrote:

> *Men with big egos*
> *Don't find the earth too large*
> *Men with small egos*
> *Have to look at a map*
> *to find their bed*
> *And the hole*
> *Where the mouse hides.*

See you soon, I hope.

ALEXANDER

Dear Myron:

We've never had much chance to talk in school except at recess and telephones are funny: you do a lot of talking but it's more like gabbling. I don't mean you, personally, but I can't stand "*one* does." You can't arrange your thoughts on the phone, at least *I* can't. If you were Jack Bunnell or Steve Rickert or any of those athlete-politicians we sit alongside of in school it would be different. It doesn't really matter how you put your sentences together for them as long as you make sure they know you realize they are the student leaders.

You and I, I guess it's clear, are the barely tolerated ones. We don't join in, we don't play basketball and we don't bring apples to the teachers.

Around my house no one blurts out the truth unless they're angry. So I'm not used to being bluntly frank; I'm afraid I'll offend or turn people off. I only have one close friend so anyone I become fond of I'm likely to treat overcautiously for fear they'll vanish.

But the thing about you, Myron, in case I've never told you, is that you listen and when you do, you sympathize and understand. I don't mean that I want to talk all the time; it's just that being listened to seriously is such a luxury for me I can't help but take advantage of it.

You seem much more resigned to all the evil in life than I am. Is it part of the heritage of being Jewish? Or are you simply more grown-up than I am? I admit I'm very confused. I laugh so much that a lot of people think I'm just a happy-go-lucky lightweight.

The laughter's genuine enough most of the time but some of the time it's just to cover abject fright. My family is probably a perfectly fine one as families go except for one nightmare problem I may tell you about someday. But they all act as if I were a close relative whom they'd never seen before, lately arrived from New

Zealand, whom they are too polite to be impolite to. I feel tolerated rather than accepted.

In a way I'm sorry for them. God knows I'm only fourteen, but they seem unable to see farther than the neighbor's window through which they'd be much too proper to look.

I'm pretty dumb, I guess, in anything that requires real mental gymnastics like math, and I certainly don't understand Shakespeare or philosophy. But I have read a lot of books and I don't mean the Rover Boys (although I've read every one). But intellect, real logical thinking, is something I simply stand in awe of. I guess what I have is something only women are supposed to have, intuition. (By the way I don't know any females who have any except my mother and sometimes she's spooky.)

Anyhow, the real point of all this is that, you'll just have to believe me, I do really suffer from all kinds of fears and confusions. I even got religion last summer and went around with a Bible boring everyone to death. That must mean that I felt like a sinner. But how have I sinned? By letting the bath water run full force so that it made my you-know-what tingle? By not loving my mother enough?

What *am* I saying? I'm babbling. I guess what I'm trying to say is that I want a wonderful world to open up before my eyes, the kind of world you begin to believe in when you've seen a great play or read a great book. But then something terrible happens like all that nightmare stuff at Lawrenceville or being scared by the bully boys or by deciding that you (I) are (am) nothing but a coward and a silly, empty-headed jackass. But, Myron, I respect *you* and *you* don't treat me as if I were an idiot. You laugh at my foolishness but then sometimes you make me believe I've said something original or anyhow, intelligent.

You may think I'm trying to get sympathy I don't deserve when I tell you I've even thought about killing myself. But it's just like running away: I'm too much of a coward to do it. In fact every time I get any kind of courageous idea that might lead me to some kind of peace of mind and real joy, I do nothing because I'm really a disgustingly timid person.

Would you mind very much if I asked you to write me (for God's sake don't tell me to my face!) what you really think of me? I won't mind how terrible it is as long as there's even one nice trait you admire about me.

ALEXANDER

Dear Myron:

It was very kind of you to write such nice things about me. But you make me out to be something much more than I really am.

I've never admitted this before or even thought about it, but when I started growing taller than I expected to be I used my tallness to take the place of muscles. I've always been scared of fights and even being knocked down a lot doesn't make me want to fight back.

I asked for an oak bar to hang up in my bedroom doorway and I've been chinning myself every day for two years, but I don't notice any bulging biceps. I even bought an Earle E. Liederman contraption of rubber straps you attach to handles and pull them out as far as you can. But nothing happens to those muscles in back of the biceps.

Being tall helps a little. Besides this my sister says I have big expressive eyes and soft hair, so I keep acting as if I were being modest about being handsome. The only trouble about this is that my idea of handsome isn't what I see in the mirror.

So you see I've had to think of even another trick to meet people without acting frightened. And I'm sure you realize what it is although you're much too polite to say so.

I make remarks that people aren't supposed to. What I do is admit weaknesses and stupidities and it makes people embarrassed at first but then, when they see that I think my weaknesses or stupidities are funny, then they laugh. As a result I feel less scared.

When I read that back it sounds as if everything I do is calculated. Well, that's not true because most of the time I get so nervous I just babble and interrupt and mess everything up.

What I'm trying to tell you is that your compliments about my "charm," as you call it, really isn't charm. It's more like dodging. Of course, when I'm with you and a few others who aren't muscle-flexers, I relax and behave, I hope, like a sane person.

I only wish I knew what was going to happen next. In a couple of years I'll be expected to go to college and I'm positive nothing outside of force will make me go. I have great respect for learning, and literature — not science — but even knowing that there are great teachers in lots of colleges doesn't make me want to go to any of them. I'm sick of being around most people my own age. I can't find any common ground with them.

As for girls, sometimes they make me feel funny and I want to rub around them. The whole boy-girl business is pretty strange to me. I guess I'm curious about their bodies and all that but really, Myron, I only think about them for short periods of time.

There's a Pianola in my uncle's house in Geneva and in one of the downstairs closets there are stacks of old piano rolls. All the labels have titles of pieces I never heard of and only a few are familiar to me, composers like Chopin.

When the roll gets going, a red line starts on the right-hand side of the roll. There's a metal arrow on the Pianola which is supposed to follow the red line. You guide it with a lever. Its purpose is to speed up and slow down the music. I dragged all the rolls out of the closet, blew the dust off them and ran them on the Pianola. You have to pump and when the red line veers to the left it not only slows up the music but makes you have to pump harder. I can't figure out why. Sometimes I would get exasperated and ignore the red line. But then the music would sound wrong so I'd go back to the red line.

The reason I mention all this is that this music is like nothing I've ever heard before. Some of it's very flossy, but some of it's strong and emotional. When I'm not using the metal arrow, I put my fingers on the keyboard (which depress when those notes sound) and pretend I'm playing the piece. I've only known popular music so it's been an unusual experience. There's something so exciting about it that I wonder if I could get mixed up in the world of music. The best thing about it would be my getting out of going to college by saying I had to study music.

Of course the only trouble with that is that my mother would say, "Well, I think it's very peculiar for any member of our family to want to study music. But if you really want to, then you'll have to go to a music school."

But I don't want to go to any school of any kind. In fact, I've had nightmares about algebra and French this very week.

Do writers of words have to go to college, too? Can't they just write? I'm sure O. Henry and Shakespeare and Keats and Shelley never had to study writing before they wrote.

You see, Myron, my problem is that I don't know how strong my desire to be a creator really is because it seems more like a way out of becoming a banker than anything truly creative.

I won't bore you with any more "I, I, I's." They must drive you crazy.

See you on Monday where we can be fulfilled by the glory of the Gallic Wars.

ALEXANDER

Dear Myron:

I was so eager to get to Europe that I took advantage of a situation which occurred in rocking chairs on the porch of the summer hotel my family goes to. My mother happened to be rocking next to Mrs. Wilkinson whose husband owns a wholesale grocery business in Newark. The entire Wilkinson family is (are?) slobs. But they *did* stay at the Bluffs, thereby making them acceptable to my mother, and they *were* going to Europe the following summer.

I knew it was a mistake but I also knew it was the only way I'd get there at the age of sixteen!

Well, I'm in London and already working out a plan to stay in England when they go to France and to meet them there later. Fortunately they are too dumb to realize that if they are supposed to be responsible for me, they shouldn't risk letting me get lost on the Scottish moors.

I don't remember if you told me you had been to Europe or not. But it's a revelation to me. Everyone is so much more polite and attractive. Maybe they aren't really, but they certainly seem to me much more open and friendly, people in stores, restaurants, small towns, everywhere.

They make me feel as if I were a dignified, civilized young man. And it's not because I have a lot of American Express checks; they're simply nicer people than most of those I've met in the Eastern United States.

And books! Why, they're everywhere! I'm sending home great bundles of them. There's a Tauchnitz paper cover edition, very cheap, of every great book I've ever heard of.

And the countryside is enough to make you cry. In fact I did cry when I snuck a trip to Devonshire. I couldn't believe the beauty of it, the hedgerows, the gardens, the houses, the old, old, old churches! Myron, what are we all doing in that monstrous marketplace of New York? They keep saying how exciting the skyline of New York is and how beautiful Fifth Avenue is! You can have it. I prefer the winding streets of London, the tradition, the endless living history of it, the gentle people, the cared-for land and the cleanliness.

As you can see, I'm spinning like a top. And it's partly because for the first time I've started to think of myself as something more than a frightened kid. I even find myself thinking seriously about being a writer, even though I haven't the faintest notion what I'd write about.

I've got to meet these terrible Wilkinsons in Paris and I'll bet that everything I've ever dreamed about that city is cheapened and distorted just because of their presence. My French is too sketchy for me to escape from them but maybe they'll depress me so much I'll risk a few early-morning walks or a few trips to places like Chartres. I know what they'll want: to take charabanc trips to the battlefields and visit champagne cellars so they can get free drinks.

Wow! In spite of them I have a marvelous feeling that I'm growing up and that if I am, I may wind up with a little self-respect!

See you in about a month! I hope you're having a pleasant summer.

ALEXANDER

Dear Carroll:

I managed to persuade my mother to let me come to Italy with my Aunt Clara and Uncle Michael. We had a beautiful trip there with no bad weather, midmorning soup, lots of laughter and a lovely daylight passage through the Azores.

Italy is absolute magic. I got up early when we were due to land at Naples and I'll never forget it. In spite of your suggestion that I try to become a writer, I realize that I don't really know how to, for if I did I could convey to you the extraordinarily mystical experience of a slow-moving ship slipping past unreal islands with Vesuvius slowly emerging in the early light, the blues and greens of the water, the tenderness of the sky and the breathless anticipation of a true miracle about to occur where miracles should occur.

The old hotel we went to in a horse-drawn carriage, the heartbreaking Neapolitan tune drifting in the window from a hurdygurdy down in one of those streets festooned with flower stalls, the orange-blossom honey from Sorrento!

No wonder these people sing all the time and scream and grin and burst with life! The very air itself demands that life be a miracle and that you damned well better live it!

ALEXANDER

Dear Carroll:

How am I going to be a writer of words when everything in this country is music? I know that's not true when I come back from a day moving in and out of the glorious churches of Florence, seeing the breathtaking sculpture and painting, but something keeps shouting at me to look deeper and deeper into music.

I've heard no concerts, heard no music but that of countless people singing in the streets. Yet I've already started buying stacks of music, in fact I've even rented a piano. I don't know beans about music, don't play worth a damn nor read well, but ever since you took me to that concert at Carnegie Hall and I heard *L'Après-Midi d'un Faune* I've got the bug.

I've even written a piece of music that's not just a tune. I don't think it's good, but it is *something* which I wrote. And it's the *first one!*

I don't want to leave this country! I've been studying Italian and the more I can communicate with Italians the more I feel really, for the first time, at *home!*

I've even met a girl here at this *pensione* who treats me with respect and she listens to me gravely and as if I were grown-up. She must be in her early twenties and I'm sure she's aware that I'm very naive and uncivilized at least in terms of her civilized background. Yet she makes me feel like a grown man. Her name, of course, is almost enough to make me love her. It's Luciana Aloisi. How lovely it sounds when pronounced by an Italian.

As you know, I was writing words every day for nearly a year in that room you had down on Fourth Street. And as you know, I wrote a stack almost three feet high of manuscript. Yet in spite of all that concentration and diligence, I find myself veering off into a world of sound.

I know what you'll say: "Oh, you have all the time in the world ahead of you! Don't worry!" Yet I *do!* I know I'm very young but I feel as if I must hurry! It's not that I'm back in my suicide state but I have, not so much a presentiment of doom as much as the sense that I must start building my own world as quickly as possible.

I know no matter how it turns out, it will all be a dream, an illusion. But, Carroll, dreams can build sturdy walls that keep the goblins out and I must start building them!

We're going to Venice and I don't know if I'll be able to stand it, the absolute magic of it, sewer smells to the contrary, plus no longer being able to know I'll see Luciana every day.

I'll write you from there if I'm not in such a fit of awe and wonderment that I can't sit still long enough to put words to paper.

ALEXANDER

Dear Carroll:

I can't possibly describe Italy to my mother, and its storybook magic. She lives in a world of little imagination, conventional American concepts, little-girl dreams which never flew farther than a Newport ball.

So how can I tell her about the shadows of the water dappling the ceiling of my rooms in Venice, on the Zatterie where the wood boats anchor and the boat-dogs' barking wakes me at dawn?

How can I tell her of the romanticism of having my own piano in my room there, making me feel like a true continental adult composer — when I've only written little Chaminade Scarf Dances?

How can I clarify the sensation of being young in an ancient land, with the callow dreams of becoming a part of the world of creation, moving about a country where every object and every view is venerable and a reflection of the eyes of master painters and sculptors, where great music flows as casually as mountain water?

How can I tell her of the sound of steam engines pulling up the long hill out of Firenze in the night while I'm lying in a feather bed watching the flickering light from the fragrant fire of pinecones in the fireplace across the room?

How can I tell her of my walk from Numero Otto Via Tuorbuoni through the ancient streets to my language lessons at Berlitz, stopping to eat fresh, hot brioches at roadside bakeries and sitting in a vast plaza after the lesson at a street café drinking chicory coffee mixed half-and-half with warm milk?

How could I tell her of slipping notes under the bedroom door of that girl who treats me with such tender affection, whose name sends me soaring, Luciana Aloisi?

How could I explain that there is no place for me in a world of ugliness, facts and figures, condescension toward the artist and hatred of the ungregarious and the noncompetitor?

I, with my few little awkward pieces of music, I am called in Italy and with solemn respect, a *compositore*.

How on earth can I ever persuade her to let me come back here to live? She'll be sweet and half-listening and even a little patronizing. But she'll never let me have that money my father left me!

Oh, dear!

To think I might have never known this beautiful land so filled with childlike love and *simpatia*, so fair to look upon!

That day I wandered down the narrow, dirt, walled roads of Sorrento sniffing the oh so sweet orange blossoms wafting over the walls from the ancient groves, the two-wheeled donkey carts, the earth-brown faces of the smiling countrymen!

The long walk up through the vineyards of Capri, led by a beautiful almond-eyed little boy who told me to scramble over the fence set up around a tiled yard of Tiberius's castle! I, too stupid to realize I was disturbing and stealing tiles laid down two thousand years ago, did as his generous vandal heart suggested and have now in my suitcase no less than twenty of those tiles! I'm ashamed of myself!

Those walks in Napoli, the sounds of the city, the very special sounds of the barrel organs playing Verdi tunes, the streets of endless steps and seeming miles of fresh flowers for sale.

The blue nuns striding through the fountain-filled parks of Rome, the nightingales in the garden behind my hotel room, getting lost wandering through Firenze, Siena, Padua, and finding walled gardens down strange narrow walks over humped bridges in Venice.

How can I explain the pigeons in the Piazza San Marco and the string trio playing "Valencia" as I drank my first glass of Orvieto?

The hill towns, oh, those adorable clumped-up, red-tiled hill towns at the top of those precipitous winding roads, the laughter, the singing, the respectful bows as I, seventeen years old, am introduced as *il compositore!*

No, I'm afraid it's back to the gas stations and the sounds of business as usual, the droning talk of who she was before she married so-and-so, the flowerless yard, the bookless shelves, the bullying boys.

But I'll tell you one thing: I shall continue to be a composer and I shall make myself an inner world that's as much like that outer Italian world as I can make it.

ALEXANDER

Dear Mother:

I have already, as you must have heard, broken away from Clara and Michael and Vernam. I suppose I must come back to America to explain my present rude refusal to leave Italy. It has made Clara very upset and as you know, Michael is already a neurotic wreck.

Italy has had such an extraordinary effect on me that I want to come back here to live. I have learned the language, I have met an older girl whose name is Luciana Aloisi. She's not pretty particularly, but she likes me and is kinder to me than any girl has ever been. It isn't that I wish to marry her; I couldn't, as she is already engaged to a very handsome Italian boy her age. Everything about Italian people, their respect for art, their landscape, the language itself all make me feel that Italy is my real home.

I know you will assume that I'm just having growing pains, that I couldn't possibly have a clear notion of what I want to make of my life at the age of seventeen. Yet, strangely, I do know.

But I realize I must come back in order to make it clear to you.

I'm very sorry to have caused Clara whatever consternation I have caused. I love her very deeply and wouldn't consciously do anything to hurt her.

I'll be back on the *Bremen*, which docks in New York on the 14th.

I'm sorry to have caused all these cables and confusion.

ALEXANDER

Dear Carroll:

You have been very patient with my weathervane shiftings. After all your kind encouragement to write words I veered about and started pointing the arrow toward music. Of course you were somewhat forewarned by those crummy tunes I wrote and by that dreadful "tone poem" I played for you and Lavinia. (I'll never forget the sound of her giggling while I was struggling through the damned piece! I didn't know she was laughing at something else.)

When you gave me that Kipling poem to set to music, I was very much honored that you thought I could do it. Frankly the whole experience was one long drip of perspiration! But I did finish it for some kind of chorus and some kind of orchestra. Parenthetically let me say I can't understand my stubbornness and stupidity in deciding to compose music with no training whatsoever outside of a few piano lessons and listening to a few orchestra pieces. Why on earth do I so resist study?

Or, I should say, why *did* I?

That's the point of this letter.

As you know only too well, I've had a continuous problem trying to clarify my maverick, unconventional character to my very conventional, conservative mother. When I failed my entrance exams for college, it was as catastrophic as contracting a venereal disease. And now that I've moved to Rochester, I've had to save her face by having a reason other than not being able to tolerate home life. As you know, when I asked for the money my father left me, my mother acted as if I had rejected her totally. I'm sure she was sitting on the inheritance only because she is aware of my perhaps impractical generosity. (It's very possible that I'm not really generous at all but simply wish people to like me. Am I just trying to buy affection? Christ, I hope I'm not that callow!)

Anyhow, now that I have my own money I can move about as I please and though Rochester has few fond memories, there is one family I grew up across the street from with whom I've established a very warm relationship.

One minute's walk from my hotel is the Eastman School of Music. And so recently, after cudgeling my brains to find an adequate reason for staying on in Rochester and after looking over that Kipling cantata, I went to the school and asked if I could consult with a teacher, or I guess I should have said "professor."

After a very muddled and embarrassing attempt to explain what I needed, which, put simply, was compositional advice, I went to a fourth-floor studio and met a marvelous, twinkling man by the name of Inch. He teaches theory (I haven't yet figured out exactly what theory is) and counterpoint.

He's rather a timid man and in my own nervousness I roared and ranted and carried on like a demented clown. So the first fifteen minutes were touch-and-go. The poor man couldn't understand why I was there. Why didn't I go through proper procedure and apply in the approved way to become a student of the school? What on earth could he do for me when I was (he didn't say so) a musical ignoramus?

So then I showed him my Kipling cantata and oh, was I sorry for Mr. Inch! For I could see he was appalled by my idiotic notes and much too timid and too polite to say so. So I helped him by admitting my ignorance, but also made it as clear as I could that I wanted to learn.

Then it turned out that he had never taught composition. (Why had I been sent to him?) But he suggested that if I liked he would be happy to teach me beginner's counterpoint in private lessons. Then he suggested I see a Mr. Royce who *did* teach composition.

I asked him why I needed to study counterpoint as well as composition. And he made such an impassioned speech about the glory of what he called "linear writing," the glory of the baroque composers whose work was practically entirely counterpoint, that I decided I had to study it with him.

It goes without saying that the Kipling cantata went immediately into the trash basket. It was simply a hopeless series of meaningless notes.

But the whole point of this endless letter is that I would never have arrived at this sensible state of affairs if you hadn't persuaded me to try my hand at something of a larger canvas than songs or shapeless "tone poems."

So now I'm not only studying counterpoint with Mr. Inch but composition with Mr. Royce. God, I'm dumb! What I don't know! It's been a shocking revelation but for some stubborn reason or other I'm not going to quit. And it isn't simply because if I were to do so I would no longer have an excuse for living in Rochester.

I'll write you soon about the strange world of musicians I'm beginning to become acquainted with as I sidle down the corridors of the Eastman School. A world I never knew existed! And, I'm beginning to see, a beautiful one! No banks, no dull talk, no keeping everything you say within the limits of propriety and prissiness. No, it's the wild, free, searching, roaring world of young people who know what they want, know what they have to sacrifice to get it, do all kinds of menial work to get the money to go on with it, and Carroll, they really laugh! And they curse and pound the table and argue and my God, how they love music!

ALEXANDER

Dear Mr. Inch:

You have been very patient with my slowness in absorbing the elements of the flow and balance of independence and interdependence in counterpoint.

You may be certain that I am possessed by counterpoint and angry at myself for discovering it at such a late date. Your teaching methods are marvelously revelatory and, as I said, patient. If I am slow in coming to grips with it, it is because I came to you last fall a true musical ignoramus.

I don't wish to embarrass you by speaking to you what follows.

So I'll write it. I have the impression that you are puzzled by a boy (?) man(?) nineteen years old starting out in music by studying counterpoint as a private student. I can imagine your asking yourself, "What is this young man up to? Why isn't he enrolled in the school, taking the regular courses? Why just counterpoint?"

Well, I can answer that. I didn't enroll because I'm afraid of groups of people and can't concentrate among them. As far as counterpoint is concerned, little as I know about it, I'm convinced that it is the bones of music. Harmony and rhythm are fascinating but to me they represent flesh as opposed to bone. And without the strength of interdependent lines, the musical building may collapse. Such a statement from a beginner may sound sententious but I want you to be certain that it is no casual impulse that brought me to study with you. And though I hear less and less counterpoint in contemporary music, I wish always to keep it an integral part of any music I write (if, God willing, I ever learn to compose!).

Undoubtedly I'll be sorry not to have taken ear training and theory but at least I am trying to comprehend the nature of composition from Mr. Royce (also privately).

Confidentially, my principal problem with him is his obsession with logic. Everything must be foursquare. I certainly am all for order and discipline and control but Mr. Royce has me in almost a musical straitjacket. He too, I think, is puzzled as to why I'm there and why I want private lessons. He is, I've learned, the son of Harvard's famous logician, Josiah Royce. It shows.

The other day he showed me his notebook (not for notes but for words) in which he stated precisely what he was going to compose in his new piece, "Far Ocean." Along about measure forty, after explaining in detail everything he would write up to that point, he wrote "allow thirty measures for inspiration."

Well, really, Mr. Inch, how can you determine the precise point where you're going to be inspired??

In any event, I'm writing what he tells me to as best I can, none of which, I'm afraid, is better than kindergarten stuff. But anything is better than nothing. I trust my counterpoint exercises are better than what I'm doing for him, which by the way is without counterpoint. I don't know if I've mentioned I was also studying with you, but Mr. Royce has up till now said nothing about counterpoint. He seems almost hysterically enthusiastic about Beethoven, whose piano sonatas he has persuaded me to examine. Obviously I can play only the slow movements and not even the whole of any one of them.

I like these slow movements, and though I can see that Beethoven had an orderly mind, I'm not nearly so enthusiastic about his music as Mr. Royce would like me to be.

Forgive the sacrilege (since they employ little or no counterpoint) but I admit to great affection for Debussy and Ravel — particularly the Debussy string quartet, Ravel's *Daphnis and Chloé*, and what I've heard on records of Debussy's *Pelléas and Mélisande.*

But please don't think that means I'm unconcerned with counterpoint, for I believe Johann Sebastian Bach to be the greatest genius of them all!

ALEXANDER WILDER

Dear Mr. Royce:

I know you must be in a constant state of irritation trying to pummel composition into my head.

I realize I'm going at it backward, but as I think is apparent, I'm on fire. I should be taking conventional courses, conventionally, in a classroom instead of studying privately simply because I can afford to.

I only know that there is a very violent hunger in me to create, and every piece I hear that I like makes me more eager than ever, even though I realize I'll never come close to the creations of the composers I admire the most.

I know I should be more excited about Beethoven. I know he's a master and yet there are others who seem to reach inside and wrench my gut. Bach and Ravel and Moussorsky — oh, I don't know nearly enough about music to say anything. Nor have I *heard* enough. There are so many composers with whose music I should be familiar. I should spend all my spare time listening to records. Yet I admit I'm afraid to, afraid that if I hear too much great music I'll give up practically before I've started.

I beg your patience. I truly do wish to learn how to solve the awesome mystery of creating something out of nothing. I can think of nothing nobler or more rewarding than being able to compose worthy music.

ALEXANDER WILDER

Dear Carroll:

I don't know if I'll ever be a composer but I certainly have learned an enormous lesson about people.

If I could have peered through a window at these young men and women milling about the main hall of the music school, I would probably never have dared open the door. When I actually did walk down that hall the first half-dozen times I was scared silly. Some would stare at me, even gape, some would call out "Hello," some would even turn around after they had walked past me. I think if I weren't tall I'd have fled.

One day a boy with carrot-red hair came roaring up to me, told a terrible joke, and burst into hysterical laughter. I suddenly stopped being scared and bellowed along with him. It broke thicker ice than anyone but you could believe.

He told me he was a French horn player and I told him I was trying to learn something about composition. When I told him I was studying privately he asked me straight out where I got "that kind of money." I was embarrassed when I told him I had inherited the money because I realized that he was from a very poor family.

Since I met him I've met others through him. And they're all poor. Not only poor but tough. I could sense that they had grown up in the street and that fighting was as commonplace to them as sleeping.

But they all seemed to like me; maybe as they might have liked a very unusual animal in a zoo, but at least none of them has been hostile. And the reason, I'm positive, is the common bond of music.

If nothing else comes of all this at least I've found out that I don't have to assume that practically every young male person is my natural enemy. I honestly believe that if I hadn't come to this school, I would have retreated farther and farther into my shell and have wound up even more peculiar than I already am.

On the other side of the coin (should I say the "tail" side?) the girls here are very direct, outspoken, some of them very pretty, and I have the impression that they are far from inhibited. They keep eyeing me as if I were some kind of freak and a few of them have walked right up and asked me a lot of questions, some embarrassing, some just plain silly, but none of them without suggestiveness, if I may use a frumpy word.

I'm polite to them and get along well with a few but I'm petrified of any involvement. Frankly the whole sexual world is a mystery to me and I limit myself to you know what.

So thank you again for the Kipling cantata!

I've reached the point now where I can write a little counterpoint. (I even tried to write a fugue based on the second theme of Gershwin's "Rhapsody In Blue." It was a bust!) I also have written some short piano pieces for Mr. Royce and I've found that the poems of James Stephens make great songs, not that my settings are so great, but it's marvelously exciting to set them, partly because the form is created for me by the poems themselves. I even set *Annabel Lee*, by Poe. It gets weaker as it gets into the later verses but there's something rather touching about the first verses, that is, in the music.

I've met more people in the school and have begun to write short pieces for flute and for cello. The wildest notion yet is to orchestrate a group of songs. For full symphony! I must be out of my mind, as I've studied no orchestration and done no more than read Cecil Forsythe's book on the subject. He has a footnote that says something like "Remember, gentlemen, the orchestra has no sustaining pedal." That hits home, as my ear isn't good enough to compose away from the piano and you can easily be fooled by piano sounds if that pedal is depressed. For the sounds you have just played may linger but they won't linger if an instrument in the orchestra stops playing them.

It's a glorious dreamworld and I'm finally sure it's the only one for me. Even my mother, I think, realizes this and is resigned to the embarrassment of having to tell her friends that she has a son who is a *MUSICIAN!* I'd be better off as a professional baseball player!

I still write pop tunes and struggle with lyrics. A few of the students here, and only a few, like that side of music. Most of them act as if it's beneath them. Naturally my model as a pop singer is Ethel Waters. So I write everything with her in mind. God knows I'll never meet her. But it's fun. Also, I've been listening to a fellow who's part of the Rhythm Boys. His name is Bing Crosby and I find him wonderful. So I write the male songs for him. He's supposed to go out on his own soon. I think he is to be a soloist on the Cremo Cigar radio show.

When I'm in New York next time I'd like to play you some of the tunes. I can't demonstrate the "art" songs as I can't play the piano parts or sing the voice lines.

ALEXANDER

Dear Sam:

Until I met you I had known only two boys of my age of whom I hadn't been scared. You were the first student in the Eastman School who ever spoke to me. I've never asked you why you did and you probably don't remember. My hunch is that I behaved so oddly or at least so unlike the rest of the students that your curiosity impelled you to find out who that strange creature was.

It was a grand impulse.

For from that day on I became less afraid of boys my age. You cracked the ice, and as a result I began to understand a great deal more than I ever had before about the world and the people in it. I had never known about poverty, freedom, gaiety, wild enthusiasm and trust.

We don't see each other much these years and it saddens me, but strangely, not as it might if it were due to estrangement or disagreement.

You are one of the very few truly steadfast, stalwart friends of my life. Your loyalty, patience, devotion, are as rare as that of our beautiful friend, Louis Ouzer.

You truly opened up the world for me, brought me new and invaluable perspective and faith. So just because we're not constantly in touch, you know as well as I that my love goes on and on.

ALEC

Dear Dr. Watson:

My Aunt Clara used to tell me about knowing your mother and father. I told her how I read the *Dial* magazine every month. I also told her that although some of the articles were beyond my comprehension, still I knew the magazine was the most distinguished magazine in America.

So she must have known I had immense respect for you, as the magazine is yours, and she told me you wrote those very erudite articles which are signed W. C. Blum.

But I never came right out with it and asked if she would introduce me to you.

So you can imagine my stupefaction when Remy Wood came up to me in the Eastman School and asked me if I'd like to be in a movie that YOU were making!

I couldn't believe it. I told him so, but he, in his genial and ponderous and snickering fashion, insisted that I had the perfect look of a sex-crazed butler.

It took a lot of palaver to make me believe him. Naturally I had to explain that I knew nothing about acting. He told me you would give me a screen test and that the part wouldn't require a great deal of acting.

When I met you I nearly fainted. But you were so relaxed and you laughed at my ghastly puns. Before I knew it I stopped thinking of you as a full-time god.

I was trying so hard to impress you that I used words I had only read and one was a pip. I said that a situation was absurd and "farcial." To which you replied solemnly, "Like a fart?"

Then I tried to walk pompously about as I imagined a self-important butler would, and after the film had been developed you told me I would be all right for the part but that you had never seen a butler with a mustache.

Well, Dr. Watson, I don't know if you ever got a hint of what the loss of that silly spatter of hair meant to me. I had grown it because the only adult friend I ever had wore one. I even put Vaseline on my lip at night to make it grow.

And when that really dreadful little French barber down at the Sagamore shaved it off, I felt stark naked. Worse than that, I was certain I had the longest upper lip in the world.

But that's what you wanted and by shaving it off I knew I'd have a legitimate excuse to see you sometime every single day.

ALEXANDER WILDER

Dear Victor:

I can never redeem myself for my long years of silence, for my failure to live up to my (somewhat amorphous) responsibility as your daughter's godfather, for all the trips I promised to make to Vermont and never did.

You were very kind to me in my callow youth. You and Carroll Dunn listened without even a blink of amusement to my outlandish ideas and asinine attempts at poetry. I owe you a great deal and all I really ever did was help you minimally to get to China to interview Sun Yat-sen. You stopped off in Rochester on your way to San Francisco and the Orient way back when I was at the Eastman School.

God, what a self-centered idiot I was! There you were, miraculously making your way through China to visit a famous man who could see all that lay ahead for his country! You even came back with the Tanaka Memorial, that master plan of Japan to annex Manchuria!

And no one would listen to you! No paper would publish you! Even I never read those endless letters you sent me from China, not only because I was too filled with the raw juices of growing up, but because I wouldn't take the time out to decipher your I must say very difficult handwriting.

Christ, but the young are such fools! Somehow I inherited a metal box filled with letters written by my great-grandmother in New Orleans to her relatives in the North long before the Civil War. Did I bother to read them? No! Did I keep them? No! I gave them to that dear superintendent of service at the Algonquin (why? why? why?) to see if he could get some money for them. From whom? Why turn them over to him? Why didn't I read your letters? Why didn't I visit you? Why not read your books?

And I can't blame youth for half of it, for most of my sins of omission have occurred way into middle age!

I can and I do wish you well, Victor. I don't think it would help any if I were to try to rebuild the bridges this late. The roads lead nowhere anymore. We'd sit there muttering about the past, talking mostly not to each other, but to ghosts.

ALEXANDER WILDER

Dear Evelyn:

When I met you yesterday in the Eastman School lobby and you laughingly told me you thought I was in need of a little release, I didn't say anything, out of sheer shock, but I assumed you meant sexual release.

You said flat out that you were coming up to my boardinghouse that night to administer to my needs. Naturally I assumed you were joking.

So I was considerably shocked when I arrived back from that speakeasy over the top of Jesus Lighthouse, to find a note from the landlady saying a young girl had sat for about an hour waiting for me.

I honestly thank you. I can scarcely believe you did it, but since you did, I'm very impressed. I suppose it's a high compliment to be called upon by as pretty and sexy a looking girl as yourself.

But I'm writing this to say that when we meet in the school, as we inevitably shall, please don't assume that I'm ungrateful or being snotty if I don't thank you and also if I make no attempt to further this great opportunity to learn more about sex and, not incidentally, to get that great release.

I'm not a homosexual. I wish to make that clear. So how do I clarify my rejection of so alluring a prize?

All I can say is that I'm not ready yet, indeed I don't know if I ever will be. My personal life is a solitary one and my most intimate secrets are transmuted into poetry and music.

I feel insecure sharing intimacy with another unless that intimacy is limited to words. The total revelation of self that results from sexual fulfillment is simply too far out of my protected area for me. I'm a coward, I'm terribly vulnerable, and I think I'd go to pieces if I were to stand (or lie) revealed totally in another person's presence.

But that is not to say that I'm ungrateful for what was obviously a most generous, healthy, affectionate gesture.

ALEXANDER WILDER

Dear Mr. Smith:

I gather from your remarks last night in Seidel's speakeasy that you found the somewhat hysterical, semi-drunken behavior of Frank Baker and myself to have been faggoty.

Well, Mr. Smith, neither Frank Baker nor I are faggots. We're simply a couple of guys who love music (we go to the Eastman School) and we love to drink and to laugh. If we offended you, I, for one, am very sorry. I've heard marvelous stories about how you can hold a batch of tickets up to your ear and riffle them at top speed, stopping at whatever number someone has suggested. That fascinates me.

But more than that I've found out that you used to manage a burlesque house that my father, a banker, inherited as the result of a bad loan, and my mother has told me of the marvelous job you did managing it.

So I hope somehow we can mend whatever was broken last night; in fact, the next time I see you there I'll ask you to have a drink and I hope you'll accept it.

ALEXANDER WILDER

Dear Mr. Royce:

I'm writing this to let you know that I am humbly grateful to you for trying to show me how to use dexterously the tools of musical composition.

I can't be blamed for misrepresenting myself. I'm certain I made it clear when I came to you to ask if you would consider teaching me privately that I was a total musical ignoramus. I also told you that Herbert Inch was trying to teach me the rudiments of counterpoint, also privately. You were even kind enough to give me some piano lessons, since the piano teacher who had been recommended to me behaved like such a bloodless dud that I could learn nothing from him.

I realize now that you must have revered very highly your famous father, the Harvard Logician. For your method of conveying the basic elements of composition to me was so logical that I felt absolutely no freedom or air space in which to try to stretch my creative wings.

Very probably you were right to keep me on such a tight rein.

But, having only yesterday looked over the notebooks containing the puling efforts at composition I managed to get on paper while studying with you, I find only logic and damned little creation.

Please believe me when I insist that I am obsessed with order, self-discipline and clarity in any creative effort. I am revolted by anarchy or license in any form (or should I say "nonform"?).

But when logic hamstrings the joy, the ebullience, the wing-stretching, then I'm unable to function creatively.

May I also make it clear that I have very little confidence in myself and am by no means sure that I have what it takes to become a composer. A few years ago I wanted to be a writer of words and stopped trying when I realized that besides knowing how to write, a writer has to have something to say.

Perhaps I have nothing to say musically or if I do, it is all so derivative and imitative as to be as shallow as a housewife's attempt to write a Shakespeare sonnet.

All I know is that in spite of the trash I turned out for you, I still want to write music. God knows you tried and I'm very grateful for your patience and affection.

If I go on, as I expect to, studying counterpoint with Mr. Inch, that won't move me any closer to composition but at least it will make me feel like a sculptor who has learned the muscles and skeletal structure of the human body.

I have a hunch that I'll go on pretty much on my own, taking forever to learn orchestration by listening instead of studying, and stumbling around like someone in a dark room looking for the light switch in my efforts to find *my* way to compose.

The fear instilled in me during my childhood of people my own age makes it impossible for me to study in a classroom with other students. I'm not arrogant, simply scared.

Who know? I may wind up a rose hybridizer, or an authority on raccoons.

I truly do thank you and none of it's your fault or, I hope, mine.

ALEXANDER WILDER

Dear Mrs. Harlan:

I ran into an old Eastman School student I hadn't seen in thirty years, Sy Karasick. He, in case you don't remember, was a trombone player, likable and intense.

We performed the customary formal dance of what happened to whom, in the midst of which he mentioned that you were married for the third time and lived in Lima, Ohio (where, unromantically or romantically according to your love of railroads, steam locomotives were once manufactured).

I wrote a song for you once called "Will I Be Upset" in which you sent your husband off to business as in a child's game. The illusion of your smallness, as you may remember, was created by means of very large chairs and tables.

You were a darling girl. A few days after the last performance (how many were there? three? two? surely more than one!) I took you to the toy department of a department store and bought you a hoop which you blithely and sweetly rolled down East Avenue. I thought you a darling child, God knows a virgin! I wouldn't have dreamed of making a vulgar remark in your presence. In your little-girl clothes on stage you were cute as a button and, I have to admit, very desirable, as sometimes a precocious little girl can be. But my slight lust I quickly dampened because it seemed almost sacrilegious.

And then I found out that for four years you'd been passing it out like penny candy. Now, in your old age, lovely body gone, lovely face long since destroyed by time, the brassy cynicism induced by three marriages conditioning your spirit, you may recall this small episode in a long life as so much sentimental twaddle. And also you are probably, if you have reached this line in the letter, making a grimace of elderly distaste that any man of my age could be so undignified as to dredge up such a trashy memory of youth.

If, however, you remember all this with the same delight as I do and also can't remember one of the names of those to whom you offered the use of your adorable body, then perhaps you see why I have written this letter.

I've never seen you since a week after the show, when you grad-
uated. So I still possess in my very well-guarded memory the
image of a lovely young laughing girl rolling a hoop in and out
among the midday lunch crowd of Rochester, New York, in
May of 1931.

Goodbye, dear little girl!

ALEXANDER WILDER

Dear Dr. Watson:

This is an interim report which I'm writing because I find my
reactions to the situation so strange and unwilling.

Leopold Mannes, who as you know has been in Rochester for
some time, developing color film, saw the show I wrote and produced at the Eastman School of Music, some of the songs from
which Frank Baker sang for your mother and father. I made the
mistake of starting him off with a song of proposal of marriage
oddly entitled "Howdy'a Like My Name on Your Tombstone?"
Your mother's reaction was, "Isn't it just a trifle macabre?"

Leopold knows a lot of theatrical people in New York and was
so excited by the score that he set up an appointment for me to
play it for one of them. I wrote you recently about this prospect.

I took Frank Baker along to sing them. When we went to the
appropriate office the large, aggressive lady at the reception desk
informed us that the man we were to have played and sung for
had left on an emergency trip to the West.

We turned about and returned to Rochester. We found out later
that the man's assistant had been told to listen in his place but
he'd forgotten to tell the reception lady.

And now for the point of this letter. Why did I make no
further effort to have Leopold make another appointment? It goes
without saying that I was scared and unsure. But that's too flimsy
an answer.

Was I so embroiled in growing up, in trying to write more
"serious" music, did I have second thoughts about the score and

conclude that while it might work in an amateur production, it would bring yawns to a New York producer?

Or did I sense that it just might meet with a favorable response and I therefore might be catapulted into the aggressive world of the commercial musical theater? Did I distrust those slick, hard-eyed men, did I not want to run the risk of failing or of succeeding in such an alien atmosphere?

Would you hazard a guess?

I suppose, in my confused state, I'm asking a question: should I enter the lists, should I move into the musical marketplace?

Of course I'm old enough to make this decision myself and am probably using this situation to persuade you to give me a parental pat.

Besides, all I know how to do which might make money is write songs.

If I make the move I shan't desert a single principle, I swear, and I'll constantly send you poems to prove it.

ALEXANDER

Dear Dr. Watson:

I haven't been in touch nearly enough and I sorely miss seeing you as often as I used to when we were working on those films. The prohibition rye in the glove compartment, the endless nonsense in the studio, the picnics out on Cheese Factory Road, that marvelous trip up to the cabin in the Rangeley Lake mountains, even the pistol shooting at targets you used to make me try my shaking arm at.

Those summers on Hildegarde's farm, that crazy Stutz Bearcat we bought and you had souped up, the endless patience with which you read my tales of woe and my poetry and most miraculous of all, the money you would send me as if you could see my checkbook. For your gifts always arrived on the days I didn't know how to face the hotel manager! How could you have known? I know I drank too much but I would remember if I had written you for money. And I never did!

The cryptic letters you've written me, much of the contents of which I didn't understand because of their literary and linguistic allusions but which I'll keep all my life!

Well, the reason you haven't heard from me oftener is very simply because I'm in a state bordering on hysteria and panic trying to make a living in popular music, writing songs and orchestrations (called arrangements). I have to deal with people you would have to meet to believe they exist.

I've tried to learn their language, their tawdriness, their total absence of ideals, their dishonesty (I won't join them there), their greed and sleazy, wholly unromantic attitude toward women.

Yet I know no other way to survive. I don't know how to do anything but write music and what I *do* write in most instances is greeted as if I had tried to sell them a batch of Schubert lieder.

I must make it clear right now that this letter is *not*, definitely *not*, a roundabout plea for more money. I love and trust you so much I promise I would holler if I were on the edge of disaster. But up till now I've been able to get by.

In a way I think you'd be puzzledly proud of my insistence on functioning in an alien world without deserting my principles.

My very best to Hildegarde and yourself.

Please tell her I ran into Mr. Cummings. He sent you both his best.

ALEXANDER

Dear Mr. Copland:

You were very kind to take the time to look at my string quartet. I'm not surprised or hurt that you said I was more interesting than my music except that I do believe you could have said the same thing slightly more politely.

I realize that you are highly respected as an American Composer, an accepted member of the musical hierarchy and so I am further impressed by your kindness to one such as myself, a beginner and, if your words are an indication, perhaps not a talented one.

I have clung to that quartet overzealously probably because it's the first long piece I've ever written. It "looks" interesting perhaps because I desperately employed as many contrapuntal devices as I could, but I'm aware that it's only a bumbling burst of joy over having discovered the marvel of music but with no technique or sense of direction to guide my hand.

I shan't quit no matter how much more interesting you may find me than what I'm doing. Nor shall I make a career of being "more interesting."

I doubt if I shall show any more of my music to any but my close musical friends. It's too risky showing personal creations (no matter how amateurish they may be) to kindly strangers.

It is as dangerous as counting on a pediatrician agreeing that your first baby is beautiful.

Nevertheless, we had an entertaining dinner in the Don Juan, didn't we? I'll miss speakeasies when the Volstead Act is abolished. When again can I sit at a table next to Katharine Cornell and her "friend"?

Thank you for taking those tinsel stars out of my eyes!

ALEXANDER WILDER

Dear John:

Now that I know you're in New Haven and where you live, I may surfeit you with the sobbing confessions of a would-be songwriter and accounts of the sinful and depressing world of commercial music.

I don't know if I ever told you that my meeting you and Sam and Frank and Mitch in the Eastman School quite literally saved my sanity and possibly my life. I had never known that such dedicated and compassionate people existed. I'll never be able to pay the debt.

But now I'm in the midst of the goblins. Songwriters, generally, and publishers, totally, are a frightening, agate-eyed lot. I might as well be dressed like Little Lord Fauntleroy, golden locks and all, as be myself in this stevedore society. As hard as I try to introduce the word "fuckin'" into every other sentence, as hard as I try to avoid any word of more than two syllables or admit I've ever read a book, it's impossible to convince them that I belong in their offices, rehearsal halls or night spots. Even the waiters in Lindy's know I'm suspect.

Why don't I quit? After all, I ran away from school and hid from the kids in my block all through childhood. Why be inconsistent? Well, the money I treated so casually has begun to run out. So money is one reason I'm sticking.

The other I mentioned in another letter, simply that I lack the confidence to try to write more complex music. Of course it would be jim-dandy if I could write successful songs and make enough money to continue to try to improve on a more demanding level.

You say you've been offered a playing job with the Minneapolis? Are you certain that orchestra playing is what you want? I always thought of you as a chamber music player. But I suppose once again it's the money. My assumption is that chamber music is the bones and truest spirit of music but that unless you're the cellist of the Budapest String Quartet you'll never make a living out of it.

Oh, how I'd love to be rich enough to underwrite you and every other great musician so that you could do what you want to do and should be doing!

I heard you were composing. If so, I'll bet the results are great!

ALEXANDER

P.S. For popular music I'm shortening my name to "Alec" as Alexander looks so pompous.

Dear John:

You don't sound exactly ecstatic about orchestral playing. And yet Mitropoulos must be marvellous to be around from all I've heard. If you decide to move, please, for God's sake try to come to New York!

At last I've stuck my nose out of the mousehole and started writing more than songs. I've been writing short pieces with elements of jazz in them. Curiously enough, I made the move because of arranging for recording singers. Arranging, after all, is a euphemism, for it includes composition as well as orchestration. The introductions, countermelodies, transitions, reharmonizing are all more than just orchestration. But by using the word "arrangement" they get two skills for the price of one.

Mitch Miller managed to con some pathetic fellow who knows

nothing about popular music but wanted to conduct into believing that I was the perfect person to do the arrangements for his new radio show. It had a thirty-five-piece band. So I began doing some weird things, weird, that is, for commercial radio. I did a swinging transcription of Bach's little G-minor Fugue, kept every note but had everyone play dance style. It sounded great but brought a flood of perplexed letters. Then I did a really pretty arrangement of Ravel's "Pavane" and a lulu of Debussy's "Golliwog's Cakewalk." I even did Kreisler's "Tambourine Chinois." They all worked fine, made the players very happy but elicited black frowns from the men handling the advertising account.

The reason I mention all this is that it made me realize I had more talent than I thought I had. So it kicked me back into respectable composition. And, not incidentally, I'd never have been able to get into the arranging end of music if I hadn't had the help and advice of Jimmy Caruana. You remember him at Eastman. He's a short, smiling Italian boy who plays exquisite jazz clarinet and not as good trumpet. He's very even-tempered and marvelous to work with. He taught me a great deal about dance band orchestration.

His name rhymes with "marijuana" so he changed it to "Carroll."

Now that I look back I realize that what encouraged me to try my luck in the pop music field was that show I wrote the last year you were in school. You should remember! You played the part of the iceman in that skit with Alice George! Remember?

One music publisher is beginning to be interested in my songs even though they are not typical of the marketplace. He's Benny Goodman's brother, a former bass player. Thank God somebody will listen past the first eight measures! You realize, I suppose, that I have to play the piano and also sing the song! Since I both play and sing badly, it's quite a sound!

I would never have believed five years ago that I'd have had the courage to deal with these rough-and-tumble people. Of course a little booze before one of these confrontations doesn't do any harm. I've even been known to smoke "grass," as they call marijuana — they sometimes call it "shit." Charming, eh?

I don't know what my mother would have made of this life I live, but she died, poor lady, back in thirty-two. My brother, who is totally unlike me, accepts on faith what I tell him about the song world. I don't think he really has any notion what it's really like.

I manage to make a living of sorts from arranging, and I just may wind up making something from songs.

Whenever a check comes in from my mother's trust fund I ride trains, ride them all over the country and Canada, sometimes for as long as three weeks. It's another sanity saver and, as well, I've begun to see the enormous mystery of this romantic, raw, brawling, bigoted, innocent cauldron of a country.

Remember, when you leave Minneapolis don't go back to San Diego or Chicago! Come to New York! There's lots of chamber music here and some incredibly fine players!

ALEXANDER (ALEC)

P.S. I'll write a horn piece for you yet. And after I do I have a hunch a flood of legit music will pour out. Better late than never!

Dear Dr. Watson:

Well, I went and did it. Not the dive at the deep end of the pool, that is, not playing the show tunes for the producer, but I've gone and got my feet wet: I've sold a song.

That sounds reputable enough but already I can see the sort of life one must lead in order to be a successful songwriter. (By the way, much as I unabashedly love good pop tunes, I really would like to be a composer of somewhat more complex music.)

One must learn a new language or at least *I* must. One must play games, be prepared for slobby insults, be willing to change one's most cherished phrase. One must not simply visit the marketplace;

one must virtually live in it, appear to be deeply interested in the gossip, the status of all new songs. One must laugh at ugly, unfunny jokes, one *should* have lunch at either of the Lindy's, one must be prepared to allow bandleaders to "cut themselves in on" a song, get a percentage of any song of yours they play, along with their name on the cover. And more.

In this instance the boy I write with (*my* lyrics in this song) managed to get to the producer of a new show called *Three's a Crowd*. The score is obviously not by a single team of writers. But one of the well-known lyric writers has an interest in the show and, though he liked the song, he felt one line should be changed. Before I could think of one, he did. As a result his name is on the cover and he shares a part of whatever lyric profits may accrue. And for a single line! It consists of three words: "Smooth my path." Irony?

But I suppose I must somehow adjust to this dreadful world. The money I've inherited is fast vanishing and I must earn some. I believe I literally would have a breakdown if I worked in any kind of office job. Not because of the daily grind and having to be there from nine to five but because I still am terrified of everyone but my tested friends. In an office I'd be unable to get away from the other people. As a free-lance songwriter, however, I can at least walk away from the worst of them.

When and how am I ever going to have the time and peace of mind to continue to compose? Am I fit to be a composer or was my minimal training at the Eastman School inadequate apprenticeship for any art as complex as so-called serious music?

I don't expect you to answer any of these questions, but to put them down on paper for your eyes gives me a feeling of comfort and security. At least someone I love and trust knows and I'm sure, understands the hurdles that one with my cowardice and polite background must leap if I am to make a living in commercial music.

Ironically, the publishers for whom I have played songs reject them on the grounds that, as one put it, "we can't sell any of that Juilliard shit."

I'm not a composer and yet my songs are too complex to sell. More irony?

ALEXANDER (ALEC)

P.S. I've decided that "Alexander" looks much too pompous printed on a piece of sheet music, so I've made it "Alec." Why not "Alex" I don't know. There must have been an Alex I disliked in one of those ghastly boarding schools I went to.

Dear Mr. Goodman:

The arrangement I made for Mildred Bailey of "Sleepy Time Down South," as you know, had eight measures set aside for a solo by you since your band plays for her on the Camel show.

Your complaint about the unexpected harmony I used not only embarrassed the men in the band, Mildred, and myself but just maybe reveals one of your better-known weaknesses: a bad ear.

I'm not saying that the harmony was the best; I'm simply saying that you would be the last musician to know if it were the worst!

The fact that I studied music for much longer than you did does not make me a better musician than you. But it does imply that I would be less likely to write down a bunch of unmusical harmonic sequences than someone who had studied nothing.

Has it occurred to you that Mildred Bailey is in a position to have her pick of the arrangers? Why, then, did she choose me, if I'm so lousy?

I find your manners detestable, but if you can possibly curb them, I'd be willing to give you a few harmony lessons — yes, give — for free — so that next time we have an eight-measure crisis you'll be able to stumble through it with not only skill but grace.

ALEC WILDER

Dear Mildred:

Maybe I should apologize for the odd harmony I introduced in the release of "Sleepy Time Down South." At the same time I want you to know that I was only trying to make it a little less obvious and cliché. I noticed that all the guys in the band were on my side when Benny started being embarrassingly rude about my harmony.

But if I went overboard and it in any way caused you embarrassment or trouble with Benny, please accept my apologies!

As you know, I have infinite admiration for your singing and deep affection for you personally. Every song I write I hope you will approve of, not because I'm after you to sing it but because I have great respect for your judgment and taste.

You don't know what it's like to come from the boondocks into the wild world of the music business, and have one of their heroines offer her friendship and her encouragement! It's been a marvelous stimulation and a great stabilizer for my wavering self-respect.

If I arrange any more tunes for you with the Goodman band (or will Benny refuse to play them?) I promise I'll tiptoe on musical cat feet.

It's a great honor to know you and to be your friend!

ALEC WILDER

Dear Eddie:

Bumping into you in Asheville last month called to mind so many memories I had assumed to be lost in the ash heap of the past.

I've been fruitlessly trying to remember where we met. My brother George would probably know: he remembers everything. We didn't go to school together and I didn't meet you in a publisher's office, for I hadn't ever been in one at that time.

I must have been about twenty. Prohibition was still a romantic failure and I think I had been studying at the Eastman School. You lived at the Sherman Square Hotel with your cheery mother. That was on 71st Street but, though I keep thinking I still lived at 235 West 71st Street, I couldn't have as we moved from there when I was about fifteen.

My mother liked you because you looked "clean-cut." I remember her saying, why I'll never know, "Eddie Brant, Eddie Brant, Eddie Brant," over and over again.

You knew Henry Kiselik and played two pianos with him over at WOR in Newark. I wrote you some terrible piece and I think you performed it on the air. Henry had halitosis and, in spite of it, became a very successful bandleader under the name of Henry King.

When we met in Asheville thirty years later, you told me you were working for a laundry. Why, for heaven's sake? The last time I heard of you, you had a very successful band in the manner of Fred Waring.

I wrote lyrics to your music and had very little to do with the shaping of the tunes. Why was that? I wasn't particularly interested in lyric writing. And God! Did I write some horrible ones for you! Do you remember "Life's Just Funny That Way"?

> *I don't want a lot of things*
> *Ermine furs and diamond rings*
> *All I want is what love brings*
> *But life's just funny that way.*

What's so funny about not wanting diamond rings? I consider it highly impractical and not wanting them by no means makes life funny.

Then I wrote one I can't believe you could have set a tune to. Believe it or not, it was called "Yes, Today! No! Yesterday!"

What in God's name was that about? I remember the following line. It was "Which is it and why?"

But then we did write one that got published and laid there

like a dog in summer. It had a good tune. It was called "Day After Day."

Then we got lucky for a while with "All the King's Horses," getting it into that very successful show *Three's a Crowd* with Libby Holman, Fred Allen and that ghastly dancer, Clifton Webb.

And if it hadn't been for the song from England called "The King's Horses," we'd have had a hit, I'm positive!

Remember that cocksure young man who had a meaningless song in the show and got furious when it didn't appear in the overture? He changed his name later and became a very good and very successful songwriter. No names, no pack drill!

As I look back on that strange time, I can't help using the word innocence. Of course I'm sure it was the starry eyes of youth and nothing like the truth. But still, my memory of you playing upstairs in that East Side speakeasy with your trio was as innocent as musical theater. That hood on the door who later worked at the Copa! One night I saw him peel off thousands of bucks to stern-faced business types down in the lobby of the speak. They were obviously revenue agents who couldn't have cared less who saw the payoff. Then there was a night when Helen Morgan attacked some poor half-loaded debutante in the ladies' room: sheer innocence! Oh, I knew it wasn't but it had the air of theatricality and therefore unreality.

Then there was that exquisite young girl I found sitting outside the place on the curbstone, reading the Sunday comic strips. And I swear she wasn't drunk. I remember she could put the booze away but I never saw her loaded. What more perfect vignette of the twenties than that curbstone rendezvous!

I've never told anyone before, but when I wrote a show up at the Eastman School, I ran out of ideas for tunes and used two of your tunes without giving you any credit. That was, I readily confess, rotten of me, no matter what my age or what the situation. One was the closing number. Was the original title "Here Today, Gone Tomorrow"? Anyhow, it worked perfectly. The other had a title like "Wastin' My Time" which I arranged for a trio of girl singers and it, too, worked perfectly!

And damn it! I didn't have the common decency to see that your name was listed as the writer of the music! That's not only dishonest, it's mean and petty.

Did that TV station ever open in Asheville? I remember you said if it did you were going to do a spot and call yourself Mister Eighty-eight. Well, good luck to you Eddie Brant, Eddie Brant, Eddie Brant.

ALEC WILDER

Dear Morty:

The morning you walked into that mittel-European apartment where we were about to play a piece for the head of a recording company (some uncle of yours) I felt less frightened of the outcome.

Looking back I can conclude it must have been the literal loving light in your eye. It certainly wasn't your clothes or your remarks, your presence or any signs of reassurance — except in that bright, almost raccoon-bright mischief in your eye.

I found out in short order that you had come along because your uncle knew nothing about music. But thank God, you did, and you liked that sample piece scored for legitimate woodwinds, harpsichord and rhythm section.

As a result of your enthusiasm, I wrote, and there were recorded, about twenty original pieces. And you ran all the recording sessions. You even came up with one of the best titles, "Sea Fugue, Mama."

And then you wangled recordings of tunes I had written, the first decent recording of "I'll Be Around." Cab Calloway, as I recall.

And then, finding out you were a good fiddle player and had lots of melodic ideas, I wrote with you and the results were "While We're Young" and "Moon and Sand." We used to fool

around by the hour with all kinds of marvelous notions, which I
was too damned lacking in hope and self-respect to put down on
paper.

You were, bless you, a godsend! There were damned few
people who cared about me or my songs in those days. You introduced me to all kinds of wonderful people: Sinatra, Peggy Lee,
Ella Fitzgerald, Buddy Clarke, all the great recording musicians.

Then, when you went to work for Decca, something got
twisted. As I remember, you became kind of full of yourself. You
had a coterie of people I couldn't stand. We never met and it
was almost impossible to get you on the phone.

But it all cleared up later and I saw a lot of you in Los Angeles.
We sure as hell laughed a lot.

Then there was a slump. You were out of a job for a long time
but finally got one with a small, somewhat scruffy recording
company. You found an awful singer and made a star out of her.

Then that folded. I didn't see you for a while. When I did you
were very bitter. No more laughs. You had remarried, a very
sweet woman. You were painting for fun.

There had been some strange heart ailment back in California
which I had never taken very seriously. I thought you were
coddling yourself, looking for sympathy. You were always
kvetching (the best I can do with that marvelous Yiddish word)
and to the wrong people, those who'd run and tattle to bosses.

I knew your mother had spoiled you rotten in your youth, but
I hated to see you getting a persecution complex.

I admit I wasn't nearly a faithful friend, and I'll never forgive
myself for it. I've been pretty good at friendship most of my life,
except for my occasional drunken viciousness, so the only reason
I can come up with is that I must have been terribly disturbed
about myself and therefore completely egocentric.

Then a miracle occurred: Sinatra had finally decided to open
up a recording company and you were his favorite recording
man.

I remember your making a trip to Los Angeles to discuss the

details with him. Everything was happily settled and you came back to New York to wait for the job to start.

Then that heart weakness I had jeered at grabbed you and I suppose it was a serious heart attack. I've always thought it occurred as a result of the joy of at long last finding the perfect job.

I went to see you. You were cheery and very casual about whatever had knocked you out. You were making plans and you were looking very chipper.

Then, totally unexpectedly, you died.

Damn it, damn it, damn it! What a ball it would have been for you, working for Frank, who so truly respected and loved you! After all that long rejection and miserable series of disappointments, to get precisely what you'd always wanted — and then, death!

Forgive my temporary faithlessness and thank you, dear man, for all you did for me and for all that glorious laughter!

ALEC

Dear Dr. Watson:

I admit I'm terrified of being drafted. And it's not the danger, it's the men. Here I go again: it's boarding school all over again, summer camp, all the bullies, except this time they'll be big red-faced slobs, foul-mouthed, trigger-happy and all the rest of a slob's conception of being a real man. Communal showers, toilets, barracks, no privacy, and you can be certain endless cracks about needing an oyster fork to get it out of my pants, cracks about being physically weak, about using big words. You can imagine. And then the overlords, the so-called brass, shouting and jeering and humiliating everyone who isn't the perfect slob!

I admit it, I can't take it. So I've decided to go to a psycho-analyst and, being the same coward I've always been, I suppose I won't have the courage to tell him or her my real reason for being there. My hunch is that I'll lay it on so thick about my inability to adjust to society that perhaps I'll be lucky enough to have a professional opinion from him or her to take to the draft board.

I know damned well I'll never summon up the courage to come right out with it and confess the real reason I'm there. I'm not making any excuses (particularly to you!) but I must admit that I could never, with no matter what conditioning and impersonalizing, become a useful member of any fighting force, even in a noncombatant position. My fear of those people whose egos and aggressions have made it possible for them to function in groups and organizations as a matter of course and without fear or panic, is so deeply seated that I become a nervous wreck and incapable of fulfilling the slightest assignment while in their presence.

Forgive the melodrama, but I honestly feel as might a single creature from another planet feel upon finding himself suddenly teleported to the Earth. I consider it a miracle that I've managed to function as well as I have, to have actually made a living out of songwriting and arranging as I have these last few years in the midst of a totally alien section of human society.

I profoundly hope you understand my plight even though you may not be able to bring yourself to condone or sympathize with it.

ALEC

Dear Aaron:

It's oh, so long ago, but once upon a time, not the time we had dinner in the New York speakeasy, but later, up in Rochester at Bernard Rogers's house we met again.

I had written a cello concerto of most uncertain merit. Indeed, it was a living proof of your suggestion that I was more interesting than my music. I had been so entranced by having composed a large orchestra piece (my very first!) that I had it bound in a hard cover which had on it not the title of the piece, but my *name*. Very odd, indeed! And in binding the edges of the score, pages had been trimmed so that the instrument names along the border were in some instances beheaded.

I had brought it to Bernard's to show you in spite of your earlier indifference. You politely turned its pages and finally asked me casually, "What's an ASS DRUM?" (The "B" had been trimmed, page after page.)

To this day I've never heard the piece. The man I wrote it for never got around to it any more than he had got around to the string quartet I showed you. But much later another cellist asked for the score and parts. I was in New York and couldn't get to Rochester. I sent the music up and shortly afterward the cellist phoned to say he had tried it out with the orchestra and liked it. He also added that the score and parts had vanished.

All manner of searches ensued, to no avail. So after a few years I came to think of it as the best piece I had ever written and, possibly, ever would write. I think I was more nourished in a perverse fashion from its loss than from a performance by Piatigorski.

Then ten, fifteen years later it turned up. It's hard to believe but where no one had ever thought to look, in the music library.

It was sent to me, score and parts. By then my music may not have become as interesting as myself but it had improved considerably. So when I looked through my precious "lost concerto" in its elegant binding with my name embossed in golden letters (with its procession of pages reading "ASS DRUM"), I realized that it was a total dud.

The scoring was infantile, the composition nonexistent; a provocative idea here and there but no, my adored concerto could no longer be adored and lamented in its glorious "lostness."

So I dumped it into the trash where it should have been dumped years before.

My greater loss is never having discovered why the cellist who had tried it out liked it so much. For some mysterious reason I never asked him. He was a highly competent musician but he gave up music, became a gag writer in New York, and died. (Laughing at his own gags?)

ALEC WILDER

P.S. Thank you for recommending me on several occasions for music projects in New York! I hope I was gracious enough to thank you then but if I wasn't I apologize all these years later. I trust all goes well for you.

Dear John:

Naturally I hope all goes well for you in Minneapolis, but I wish you were in the East as I truly miss you and your mountain-water clarity about music.

You knew when you were at the Eastman School that I wanted to write "concert" music as well as pop songs. Well, I haven't dug nearly deep enough since we last met, mostly because of the need for money. My inheritances have all been dissipated and I have to scrounge around the marketplace (in my case, the Brill Building, the center of pop music publishing). But I still have the hunger to get at music with deeper roots, longer lines, more extended forms than songs. There's nothing wrong with songwriting. It's fun and very rewarding to find unusual melodic patterns. But I feel literally guilty about not giving more time to the other, almost as if I were not fulfilling a promise to a trusting child.

I am going to attempt some short pieces which stand a good chance of being recorded. They'll be an attempted union of legitimate and jazz ideas for legit woodwinds, harpsichord, bass and drums. Mitch Miller has found the players for me from the CBS staff and they're all willing to rehearse lengthily for no pay. A marvelous guy who works for Brunswick Records as a kind of record producer has okayed a session for which I've already written four original pieces.

I'd like them at times to swing more than they do but even with Jiggs — who plays glorious clarinet — even with him playing lead, it's not in the bones of Harold Goltzer on bassoon or Mitch Miller on oboe to play a jazz phrase. Besides which they have the very tough problem of the unswinging double reed.

The harpsichord turns out to be a most colorful and properly percussive background for attemptedly swinging legit woodwinds. I doubt if these records will do much more than tickle the fancy of a few gentle-hearted musicians. But they're fun to write and the guys in the group are a bunch of laughers and hard workers.

I'm going to use nutty titles which are just attention-getters, having nothing to do with the music which is distinctly non-programmatic. Some of the titles are inside jokes like "Sea Fugue, Mama" (based on a lick from that Andrews Sisters record "I Want Some Sea Food, Mama"), "The Children Met the Train" (Kay Thompson gave me that one), "It's Silk — Feel It!" (Sam Richlin gave me that!)

But I still want to dig in deeper. If you ever decide to move East, my first step will be to write something for French horn. For some reason I can't write it *here* and send it to you way out *there!*

All my best to you and I hope you don't stay there too much longer!

ALEC

Dear Phil:

I was very happy to hear from Sunny Blake that you are still in the land of the living. He gave me the last address he had of yours and so I'm trying it.

You undoubtedly wouldn't remember me from all those thousands of kids on the beach at Bay Head. You were an honest-to-God lifeguard, not lolling back in an elevated beach chair, horsing around with the girls. You walked up and down the beach seeing to it that we kids didn't get sucked down by the undertow or get boiled by a sudden breaker. You kept on your feet, not only because you took your job seriously, but because in those wonderful years they wouldn't have dreamed of putting a lifeguard up on a platform.

And, forgive me for saying so, they probably wouldn't hire you in these times, as they only want fancy-looking young men who give sexy smiles to the old ladies and wear tight swimming trunks.

As I remember, you had been a wrestler. God knows you had terrifying muscles. You had a kindly face, but it wasn't one for competing in beauty contests.

The reason I'm writing after all these years (is it fifty?) is that you saved me from drowning one stormy morning and I'll bet I never even said "thank you."

All I remember is that I kept trying to swim to shore and couldn't make any headway. I kept getting more and more exhausted and then a wave broke right over my head. Next thing I knew I was being picked up by a single giant hand.

It was yours, Phil, and I'd never even seen you do anything but walk up and down the beach.

My friends (I had two of those that summer plus ten bullies) told me that you shot into the water as if out of a gun, and that you swam like a bullet.

You had a Brooklyn accent and I have to confess it: I used to give terrible imitations of you trying to make conversation with my mother. I'm very sorry about that and have been for years.

Nowadays your picture would be in the paper, and you'd be given a gold medal. In those days people simply did their duty and thought nothing more about it. Thank you, Phil Campon, fifty years late.

ALEC WILDER

Dear Mitch:

Thanks very much for asking me to write that oboe piece. I've needed to be asked by someone who plays as well as you and who isn't a stranger, to write something more ambitious than the tentative pieces I've been writing.

Since hearing you play the piece I've become inspired to write a series of pieces for solo woodwinds and strings. God knows who will ever play them but it certainly feels great to be back in the kind of music I went to the Eastman School to learn how to write.

When I get through with that suite (for flute, bassoon, English horn and maybe woodwind octet and strings) I plan a much larger piece; an oboe concerto for you. I don't know if it will be worthy of you or if it is, where on earth you would get a chance to play it.

By the way, I've been seeing a lot of Frank Baker lately. As you know, he has a house out in the Ramapo Hills near Suffern. As a result I've been writing a lot of "art" songs. He is such a great musician and besides he can read them straight off my somewhat untidy manuscript.

Among other things I've done is a setting for voice, harp and English horn of lines he chose out of The Song of Solomon. When I copy the parts, maybe you could suggest a harpist and run it down with Frank.

I can't thank you enough for bringing all those great guys together to form the octet. I would never have been able to find them or ask them myself. As a matter of fact you were the one who got the whole thing under way. You got hold of Yella Pessl's harpsichord, you persuaded her to let us rehearse in her apartment, you brought Morty Palitz up from Brunswick Records to listen to the group. If it weren't for you I would never have written all those crazy woodwind pieces.

They're too special to make any money but they do seem to be attracting some attention. I was astonished when Brunswick asked me to write some more. After the first session with all those "legit" instruments and semiserious counterpoint I assumed Brunswick would have had its fill. But evidently the pieces must have some kind of *prestige* value.

Well, thank you once again! For you did the whole thing!

ALEC

P.S. I'll show you the first movement of the concerto as soon as I finish it. By the way, can you get me an "air check" of the oboe piece you played? It was broadcast in England. Does that make it difficult to get an "air check"?

Dear Frank:

I haven't read enough Freud to speak knowledgeably about night dreams. But I know all about daydreams and for a very good reason: the less that happens in anyone's life, the more daydreams they have. At least it's so in my case. And while my life hasn't been wholly without incident, there have been only a few pleasant ones. Mitch Miller was responsible for my getting all those octets recorded and for a while I didn't even have time to daydream.

But in the wildest of those dreams I couldn't have made up anything as marvelous as what you have done for me. It was only by chance that I brought that "air check" of the piece Mitchell broadcast up to your dressing room at the Paramount. And I'll bet it was also by chance that you played it.

As a result you have made possible a whole album of original pieces and even more miraculously you have conducted the whole kaboodle! I'll be in your debt forever!

Talk about coincidences! It was only because the piece I wrote for Mitch Miller turned out well that I wrote all the other pieces! And finished them precisely at the time you asked me if I had any pieces like the record I had left in your dressing room!

You don't know this, but I was in the office at Columbia Records when you called up from California after seeing a copy of the album cover and raised hell because my name wasn't in as large type as yours! That was damned considerate of you and so I bow deeply once again.

My very best to you in your movie making out there and all the best to the Nancys, senior and junior!

ALEC WILDER

Dear Dr. Watson:

I must really need music because I keep trying to write it.

I've been living in Rockland County down the road from the Mitchell Miller family in an old barn remodeled by the fellow who writes lyrics for tunes of mine.

We've written a very comic one-act opera based on the Chicken Little story and I've written two other one-act operas with another fellow for publication. If I were what is known as a "hustler," I'd have had everything recorded and I'd be fairly well-known.

As Mr. Miller gets more powerful in the recording industry he keeps getting rougher with me about "adjusting on a lower level," except in his mind this means accepting corruption and being willing to work in a pussy environment (pussy as in pus).

I won't do this and therefore remain unsuccessful and a puzzlement to the competitive music world. I'm no longer interviewed, which suits me fine, still drink too much, still dally with emasculators, still write verse, still travel on trains but still write music (nonpop).

I've even written the scores for musical comedies which no one wants.

I keep losing teeth and still don't dare go far from my dentist for any length of time. I begin to realize that three elements control my life: lack of self-confidence, fear of everyone but a proven friend, and fear of losing teeth.

I found a word: pantaphobia — fear of everything. I'm not quite that badly off as I'm not afraid of mice, flowers, butterflies or the moon.

I was the most scared of my childhood contemporaries, slightly less of those in high school, not at all of music-school contemporaries, but petrified of these music-business bums.

Anyway, what I'm trying to say is that it's a precipice walk, always has been, always will be. And I had better become expert at it since it will be a permanent locomotion. I guess that's why I prefer giving to receiving, as when I give, I'm in charge. When I receive, I'm wholly vulnerable and on the edge of a cliff.

I was ready for death at seventeen, again at thirty-two (who'd want to get any older?) but not now. But what on earth am I waiting for? A miracle? A miracle in what form? A fantasy turned into fact? What kind of fantasy? One of power, position, notoriety, wealth, fame? No. A perfect girl? No.

Perhaps just to keep in my head the teeth that are left and to write well enough for me to be able to say (only to myself) "Now then! That's better!"

Whom do I envy?

People who don't doubt, people who look in mirrors and nod imperceptibly in recognition of their admirable images, people who speak to others firmly and don't have to resort to pretense to sound firm, people who enter crowded rooms with confidence, people who are ready and willing to fight with their fists — people who don't doubt.

Can you believe that I wrote, during the war, a piece of music for an antiaircraft battery on Okinawa called "Ready, Willing and Able"? I'm told it wasn't easy to sing but it *was sung* by those large bullet-boys while I was in the Algonquin reading about the Civil War (not just to feel I was part of the general public murder but because I had been hooked by Benét's *John Brown's Body*).

Would you be more entertained if these five year (what *is* the word?) reports had more of a graph line? Like:

I don't recall what the former ones said but I'll bet the motion is circular and not even vertical (is that the adjective for "vortex" or have I wandered into another "farcial"?).

Because of my antisocial behavior, stories have started to come back to me about what I did on this or that occasion. All of them are false. Not a trace of truth.

I have met some good people, wise people, strong, odd, unpredictable — all kinds. The point is that not all are evil publishers and greedy songwriter hacks.

One especially dear man, who deals in out-of-print books, is Edward O'Malley, who keeps sending me books and never a bill. I have to send him checks, begging him to find out who owes whom what.

A wild, witty, mercurial young man who takes all kinds of pills to speed him up and slow him down. I love him but he's even more eccentric than myself. He steals only to give his thefts to friends. He played the calliope in asbestos gloves at the Ringling Brothers Circus last year and was one of those many, many people who get out of the very small car, he in a dimity frock. He has what I'm told is termed "total recall." Remembers everything everyone said in his hearing, ever — at any time. He spins too fast for a half-speed society.

Wouldn't it be sad if I wanted a great deal? Is it because I don't want a great deal that I don't try to get more? Or because I sense that a "great deal" has a way of running one's life and I much prefer freedom of motion, few commitments and no strategy for the days, weeks, months and years to come. I'd be a wreck if I knew I were bound to a plot for the rest of my life. But I suppose the plotters consider their campaigns life itself.

I've just read this over and it reads as if I had written it either half stoned or while riding on a Catherine wheel. What am I trying to tell you? Everything?

I apologize. I must learn to edit if I'm to continue plying you with letters. Or perhaps I should take a long train trip and calm down.

ALEC

Dear Eddie:

Have you any idea what you did to me when you sold that house down in Berks County? I'm well aware that it was yours to sell and that my sole equity in it was a garden. I know that you found it intolerable during winter months and realized it was wholly impractical to live in the year round.

But you *did* know of my literal passion for that garden I spent three years creating, the dry wall around it, the old French roses, the hundreds of perennials, bulbs, vines, flowering shrubs! Would it have been such an inconvenience to let me know so that (wild to contemplate!) I might have borrowed the money to meet the price you received!

I know my frenzy amused both you and Helen, my jumping out of bed in the middle of the night to run about with my storm lantern checking all those lovely growing things, my endless correspondence with nurseries, the plants arriving in nearly every mail, my hysterical shooing out of dogs and cats, my refusal to permit indiscriminate picking of flowers!

Oh, I know I was obsessed! But the garden was very beautiful, wasn't it?

When I called the man to whom you sold it and he told me he would only use the place for weekends, I could hear my heart crack. For I knew the garden would run riot, be smothered with weeds and the dream would vanish.

I'm only happy about the vividness of my memory, for in it the garden lives after all these barren years. There are misty places but I can still see most of it very clearly.

It was so strange only a few years later to be asked not only to write the music for but to act in a movie which was like that lost garden.

It was about a little boy who was told by a magic shell that he shouldn't be sad when his sand castle was dissolved by the sea as it would always live on in his memory. And man, I wrote my sad ass off for that scene, where the castle does crumble into the waves.

I don't think it matters much but it well might have been that had you kept the house, I would have given up music. No great loss, but I did learn that even those delicate little blooms, vanishing overnight, meant more to me than all the permanent stacks of music in the world—except for Bach.

It makes me sad to realize that those laughing, innocent years have gone up in smoke and can never be duplicated. But I don't miss the garden, for it blooms in my Kodachrome memory bank!

ALEC

Dear Mitchell:

I've finished the oboe concerto and I hope you like the last three movements as much as you like the first. As you know, I've scored it for string orchestra and percussion.

Now that you've moved into the recording business, God knows when you'll get the chance to play it. But I'm glad I wrote it. I've wanted to write you a big piece for years out of respect for your great musicianship and in gratitude for all you've done for me.

If I balk at some of the projects you wish me to participate in, please understand that I'm grateful for your thinking of me, but I simply cannot do good work when I have to be affiliated with people I don't respect or trust. I know I'm being impractical and unrealistic, but no matter how hard I try to adjust to those I don't like, my entire creative source dries up and all I want to do is run for the hills.

Please don't get the idea that I'm choosy or ungrateful! Just put me down as a nut, an eccentric, a maverick, but not a man without the grace of gratitude!

ALEC

Dear Madelaine:

You and I don't see each other very much any more and that really leaves something wonderful out of my life.

Heaven knows, when the Millers lived in the country and the children were growing up, everything happened that could happen. And you, I'm sure, were well aware of all of it. And I'll bet you'll never mention to anyone, even your sister Rose, the goings-on of that wild family you've worked for all these years.

And now there you are all alone in that big apartment without even Lorenzo, that crazy parrot, to keep you company.

I know that once in a while Mike or Andrea or even Mr. Miller will be there for a few days, but it has to be pretty lonely for you.

I'm writing not only to say hello and tell you that I miss you, but that I suddenly remembered that you love mangos. Down here in Key West there's a mess of them in the fruit stores, so I'm sending you a lot of semi-ripe ones.

They should be nearly ready to eat by the time they arrive in New York. All the best to you, dear Madelaine!

ALEC WILDER

P.S. Remember how we'd get to laughing over what I always called daydreams and you called "air castles"? Well, my next letter will be an air castle!

Dear Madelaine:

I promised you an "air castle" so here goes:

I'm sitting on a bench in Central Park feeling sorry for myself. Nothing has been going well, the music I'm supposed to finish won't find a way out of my head, the money's not coming in and my back hurts.

While I'm slouching on the bench I hear screams coming from up the path. Then a small, ridiculous-looking Pekingese dog comes skittering toward me, pursued hysterically by a large lady wearing a lot of jewelry, a picture hat and furs.

The Pekingese is trailing a leash so I stick out a foot and slap it down just in time to stop the dog's escape.

The dog nearly slips its collar, but I grab it and get my hand nipped. I'm standing there with blood dripping from my fingers when the lady waddles up, breathing like a firehorse and moaning about her poor little Honshu or some such name.

I'm pretty sore, having caught her damned dog and been bitten for my efforts. So I say, "Poor little Honshu, my foot! What about poor little me?"

Suddenly she sees the blood dripping, puts her hand to her rather large bosom, and starts to swoon. I've got the dog by the back of the neck in one hand, so I use the bloody one to grab the old trout by her massive waist and ease her down onto the bench.

I make her lean over, but God knows she can never get her head down between her knees, so I slap her face and run up to the nearby water cooler. Now, remember! I've still got the dog by the neck, it's yapping its goggle-eyed head off, people are beginning to gather round, and I'm trying to push the water cooler button and wet my handkerchief at the same time.

I can't, but some kind soul helps and I run back to the bench. The handkerchief is soaking wet with water but also with my own blood.

(Okay, Madelaine? So good, so far? I've stuck to the old rule I once made which is to start an "air castle" from an absolutely blank mind and let her rip.)

ALEC WILDER

P.S. I've decided to behave like a soap opera and leave you in suspense. The only difference is you may have to wait a week for the continuation of the story. I solemnly swear to keep my mind a total blank insofar as this story is concerned, until I start writing about it again. And you better keep these sheets so you'll be able to refresh your memory.

How do you like the title "The Songwriter and the Chinese Dog"?

P.S. When I called to find out if you got the mangos, you said, "It made me feel so good to know you remembered that I loved mangos."

Dear Madelaine:

Well, at last the suspense is going to be over, for here's how it all wound up:

The fainting old fat lady comes shuddering out of her faint, screams over my bloody handkerchief, grabs her dreadful little dog and then glares at me and says, "I am Mrs. Waddington and I want my chauffeur and my Bentley."

This brings a big horselaugh from the crowd which had now collected.

"Why were you clutching Honshu by his neck, young man?" she barks at me, clearly well out of her faint by now.

Some kind soul, maybe the one who pressed the water-cooler button, calls out, "Hey, lady! This fellah stopped your ugly dog from running away and got bit by him! I saw the whole damn thing! And he kept you from falling flat on your ass on the sidewalk!"

This welcome speech distracts her attention from me, so she turns to my new friend and says, "How dare you speak of me or my adorable Honshu in this fashion?"

Now a cop has shown up and a man in a chauffeur's uniform.

There's a lot of remarks back and forth and finally the cop says, "Listen, lady, I'll have to give you a summons for having a dog off its leash."

"But, officer! He *was* on his leash! But he escaped!"

"What about this man's hand?" asks the cop. "He's got a case, you know! He can sue you for that bite he's got from your half a dog."

"How dare you speak of Honshu in this fashion? His pedigree extends back to the Ming Dynasty."

"I don't care if it goes back to the Boxer Rebellion," wittily responds the cop. "You better take this man to a doctor if you don't want to be sued. And here's your summons to appear in court on the twenty-seventh of this month."

Mrs. Waddington is so mad she nearly bursts. Her face gets purple, she splutters, and Honshu pops his pop-eyes at the crowd.

"Perhaps, Mrs. Waddington," says the chauffeur in a very smarmy tone of voice, "we should drive this young man to the office of Dr. Needham?"

"That's more like it!" calls out my kind soul. "And buddy," he turns to me, "you better have that damned dog checked for rabies at the same time!"

So that's how I find myself in the back seat of a big British car with Mrs. Waddington. She has wanted me in front with Clarence, the chauffeur, but he tells her my hand has stopped bleeding so it won't stain the upholstery.

At first she looks out of her window until I say meekly, "I hope I'll be able to play piano tomorrow."

She turns in amazement as if I'd said I was the ambassador to England and says in disbelief, "Play *piano?*"

"Why, yes," I say, getting bolder. "I write music and I have to play an audition of the score I wrote for a new show."

She glares at me with her mouth open. Then she whispers, "You're a composer?"

"Why, yes, come to think of it," I say.

"Then why are you wearing those shocking clothes," she asks, returning to her old self.

"I didn't know music depended upon Brooks Brothers," I answer with rising irritation.

This stops her. Then she says, a little on the nervous side, "Could I possibly have heard any of your music?"

Well, there *was* a song she could have heard in the Palm Court at the Plaza. So I take a chance and say modestly, "Well, I doubt it, but you just might have heard a waltz I wrote called 'While We're Young.' "

" 'While We're Young'!" she repeats in astonishment. "Why, that's Warren's favorite song. Warren is Mr. Waddington," she adds as if she were saying that John was Mr. Rockefeller.

Well, Madelaine, by the time I've been patched up by Dr. Needham and that ridiculous dog has been given a rabies test, I am on very chummy terms with Mrs. Waddington, Clarence, and amazingly, even with Honshu.

So it will come as no surprise to you when I say that I spent the next six months of my life living in Shadowbrook, the Waddingtons' estate up the Hudson and working on a glorious grand piano with trays of delicious food being brought to me at lunch and teatime.

There is even talk between Mr. and Mrs. Waddington of giving me a large commission to compose an orchestra piece with chorus. The words the chorus are to sing will be — and I'm sure you're not surprised — ancient Chinese poetry.

And thus ends "air castle" number 4,568,329.

Alec Wilder

Dear Margaret:

Already I'm beginning to crawl and whimper! Why do I say "dear"? You are about as dear as sable on the one hand, and sour as clabber on the other. You've been very sly and shrewd in your stimulation of the guilt nerve. Your grotesque illogic danced so adroitly that I mistook it for worthy censure.

Now that I've managed to put a short into your brilliantly provocative lighting board and now see a bare and rather scruffy stage, lit only by an unromantic work light, I am finally able to appraise the shell game you've been defrauding me with.

Men, I suppose, are first drawn to women by desire. Well, we've been through all that and you're really about as desirable as a porcupine. You can't help your face; indeed, neither of us could get past the stage door in a beauty contest. But sex can be, I'm told, simply jim-dandy if two people let themselves rip and yet don't forget that what's stimulating them is not a fucking machine but a real live human being.

I've tried for years now to clarify to you some of the simple requirements for any honorable, civilized relationship between a man and a woman. And apparently you've absorbed nothing or, if you have, you've scorned my honest convictions as if they were the maunderings of a high school freshman.

Sorry. I'm no longer spellbound. I've rescued my self-respect and I'm almost sorry to have to inform you that I'm a fairly distinguished and accomplished man. I am not the slug you so charmingly describe me as nor am I a person who should hang his head in shame.

It is very sad that American men and women almost invariably speak such disparate languages as to be incomprehensible to one another. And yet the irony is that the man can be made to feel intolerably guilty without having understood more than a few words from a morass of illogic.

If your nourishment is the destruction of the male ego and courage, amicability and sexual potency, you must by now be glutted. Perhaps it's as well, as you'll have to live on your fat until you find another theater buff whose mind you can bedazzle with your extraordinary hypnotic Pelléas and Mélisande lighting plot.

I can only say further, "Get the hell out of the garden, Maud!"

ALEC

Dear Mrs. Collins:

I was a guest in room 1214 for the past week. While you will probably be happy to receive such a large amount for such a short stay, you may also think that I'm a little crazy.

Let me tell you first that I am not rich. So I really know the value of money and fifty dollars is not just a drop in the bucket to me.

I planned to write a note to you no matter how much I put in the envelope. But then I thought that if I left you fifty dollars you just might never forget how deeply someone felt about your great kindness, your cheerful manner, your concern that everything be done to make someone as comfortable as you possibly could.

In these "getting by" days when it's considered a joke when you can skimp on a job, get away with doing the least amount of work and still get paid for it — well, it's simply a beautiful surprise and a series of happy moments when someone does a lovely job because of conscience and pride in work well done.

ALEC WILDER

Dear Mitch:

It was a strange irony that the afternoon of the day you went to work for Columbia Records as head of their A and R department, you at last performed the oboe concerto!

When I say "at last" I don't mean that I was becoming impatient, but these last years, cutting a giant swath at Mercury as their A and R man, making stars out of Frankie Lane and many others, plunging into the squalid world of pop music, you necessarily had to move away from the kind of music which had been your life up till then. I was afraid that you would never find your way back.

Now, in spite of all the pressure of the record business, you have managed to perform the concerto with your usual dexterity, spirit and dedication.

I'm enormously grateful.

But what now?

How on earth can you keep both worlds going? How can you concentrate on two such demanding areas? Is it possible? Or have you had all you want of playing? Is the big money and the excitement of what you're doing a greater challenge to you?

How great it would be if you could put a time limit on the business side of your life so that all of us who love your playing could know that we hadn't heard the end of it!

I hope it isn't the end; I'd hate to think that my concerto was the last piece you were ever to play.

ALEC

Dear Mr. Worth:

Are you really well enough founded to be taken seriously when you anathematize a composer?

Is it barely possible that you are a frustrated composer yourself? I've heard rumors that it was suggested by a recording man that you'd do well to come to me for a few hints as to how to improve your melodic lines. Frankly, I don't consider myself that competent. After all, I'm trying hard to improve my own writing and have no theories about improving the writing of someone else beyond suggesting that they try developing good taste, true style and, not incidentally, good manners, modesty and a warm heart.

Do you truly believe that a cult of admirers has grown up around my small musics? And if so, are they deceived into believing the music is good only because of the adequate orchestration? I can hardly accept that premise, simply because I'm definitely not that good an orchestrator.

So could it then be that they really do like the music? And, by the way, why does their enthusiasm irritate you so? Surely I have made no pronunciamentos to the press about my superior talent, I have had no publicized performances, I am not advancing by leaps and bounds into the Grand Arena of Big Names.

So why so nervous and upset?

Don't worry so! After all I'm just a journeyman writer who's having some fun putting on paper some innocent, towheaded notes, not grabbing for glory or notoriety.

Well, anyhow, you won't have to worry about bumping into me at parties; I don't attend them.

ALEC WILDER

Dear Mr. Canfield:

Mrs. Truslow in the village told me, when I admired that beautifully pieced dry wall around her garden, that the man who made it was still living right here in Lisbon Falls.

So I'm writing to tell you that the sight of your craftsmanship has given me a great deal of joy and, not incidentally, courage.

I say "courage" because I, too, have a kind of piece-by-piece, stone-by-stone craft which happens to be composing music. And I think I understand a little about even the smallest stone being important. Balancing, wedging, finding keystones, flat stones. Keeping shades of color together. Yes, it's not that much different except that I make sounds and never get my hands scratched or calloused.

ALEC WILDER

Dear Dr. Watson:

As you may not be surprised to hear, there has been no Five Year Plan since I sent my last report. I believe that my only plan is to have no plan.

Since you pulled your Merlin act and whisked me out of that long line of naked men about to become soldiers and returned me to sanity I have worked hard in many areas.

Before I describe them may I say that I'm reasonably certain that my rejection was "fixed" through the good offices of our mutual friend (dare I mention his name?). But, to my surprise, I am not ashamed that skulduggery may have been used, indeed, I'm forever grateful to you. I believe that even had I been accepted, I would shortly have proven too neurotic for them. But that in no way minimizes the kindness you performed for me.

As far as my planless activities are concerned I have done the following:

1) Had some lighthearted, fairly well-composed pieces conducted by Frank Sinatra and simultaneously recorded.

2) I have had a couple of songs which have attracted some attention, been recorded and made a little money.

3) I have fashioned a very beautiful garden down in Pennsylvania.

4) I have written a sentimental cantata called "The Story of a Good Man."

5) I have written for Mr. Baker a number of concert (as opposed to popular) songs.

6) I have become involved with one more impossible woman. I truly believe I attract (I can't believe I choose them!) emasculative, vicious bitches who sense my passivity and are amused by the games they can, in their superior realistic vainglory, play with me, much as a heartless child may be entertained by the contortions of frogs in kerosene cans. I admit that's stretching it a bit, but they are certainly, none of them, what I once dreamed grown-up girls would be like.

I suppose I falsely concluded that since they were not male, they would be the obverse of the coin and therefore gentle. But they're just as rough as the males except that if it comes to a squabble I'm not afraid that they'll beat me up.

7) I've been writing more and more of the kind of music I went to the Eastman School to learn how to write. As I meet more great musicians, largely through the kindness of a good friend and a magnificent French horn player, I've come to realize that outside of the poems (?) I send you, the only other deeply personal expression in my life is the writing of music.

Some of your responses to my poems are so cryptic and allusive that I fail to comprehend them. Nevertheless, I always pretend (and pray) they're compliments.

You know of my obsession about possessions? Well, I've thrown out music, given away books, in fact, kept or tried to keep myself down to the barest essentials. But through all this throw-out I've kept hundreds of poems — poems on menus, scraps of paper, backs of letters, torn, smudged, cracked along folded edges — but kept.

I've sent you only those I've had the courage to copy out in a fair hand because I thought they were worthy of your eye (and ear).

I think I'm going to find some patient person and pay them to decipher these more often than not drunken explosions. I have a hunch that some are rather respectable verse.

I manage to make a living, which constantly startles me. I *do* drink too much, to stimulate courage. I'm told my behavior is wretched after I go blank (they don't know I *do* go blank, by the way, as I don't stagger or slur speech).

Your faith in me and your fondness for me has pulled my legs in from high windows many a time.

If I have those poems deciphered and typed, would you mind if I sent them *all* to you?

ALEC

Dear John:

Now, at long last I've written the right piece for you. And you seem to agree. Your coupling of the third and fourth movements makes everything perfect.

I think this sonata has some good stuff in it. God knows it's not great but it certainly points in the right direction, I think. Of course most of my conviction comes from your enthusiastic reception of it and as an extra, extra dividend, your glorious playing of it.

Now that you've introduced me to so many great players I

have a demented notion to try to write sonatas for all the instruments. I know I can handle the winds but I don't know nearly
enough about the strings. I'd love to write a trumpet sonata for
Joe Wilder. Oh, I'm babbling again. I'm in a state of euphoria
from having finally come into a state of musical sanity and perhaps the edge of maturity.

You've turned the key in a cell door and God knows what the
results will be. Will the prisoner walk out calmly and amble out
of the prison gates or will he come out dancing and yelling and
beating the guards over the heads with dominant thirteenth
chords?

Or will he ask for some manuscript paper, a pencil and a spinet
and go back in his cell and get to work?

Thank you, thank you, thank you!

ALEC

Dear Mr. Bundison:

Perhaps I can help clear up what seemed to be your puzzlement and possible irritation over my description yesterday evening concerning my way of living.

Frankly, I'd have said nothing if you hadn't been so persistent.
I seldom attend dinner parties or gatherings of any kind and
therefore have no need to offer conversation pieces to strangers
or casual acquaintances. I mention this by way of disclaiming any
callow pride in my unconventionality.

I guess it started with your perfectly polite question, "Where
do you live?" I could easily have answered "New York," but I
admit to a degree of perversity and so I did bait you a bit by telling the truth and saying "Nowhere."

Well, you naturally assumed I was being silly. So I amplified
my statement by explaining how I never stay longer than two
weeks in any hotel room, that I couldn't tolerate the millstone of
a lease, that I'm terrified of possessions, that I can write music
anywhere, and that I always (and granted, absurdly) have the

illusion that the next move is going to be more pleasurable than the last one.

I explained, as you may recall, that I've disciplined myself to the point where I have everything I own in three medium-sized suitcases and an overflow of books and music manuscripts in three small suitcases which the Algonquin Hotel is kind enough to let me store in a cubbyhole behind their switchboard.

Oh, yes — and three pairs of pants, three jackets and one overcoat (during warm weather) in the tailor shop.

It's true I do have a rather scuffed and weathered pair of loafers besides the ones I'm wearing. But I never travel with them.

Tax base? Oh, merciful me, one must have one of those, mustn't one? Well, that's the Algonquin. Records of my own music? I have none. Published music? I have none. Old letters? I keep none, except those I fail to mail. Old music sketches? I throw them out. Passport? In my jacket pocket. Will? In a suitcase. Stocks? I have none, nor bonds, nor real estate nor insurance.

May I add that I not only distrust possessions, I'm also as afraid of them as if they all had very sharp, unpredictable claws. And that applies to wives, children (not that they're true possessions), dogs, cats, guppies, otters, raccoons, and perennial plants.

Yet I should add that I respect and admire many possessions — of other people. Not just casually, but reverently.

ALEC WILDER

Dear Harry:

Here's an illustration of my fix about being rejected.

He'd been operating the elevator at night ever since I started staying at the hotel. He was the only employee who broke the spell created by cheerful service, good food and tasteful furnishing. For he was sullen.

He never acknowledged a greeting or gratitude. He wasn't that old, but a bellman, when I asked about the man's doleful silence, said, "Oh, that's old Dan. He's been that way for years.

Lives alone and has a chip on his shoulder. But we get along with him all right. Just leave him alone."

But I couldn't leave him alone. At the end of a beautiful spring day when everything had gone well and old-fashioned courtesy had been encountered with bellmen, maids and room service waiters, it was an irritating and depressing experience to ride with Dan in underlined silence.

When I thanked him for the ride to the twelfth floor, he gave no sign he had heard me. It bothered me so much I went back down to the lobby five minutes later asking his forgiveness for disturbing him. Not even a grunt.

But coming back up I pressed five dollars on him, thanking him for all his kindness. Needless to say he accepted the money and with the most dreadful smile I've ever seen, almost like a photograph I'd once seen of a man who had taken cyanide of potassium.

Ghastly as it was, I was somewhat relieved by the fact that he thanked me. Cringingly, to be sure, but at least he had stuck his snout out of the ice pack.

The next time I was in Boston I came in late the first night and there was "old Dan" to whom I cheerily said hello.

Nothing. No response of any kind. And I was positive he hadn't forgotten the five dollars. I had only given it to him a couple of months before and I was reasonably certain it was no common occurrence.

No "good-night," no change of dour expression.

Now, Harry, we all meet pricks a dozen times a day, natural enemies, people we know we'll never get through to, have anything in common with, not even the pleasure of exchanging sentences ending in prepositions.

So why was I so obsessed with this rancid, sour, bilious, unattractive, dumb, night elevator man? Was I going through a phase of believing myself a harbinger of sweetness and light, a bringer of good cheer to the lowly minions? I don't think so. I simply couldn't believe an old employee of a distinguished hotel could be such a sulky shit.

Was it perhaps that I represented to him a brash, sleazy new world unlike those safe and sound rich widows who lived there, unlike the famous Brahmins whose daughters had had their coming-out parties there, unlike the famous playwrights, actors, Saltonstalls, Adamses, Lodges? Must I continue on for ten more years before Dan decided I was fit to be a guest?

Obviously something radical had to be done or I would have to change hotels. This probably seems a drastic step simply because one sourpuss fails to acknowledge a greeting. I think you're more realistic and cynical than I; you accept the likelihood of most people's slobbery and ignore the worst of them.

Please don't misunderstand, Harry! I don't consider myself so charming that even sullen elevator operators should react by emerging from their shell to celebrate a meeting with Smiling Al. My obsession with such people may have to do with my inability to be in the presence of isolation. I know it exists, indeed I constantly isolate myself. But I'm deeply depressed by such demonstrations as old Dan's.

So, rather than change hotels, I pulled a stunt the next time I rode with him: I faked a faint, slipping somewhat clumsily to the floor of the scented (truly) elevator. Now, I thought, now old Dan's hand will be forced! *Now* he'll have to acknowledge someone's presence; he'll even have to do something!

But the only thing that did happen was that the elevator abruptly stopped, then reversed its direction. In the face of red lights on the floor panel (I was peeking), we plummeted to the ground floor without a stop.

I sighed with relief, for I was certain he was going for help in this seeming crisis. He yanked the door open and ran out. I waited, lying prone and peeking.

The first thing that happened was the entrance of a stuffy couple who instantly backed out of the elevator at the sight of me. Shortly after this, a room clerk appeared in a somewhat hysterical swivet. I thought by then it was time to "return to life" so I opened my eyes (all the way), expressed mumbles of bewilderment and struggled to my feet saying, "I must have fainted."

By then there was a sizable group in front of the elevator door and expressions of twittery concern from the room clerk.

I reassured him that I felt okay and that I thought perhaps it would be a good idea if I got myself a brandy at THE BAR, as it's so succinctly called. I didn't really want one, but I was very curious to see if Dan was among the sightseers.

Not a sign of him.

When I went back to the elevator it was being operated by one of the bellmen. I asked him where Dan was. He looked at me oddly, as if I were guilty of some mysterious misdeed, and said that Dan was temporarily off duty.

My God, I thought, did Dan collapse from fright? Is he lying down in the cellar with a heart attack? If my stunt had caused him a relapse I'd never forgive myself.

The next morning I asked the friendliest bellman if he knew if Dan had become ill the night before. He looked about to check if any employee were nearby and said, "They tell me that Dan ran out of here last night without even changing into his street clothes. I heard that he said someone dropped dead in the elevator."

So much for my desire to communicate.

He wasn't on duty the next night nor, I'm told, has he ever been seen since. A week after my faint, my friendly bellman told me that his uniform had been mailed to the hotel, but no message. Nor, I gather, did he ever come by for the money owed him. The occurrence had taken place the night before payday.

So I guess in the future I won't try to pry open any more oysters. I feel truly sad and guilty about the whole thing. I found out where he lived and sent him an explanatory letter in which I said I'd only fainted, that he was deeply missed, and that everyone was hoping he'd be back soon. I also enclosed a fat check.

He's never come back and the check's never been cashed.

ALEC

Dear Brownie:

If I were to tell you of my fondness for you, you'd be very embarrassed. Men are not supposed to manifest affection except when blubbering drunk or unless they can convey it by arm pinching, back slapping or vulgar insults such as "You think this big shit's a buddy of mine? How stupid can you get?"

Our evening meetings in the cubbyhole behind the switchboard, right after they made a fresh batch of coffee! Your tales about the old Willard Hotel in Washington! That raunchy old song I'd sometimes get you to sing! The hour when the bookie called up with the results of the bets you'd laid on for the waiters and busboys and bellmen! Your glorious Chaplin imitations! The times you'd come up to my room when I was depressed and miraculously bring me back to life! The story you told me about the Negro soldier with the head bandage unraveling from his head walking with the troops off the ship from the First World War smelling the rose some girl had handed him! Tears would always come to your eyes when you'd tell that story.

The laughter with Earl and Harry out on the bellmen's bench! And your accounts of all the stray cats and dogs that lived in your apartment and how you'd have to race them to your room at night so they wouldn't crowd you out of bed!

Oh, Henry Brown, you were indeed a lovely man and sure as hell added a whole bucket full of sunlight to my life.

Thank you, dear Brownie!

ALEC WILDER

Dear Sam:

You and John and Bernie and Dave and Jerry have all made me very happy. First off by playing that transcription I made of the Bach piece, then by playing the semi-jazz movement I wrote for the quintet and finally and best of all by urging me to write a full-length four-movement quintet.

I've done it and upside down, at that. I took themes from the jazz movement to form the first movement and even a fragment to use in the second movement. It was a batty way to write such a piece and as a result it will suffer from it. But you've all been so encouraging and patient with me that I feel as if I had sprouted wings.

I'll make it up to all of you by writing a second quintet and this time I'll start at the first note and proceed sensibly and, I hope, logically from there to the end.

But for you five guys and Mitch Miller, I'd have wound up being an eccentric songwriter and a half-assed arranger.

Thank you, dear friend!

ALEC WILDER

Dear John:

It's with a sigh of relief and something approaching joy that I put the double line down to mark the end of the horn concerto. Whew!

At last I've written you a big piece! It's been a long time a-borning. God knows I've wanted to write for you ever since I first heard you play. The sonata was possibly just a trial balloon.

I don't know how good the concerto is but at least I've written it. It won't be the last one I write for you either.

As I told you, I'm scoring this for double winds and strings without any violins. (Why? I simply hear it that way.)

I have no notion how to get a group together to read it, let alone perform it. If you can find the players, Godspeed!

I want you to know that writing this piece has broken even more ice than the concerto I wrote for Mitch. Not that it is necessarily a better piece but, in spite of Mitch's splendid musicianship, I feel a great deal more comfortable and even protected writing for you.

I do think at last I'm out of the egg!

Thank you for your patience and faith!

ALEC

Dear Sirs:

I don't know who else to write to but the Chamber of Commerce or the Chicago Historical Society. I'm choosing the latter only because anyone concerned with commerce would never be concerned with what I have to say. On the other hand a historical society would never consider my words worthy of inclusion in the files of the history of a city. But who else would care? Studs Terkel? You're right! After all, he did those marvelous Chicago interviews he put together and called *Division Street*.

But I have really so little to say. It's all about those lovely little lights sprinkled over the Michigan Avenue trees at Christmas time. It's the curious sensation maybe only a visitor gets of bursting health all over midtown Chicago.

It was (and now they're gone) those glorious railroad stations, Lincoln Park, Second City, before Mr. Merrick tempted them out of town and into fame.

It's the fact that walking down Michigan Avenue to get the Panama Limited to New Orleans at the old Illinois Central Station, I'd feel so free and healthy that poems about being alone would start popping into my head and I'd even stop to jot them down.

Where, oh where has that Negro traffic cop gone who used to handle the rush hour at Congress and Michigan? He was not only masterly, he was a dancer.

Poor old Mr. Werner! He may never have known how to run a bookstore but while it was there it was a good one. I met one of the best men I've ever known there, Harry Bouras, and much later his very exciting family and their dachshund, Frieda, whose toenails they kept forgetting to have clipped.

One morning I wandered up from the La Salle Street Station, found a book called *The Bad Seed*, read it in one sitting on a bench in Grant Park and suddenly was sane again.

I remember leaving New York in a literal, visible, smellable sweat of panic. So why not remember Werner's Bookstore?

By the way, if any of you at the Historical Society knows

Harry Bouras (practically everyone except Mayor Daley does) could you please let me know what method you use to get him to either answer a letter or a phone call?

I despise all the North Side rich I've met, but damn it! The Pump Room, Jean and Georgetti's, a few French restaurants, even some of those hippie Sunday morning restaurants are exciting. Is it all due to Chicago's being basically a between-trains town? If I lived there would I stop sensing its drama? I *do* feel dramatic in Chicago. I *never* feel dramatic in New York. Even this spring when Oxford University Press gave a reception for the publication of my book at the Rainbow Grill on a bursting sunlit spring afternoon and I had to stand about greeting all manner of people — even celebrities — I didn't feel dramatic one bit! I'll bet I would have in Chicago.

Certainly an interview with Studs Terkel is more dramatic on radio in Chicago than a Carson interview would be on television anywhere.

ALEXANDER WILDER

Dear Mitch:

Again I must write to thank you for bringing me into the Golden Record project. I love to write gentle, simple songs and particularly if I know the listeners are going to be children.

I have to admit it isn't easy to work with Margaret Wise Brown! She writes great books but her lyrics are not good, especially since she has no ear for tunes and can't understand why you can't put ten syllables in a second verse where you had two in the first. But I'll work it out somehow. It's too much fun writing these tunes and scoring them for woodwinds to pass it up. An eighth of a cent record isn't much, to be sure, but since they're expected to sell in the millions, maybe I'll get solvent in addition to having a lot of fun.

Thank you for the thousandth time for thinking of me and,

even more, for making something happen. If this kind of thing continues, I'll become your indentured servant!

ALEC

P.S. Do you think there might be a chance to record songs about what each instrument does, in broad child terms, and also have short solo pieces by that instrument by way of illustration? Or would it be too offbeat?

Dear John:

Here we are at last in the same city and we see each other only slightly more than when you were in Minneapolis. And when we do meet at Jim and Benny's or whatever 100-proof oasis, we get to laughing and carrying on with all those glorious players you've introduced me to.

So I never get around to telling you the things that are on my mind. I've decided that the best way to tell you is to write you.

I'm sensible enough to know that I must do many unsavory and unfulfilling things in order to make a living. The principal consolation during the less attractive recording sessions I arrange for, is the presence of the warm and competent players, most of whom I've met through your good graces.

What I wonder is, were I forbidden to drink would I be able to continue in this diamond-hard world of commercial music? For without being conscious of it, I think the release that comes from drinking after fussing and fuming with those goblins is a prize I can look forward to and so can tolerate the tedium.

What's happened is that your return to New York and the spirit you instill in me as a result, has brought to the surface of my head and my heart the absolute need to write more and better abstract, concert, legit, whatever-you-call-it music.

That was once my dream and I got sidetracked by the need for money and, I'm afraid, the glitter and whirl of the pop-music world. The bandleaders, the singers, the constant dream that one of my songs might catch on; the nightclubs, the musician bars, all the temptations emanating from the exciting world of immediacy and the dangerous, dancing shadows of possible notoriety.

No good!

Only the security from the money I make is right. All the rest is the easy way, an evasion of the challenge I set up for myself years ago. And if you'll stick with me, keep pushing me, curse me if necessary, then, damn it, I'll do everything in my power to live up to your faith in me and maybe I'll appease my own hunger.

It will be a juggling act, that's for sure. Nevertheless I believe I can compartmentalize the two musical points of view so that I won't lose the high sights I've always set for truly creative writing.

With you within hollering distance I believe I can and will grow and then one lovely day wake up to find myself an honest-to-God composer!

So I thank you for the past, the present and the future!

ALEC

Dear Kevin:

I want to thank you very much for laughing at my silly jokes and for listening to the story I told you about the baby otter.

Usually people your age don't pay much attention to people my age unless they're an uncle or a grandfather. And you weren't just polite; you were a real friend.

I don't expect you to believe me, but I remember very clearly how I felt when I was your age. I remember silly things I used to say over and over to myself and I remember being very sad when I found an animal caught in a trap with its leg broken. I wasn't strong enough to open the jaws of the trap and I kept hollering for someone to help open it up and all the time I was talking to the animal and patting his head. And then a man ran up and looked at the poor animal and said, "Ugh! What's the matter with you, you crazy kid? That's a rat!" And he dropped a rock on him and I cried for hours.

I hope I can come down to Laguna Beach soon with your father so we can have another great day on the beach.

ALEC WILDER

Dear Ana:

Your mother tells me that your name is spelled ANA because that's the way it's spelled in many different countries. I think that's very nice because maybe if you went to Sweden there would be other girls called Ana. Or Greece, or maybe Brazil.

But that's not why I'm writing you this letter. I'm writing to thank you for the heart you mailed to me. As far as I'm concerned it's a real heart even though we both know that you made it out of damp Kleenex and your mother's lipstick. At first I thought it was red crayon, but it smelled so nice I knew it was lipstick.

It honestly is the best present anyone has ever sent me. Maybe you don't know this, but when men get old they don't expect any young girls to pay attention to them, particularly pretty young girls, eleven years old.

So I carry the heart you sent me in a soft velvet watch case that belonged to my grandfather. And the pocket I carry it in is right over my own heart.

ALEC WILDER

Dear Jane:

I ran into the Backuses. They knew your married name and your address. All I knew for a time was that you had married a clarinet player and had shown up stoned backstage when the Delta Rhythm Boys were singing a one-nighter in Seattle.

Then I did see you that once when you made a short visit to New York.

It would be cruel and gratuitous to dredge up our often marvelous, sometimes destructive times together in the forties.

There's no doubt that you gave me a new and healthy attitude toward girls. By the time I met you I was convinced that all females over thirteen and under sixty were predatory beasts.

The fact that you are Irish may have a lot to do with it, for American women by and large seem bent on some kind of racial revenge. You never were, and besides, you were the first girl I ever met whom I trusted. And without making a speech, may I say that the male erection is affected as much by trust as it is by stimulation. Until your affection for me became possessive, everything was glorious. I'll admit I'm no prize and never was in terms of day-to-day reliability relating to male-female constancy.

My way of life, and probably a deep-seated neuroticism, is a need of freedom of motion. I know that there can be no honorable relationship without certain unwritten rules of behavior. And the one I can never live up to is that of being physically available or on call. The other rule is that in order to live this life of freedom of motion I can have no wife, child, possession.

I tried to make that clear to you when we got to know each other and I'm sure you accepted what amounted to my egocentricity and even understood it. But love, that irrational, violent obsession, knows no rules and it entered your heart. It was in mine all the time but not the same kind as yours.

I suppose humans are the most domesticated of all animals but for purposes of survival females are the more domesticated of the two. So, from a marvelous, laughing, wild little girl who used to love sex as a child loves candy, you became a bitter, angry woman who wanted more attention, more reassurance — God knows, even marriage!

Nothing had ever been promised to suggest more than a happy sexual frolic. It was very sad, that wrangling bust-up.

Then you came back married to the clarinet player and had become the representative of the Topeka Temperance Society. Your adorable body had vanished, your laughter had vanished, and one morning you, yourself vanished and I've never seen you since.

ALEC

Dear David:

I'm back in the Bel Air Hotel which as usual I can't afford. This time Phil Landon has given me 103 which faces the pool (who *are* those tacky people who use it?) and the back door of which has that semicultivated garden with the gentle fountain. Its plinketing is so soporific that I may not get past this page without napping.

Today the pool is made of simple blue-green folds of sun and shadow. No people — the only sounds are the fountain and the

plinking of my bobble birds against their tumbler rims (two yel-
low, one flamingo red and one Kodachrome blue. You'd have
loved them!).

No sounds of Sinatra records as there were when you lived in
the next room. I was wakened and lulled to sleep by them. You
never stopped playing them all during that stay.

I guess you loved him a great deal. God knows he has incredible charm and magnetism in addition to his extraordinary
talent!

You were a very dear man and you were always so very young.
You so loved being taken care of, treated like a child.

I remember one night in your apartment you were burrowing
around in a closet for a copy of a song Bill Engvick and I wrote
called "In the Morning." It was about a war pilot who failed to
come back from a training flight. His young wife sings "I went
down to the field where nothing grows."

I don't know why I said it but I did: "You love it there in that
closet, don't you, David?" You gave me a very strange look of
recognition and allowed enthusiastically that you did.

The crib, the protective walls, that's what you wanted.

But you were a star and there aren't any but the wrong walls
around stars. It must have been pretty damn scary, even with all
the money and the glory.

And then you had to get your face all busted up. The saddest
aspect of it was that you didn't look that much different after
they patched you up. But you'd been so damned handsome! I suppose you felt you had lost your identity. Not the public face, no,
your own private face.

So you drank and desperately reached for mother figures. You
probably had a real one but obviously not the kind you needed.

So many kind and gentle ladies tried to save you.

I can't stop thinking about those marvelous Sinatra records
endlessly filtering into this room while you wandered aimlessly
around your own room. Did you lie on your bed crying? Did you
stare in mirrors searching for your lost beauty? Dreaming of some
secret you had never told anyone?

The last time I saw you I was standing by the entrance of the old Gladstone Hotel in New York. You came along with Libby and suddenly saw me. You leaped across the pavement and jumped literally into my arms. It was no strain. You were emaciated and light as a child.

And now you're gone and from Mr. S. there is a long, sad silence. Oh, the terrible sadness of losing the dear ones, the loving ones! No wonder the eyes of the old seem to be looking at something so very far away!

ALEC

Dear Harry:

You never knew me when I would spend all my extra money on train rides. I've always been ashamed that I told some smart-ass interviewers (back in the forties when I hadn't sense enough to turn them down) about these almost mystical dreamlike trips. For they used them as ho-ho signs of my eccentricity and as a result, this many years later, old farts will stop me on the street and with fake heartiness ask me if I'm still riding trains.

How could these jackasses begin to know what happened to me? It would be like asking someone who had experienced a religious revelation if he was still having them.

I know all the areas and occasions when I learned something. They're mighty few but I won't bother you with them now except to say that I know I learned more about myself and my relationship to the world while taking those extended railroad trips back in the thirties and forties than at any other time.

I learned about the United States, about its harlequin population, about my own needs and fears and wonderments. Occasionally I spoke to people but I was by no means a roving reporter, prying and poking and making a nuisance of myself.

Of course the dreadful irony is that the only machine I ever loved was the machine that made the first monstrous intrusion into the landscape, made possible big business, big factories, and set the stage for its frightening successors, the automobile and the airplane. The very steel rails, to exist, demanded a mill with stinking chimneys, pollution, strip-mining and all the horrors a few of us desperately battle against right now.

I wasn't being a martyr making those trips alone. The few I took with another railroad lover were never as fulfilling as the ones I took alone.

Of course it was a dream and unrelated to the hard, cold facts of survival. Yet I learned a great deal about the mystery of myself and the world. I found something then that I've lost along the way. It amounted to a series of spiritual resolutions that closed a circle.

The only other revelatory time of any duration was when I put together that glorious flower garden down in Berks County in a Pennsylvania valley. And that, at least, needed no mechanical aids. For I even used organic fertilizer!

ALEC

Dear Charlotte:

I learned recently that you are alive, very much so, and living in Chicago and married to great wealth. Is he the Harvey of those marvelous dining cars on the Santa Fe? Then he can't be all bad.

When I was around ten and went every summer to Bay Head, there was a boardwalk long since swept out to sea by storms. Your family's house was one of those set behind the boardwalk facing the sea.

I used to walk past it singing a song I remember to this moment. It was really not a very good song but it surely suited my melodramatic mood.

You were very pretty and very popular. I was bothered only by the harshness of your Great Lakes voice. You knew I was smitten and when I'd hang around outside the Bluffs Hotel ballroom waiting for the intermissions when all you dancers would emerge from the heat of it, you'd spot me and whirl about with your escort pretending to be having a much better time than you actually were. I'd be perched on the railing pretending it was a normal place to be on any given evening.

I was too scared to dance or even to ask for a date.

But one night I found myself at a beach party out beyond the end of the boardwalk. We'd all collected driftwood, made a fire, toasted marshmallows, and on this monumental evening you and I held hands. That was a glorious occasion for me.

Years later in Rochester when I was going to the Eastman School of Music some red-haired girl whose name I've forgotten mentioned that you were coming for a visit.

I went out to her house and there I met a loud, brittle, carefully groomed stranger. I might as well have been meeting you for the first time.

It made me wonder if it's the ladies who are the true romantics.

That meeting was a disaster. For the cute little Charlotte Drum (any relation to that dreadful general?) I used to sing to from the boardwalk and hold hands with at a beach party had vanished and very possibly never realized she had ever existed even in the mind of a lonely, romantic little boy.

Happy Women's Lib!

ALEC WILDER

Dear Mr. Income Tax Man:

Perhaps if I met you in a beer parlor out on Route Four some Saturday night and didn't know what your job was, we might possibly get along just dandy.

As it is it seems we are forced to be enemies. This is perfectly ridiculous, all things considered. Granted the big brass will clap you on the back for squeezing a few more bucks out of me or maybe they won't. Maybe they'll just say among themselves "Signorelli's doing a good job."

Well, all that makes for security, a pension, hospitalization, and best of all, the knowledge that you represent the law and therefore have power.

People sure must be scared shitless most of the time or they wouldn't have such an obsession for power. I've never met a truly great man yet who was more than mild, gracious, even timid.

How on earth can you guys maintain daily, hourly belligerence? It's impossible to be rancorous, mean, insulting, vindictive all day long! And yet from what I've seen of you and some of your fellow workers there's no coffee break in your accusatory, uncouth, "when did you stop beating your wife" manner.

If my survival weren't at stake I'd laugh in your face. You're absolutely convinced, aren't you, that when I go to California to persuade singers to record songs that I'm really just out there to ball the chicks, get drunk, and generally have a high old time?

Will you listen to the methodology, the routine by means of which singers are brought to the point of deciding definitely to record a song? No you won't! Can it be that you're jealous of people such as myself who know all the stars and call them by their first names?

Will you believe me when I solemnly swear that I go to Key West to write music, that I've never fished in my life, that at most I spend an hour a day on the beach and then only if my work is going well?

No! It's like set concrete in your head that all people go to Key West to fish! Hell, that's what *you* would do! So what's all this shit about work?

Then there's the business of how much space I use in my room at the Algonquin when I work there. If I only sit at a desk I can't ask for as much off for office space as if I used more cubic feet. What if, in order to orchestrate, I am forced to stand up once in a while, or even to pace up and down to help my thought processes?

You told me I couldn't compose if I didn't have a piano in my room. So I told you you couldn't add figures without an adding machine! Up yours!

You're jealous of what you consider to be the freedom of the artist. You haven't any conception of the amount of energy, time and concentration that goes into creation. You see us relaxing in nightclubs. Have you ever seen us at work?

Mr. X, I'm truly sorry for you and your miserable guilty-till-proven-innocent occupation. Your mind is as tight shut as a bank vault. There's no point in discussing anything with you. So take the fucking money and get lost! It's particularly comical considering that you don't see a dime of it unless you've also figured out ways to filch.

I take it back about Saturday night on Route Four. We'd simply never make it. You'd start accusing me of diluting your whiskey!

ALEC WILDER

Dear Mr. Reilly:

Harry Celentano has loaned me a batch of your poems.

I believe they are remarkably good. The imagery is vivid and sometimes electrifying, the sentiments are warm and angry, very lonely and often wildly funny.

A poet, nineteen years old, in 1972?! Not a shopgirl versifier like that smarmy raccoon lover, but a two-balled, hawkeyed, bat-eared honest-to-God poet!

Aren't you afraid of being arrested? Or do you swear your friends to secrecy? What do your parents think? Obviously, that you're loony! Of course if you wrote about the raccoon who got hurt feelings because you didn't say good-night to it, your mother would probably fly you to Los Angeles to put you on the Carson show!

But damn it, you're a real Dylan Thomas poet! I know Harry met you slinging mailbags in that branch post office. How come you happened to tell him? He said he'd get you to drink during your lunch break, so probably you belted down doubles and spilled the whole thing. Fortunately, he happens to be on the side of the right mice, so you told the right guy.

Now — what can I do? Forgive me for muscling in, but I've been sneaking poems to an old friend for forty years — never tried to publish one — it's none of those poetry editors' damn business. *My* secrets being weighed in their ferret-eyed little brains ("Will it help my career? Will Auden approve of my choice? Will the editor-in-chief call me a fag if I publish the one about the beautiful little boy?") and so on, and so on.

Are you desperate to see your poems in print? Do you feel a violent need for acceptance, exposure, the lot? Or can you quietly continue to build up a stockpile until you reach a state a trifle less frenzied so that when you choose a few to submit you won't be destroyed by rejection?

I'm very impressed and though I'm not as good a poet as you, I continue to keep my counsel, reveal my inner life to only a very few, and move through life as poetically as possible, but as little like a poet!

God knows I'll pray for you!

ALEC WILDER

Dear Tomorrow:

Is it comfortably warm there in the Algonquin lobby? Or Indian Summer hot? Have you called the man at the Social Security office? Are you still angry about losing the $300.00 and selling that stock (the only stock you owned) at a $700.00 loss? Do you rationalize it all by considering Dr. Watson's check for $1,000.00 as balancing the loss?

Do you remember how you felt sitting in Charlie Davidson's car on the Nantucket pier a few days ago while the wind blew, rain spattered the windows, and you waited to hear if the boat to the mainland would leave the island that day?

What are you more likely to remember, if you're not in too

much pain as you lie dying? Your reading this letter, what it evokes of that Nantucket morning — or how you feel right now writing about it?

Well, you're weary of waiting around with a man who can't tolerate idleness. If you were alone it would make a different memory. And keep this always in mind: you'll always be happier, except when in intolerable pain, when you know that at any desired moment you can be completely alone.

So go for a walk alone tonight, if you're forced to stay over, and remember only it, the walk alone. I'll bet you then the whole trip will have seemed worthier.

P.S. Now, the next day, as we're about to leave, it's all I remember with the same old mysterious private joy.

Dear Mr. Long:

A well-meaning but unobservant friend sent me your review of last night's concert. Obviously my name was all she saw, for had she read what you wrote, she would have burned the review.

You said in toto "that anyone in the seventh decade of the twentieth century should have written such a piece as Alec Wilder's Suite for French Horn and String Quartet is unpardonable." That's approximate.

Now, first things first.

Do you believe that criticism of music performed for the first time should have as its primary criterion contemporaneity?

Have you never had the graciousness to review a new work which employed traditional techniques and attitudes in terms of the excellence or mediocrity of its structure and/or content?

Do you insist that all new music sound "new"? Unprecedented, unrelated to the past, underivative in any way? Are you by chance or preference a Neophiliac?

Are you one more of the believers that baroque music — counterpoint, in a word — ended with Bach, that melodic, harmonic, diatonic music ended with the nineteenth century — in a word, Romantic Music?

Are you one who insists that music and other arts be a reflection of their time — even at the risk of not being a reflection of their creator?

Do you feel socially safer praising the fashionable and damning the traditional?

I'm not so respectful of my talent that I'm inclined to defend it with froth on my lips. Yet I believe that I do have a reasonably clear and detached mind to the degree that I am able to appraise my music sanely.

It risks cleverness on occasion, but since cleverness implies evasion, I guard against it.

It sings a fair amount, though I'm well aware of the current rejection of any expression as innocent as song (except, of course, for the slogan shouters known as Rock Singers).

Some of it's rather witty. And, of course, I'm in deep trouble here, since laughter isn't "relevant" or "meaningful." Besides which life is, after all, desperately solemn and laughter insults its seriousness.

I have written a series of rather large and sonorous, even loud pieces for wind ensemble which I have called Entertainments. I have used this word not because Graham Greene used it for some of his books but because I wanted to make very certain the audience knew that the purpose of the pieces was specifically to entertain and also specifically not to teach.

I believe Monsieur Ravel was once heard to say to a heckler at a party who was accusing him of wishing to be the successor to some famous predecessor, "No, monsieur (here my French fails me), you are wrong! I am only trying to entertain!"

But, of course, I can hear you interrupting, "but that was long ago before man had begun to take on his responsibility toward the oppressed, before he became aware of his racial crimes and monstrous neglect and manipulation of minorities" and on and on, winding up, I suppose, with Kafka, Kierkegaard and Hesse.

I wonder, Mr. Long, if you screw your wife to an egg timer

and if you weigh your meals on a chic apothecary scales, read only the Great Books, listen only to the Great Music, indeed, I wonder if you aren't the personification of a word I coined, a Significator.

Instrumentalists, the very best of them, by the way, like the way I write. But I'm sure that fact, to you, is the kiss of death since so many critics and composers consider players to be reactionary, uninformed, unprogressive and terribly lazy. And of course the player is about to become superfluous in the new scientifically controlled age.

To be quite honest with you, I consider myself to be quite as civilized and sophisticated as you are, while recognizing your undoubtedly superior intellect. If I thought it would help, I'd give you some spark plugs, a few gallons of gas and enough oil to allow that beautifully fashioned motor of yours to turn over. On the other hand, I think it serves your purposes better for it to remain stationary and spotless in its daily washed show window.

I only worry about whether it (the motor) will fit into the model of ten years hence or, if so, you have been able to pass your driving test.

ALEC WILDER

Dear Dr. Watson:

This week I finished my sixth woodwind quintet. I had been working at a piano in a building on Columbus Circle.

I sat on a balustrade which surrounds a square of greenery and flowers and looked over what I had written. I would look up from time to time and notice the delicate early green of the trees in the adjoining park and suddenly (perhaps foolishly) decided to dedicate the quintet to Spring, 1962.

And all four movements are springlike and innocent. So maybe it wasn't so foolish after all.

But I'm afraid that's all I know about innocence. The world is becoming a tawdry, demented carnival. I feel the stealthy encirclement of an army of Halloween masked goblins.

It's as well you isolate yourself as much as you do. Even if you read newspapers, over or underground, magazines licit or illicit, watch television, plain or color, listen to the radio, public or university, still you won't feel this fearful pulse, see this glazed look, spot this slack-jawed jamboree, this crazed death dance.

It's fairly deceptive, being furnished gaudily, lit garishly, advertised glowingly. Its overpowered cars are shiny, its highways smooth and strung with reassuring "yields" and "do not enters," with arrows and offers of food, lodging and even fuel. Sleekness and slickness, surface sheen all serve to mesmerize the most invulnerable eye.

The young people know it's all wrong but even they are being magnetized by the affluence, the swiftness with which stardom may be achieved and with minimal talent.

They forget that the ensuing wealth places them neatly in the hands of their faceless corporate enemy, they forget that the notoriety they are tempted by is also dependent upon the power and wealth of that same enemy.

Fortunately only a minority among the young is confused to this extent. But the deeply concerned majority of them is simply not observant enough to recognize the mass madness for what it is.

They see strange behavior but quickly become so used to it, it doesn't frighten them any longer because of the simple human, only too human, mechanisms of habit.

The wife of a famous writer behaved as if her husband were insane the last weeks of his life only because, I believe, he had finally sensed that society had gone mad. It was his wife who couldn't recognize the sanity in her husband's awareness of mass insanity.

Forgive my amateurish speculations. I mention them because my view of this age should have brought all my creativity to a grinding halt. It hasn't and it won't.

My close friends, myself and music — and an occasional book
— remain.

ALEC

Dear Abby:

It's pretty damned ridiculous that you should have that name,
particularly since this letter is a "Dear Abby" plea for information
such as she broadcasts like grass seed.

But first I should make a statement. I am a passive man and any
time I become involved with a girl, I automatically assume that
she will set the involvement in motion. Yet I should keep in mind
that when I drink I become not only active but belligerent. So I
ask myself "could it be that our relationship exists as the result of
my being drunk or half so on all the occasions when we first
met?" And I speculate further. Was my condition during those
meetings so offensive (as compared with defensive) that I, the
normally passive one, set it all in motion?

I am not drinking now, that is, at this moment, so I'm aware of
what I'm writing. So I must apologize for saying to you that it
would be far better for me never to have found the crutch or
weapon of alcohol. Looking back I can see that all my relationships with women must have come into being as the result of my
fuzzy condition at the very time when I should have been as clear
as mountain water.

Sober, I want no part of an intimate relationship with women
(or men, either!). Must I blame all these disasters on a prostate
gland inflamed by alcohol? Yes, I am saying that our relationship
is a disaster. The only time it takes on any direction or objective
is when I am drinking, and obviously the objective is some form
of sexual gratification.

So, finally to the "Abby" questions.

What on earth do you expect of me? Why, when we have
nothing but gardens and sex in common, do you keep sinking
hooks into me? Why do you go to such lengths to keep me in a

state of servitude by making me feel guilty when I don't fulfill your merest whim? We don't like the same things, not even each other. So is it that your conscious or unconscious purpose is to destroy me, hating all males as you obviously do? Every male friend you have is overtly homosexual. Did you hate your father so much that heterosexual males must all be destroyed?

I suppose I shan't get shet of you unless I move so far away that you can't hover over me like a vulture. Dear Abby, why do you go to so much trouble, expend so much energy? For the perverse pleasure of turning a basically decent, fairly talented, peace-loving man into a shattered, unmendable wreck?

Or must I assume all responsibility on the grounds that my personality "in wine" is such that I must accept all that exists as having been promulgated by myself?

It happens not to be true. But because there is a trace of validity to it, you are trying to Svengali me into believing that I am the villain, solely responsible for this intolerable mess.

There's only one way I can escape your imprisonment: stop drinking, develop a workable degree of self-respect and enough true courage to walk away — not escape.

ALEC

Dear Rogers:

My first awareness of your existence was the sound of your laughter in the Algonquin Hotel lobby.

Down the years I have become increasingly suspicious of loud laughter. For with the shocking decrease of wit and its leavening acuity, loud laughter usually connotes hollow lip service to the tag line of a dirty joke by the man planning his plunge ahead into the next one.

But yours was wholly genuine laughter which clearly revealed a person who knew that, but for a few rose petals and towheaded tots, it was just "a melody played in a penny arcade." A carnival without even the dignity of forthright thimble rigging.

So I managed as quickly as possible to meet you. Probably in that sleazy Blue Bar tended by that nameless slob (and he *would* sue!).

Ever since (thirty years?), you've made me outrageously happy. Of course I've made you outrageously and justifiably furious on those many occasions when I was ugly-drunk and you have bored me with wallet photographs of your dog (having just laid to filth the father-with-the-children photographs). But over and under all you have given me great nourishment, endless laughter, unsolicited sympathy and understanding, and lived up as have very few to my autocratic rules of friendship.

I've told you to your constant irritation and anger that you were a writer. I've told you you were a great man of the theater, which you proved for a time when you had the stock companies and then directed my and Bill Engvick's opera *The Long Way* to perfection.

But damn it! You're another of those nine-tenths of the iceberg people who, no matter how entire may seem their confessions, always manage to conceal the big pain or the reason for the Blind Spot.

Of course I must consider my own Blind Spot as well. Perhaps it's a valuable one, at least for my purpose, since it keeps me composing. Yet it may be blind of me to presume that creative people should create in a quasi-permanent form.

This is not necessarily so since great chefs daily watch their masterpieces being chewed to death, housewives create peace and comfort for the families and are seldom credited with having created anything but prisons for the young and millstones for the wage-earning fathers. Oscar Wilde, Shaw, Gogarty, Voltaire probably tossed off many more witticisms and penetrating observations than have ever been preserved.

Great gardeners, at best, have that ephemeral season and perhaps some Kodachrome photographs to prove the miracles which they have planted and nurtured.

Your whole adult life has been a brilliant display of rare jewels of wit and phenomenal sociological observation. You have cheered the despondent, delighted the cynical, warmed the lonely, enspirited the hopeless.

Can a painting, a sonata, a novel do any more than that? I doubt it. The only difference is that the artworks are available for a time, they can be preserved in libraries and museums, and they have the equivocal advantage of being known as Art.

You simply live it, act it out, contribute it and only a Boswell can prove you as great a creator as The Artist.

ALEC

Dear Liza:

Such a romantic instruction you passed on to me down the line of command of your cousins: that you wished me never to see you after you grew old!

The information must have reached me twenty years ago. And I know you're undoubtedly a very beautiful white-haired, seventy-year-old lady, thin, with a ramrod back, the same elusive smile, direct glance and that ineffable mystery of your secret life which I'm certain will never be revealed.

I have been for all these years deeply touched and complimented by your wanting me to remember you only as you were in those lovely innocent years when loss was desperate and lonely but never brutal or bestial, when suffering was shattering but always contained the amelioration of a poetic principle, when love was never defiled by shabbiness or the landscape of wasteland society and when a reflected light on a highway was the eye of a raccoon instead of the glint of a discarded can.

We laughed a lot in those kindergarten times, we drank and became ill from cheap gin, we held each other in the vestibules of summer trains, we even played croquet and tried to make bayberry candles.

When you decided Duncan needed you more than I, you were

right. But you, in turn, must have needed me more than I ever realized. If you hadn't, why should you have insisted I never see you old?

But it's better this way. For had I continued to see you, I would have done what I have always done with people or objects which touched me deeply: I would have, in effect, thrown you away as I have thrown away loving gifts and deeply personal letters.

But as it stands, you remain my only true love.

So that you will know I mean this old-fashioned phrase, I'll qualify it. I'm quite certain that never before or since have I met a girl, a woman whom I desired, loved as a friend, trusted implicitly and wanted to be with day and night. "Only love." That means I would have wanted to sleep in the same bed, use the same bathroom, find compensating pleasure in domestic drudgeries, loved no less in unromantic crises — perhaps I mean I wasn't afraid of you, afraid of disillusion, disenchantment, or threatened by intrusion on my privacy.

I know myself fairly well and am not overenthusiastic in my awareness but I've worked out a bearable relationship with me. But with you I'd have been joyous, I'd have confided, I'd have wept when sad and crowed when delighted. I'd even have shared with you as much of my secret creative life as you'd have cared to accept.

Yes, "only love."

ALEC

Dear "Uncle" Howland:

I was terribly sorry to hear that you have become bedbound by your recent stroke. I do hear that they can do great things nowadays with new drugs, and I have hopes that soon I'll hear you're able to be up and around the house.

I don't know if you remember me. You were driving people from the trains at Thallman into Brunswick and I rode a couple of times with you to the Oglethorpe Hotel.

Then we met again a couple of times in the depot at Thallman when you were carrying bags for the incoming and outgoing passengers.

I worried about it because you didn't look nearly strong enough to be doing such strenuous work. Maybe you were surprised the day I begged you to take the five dollar bill when you hadn't even touched my bags. I remember you were very proud and hurt and you told me one should never accept money for services they hadn't given.

One time when I got to the depot real early, Mr. Appleby, the station agent, told me how you used to work up on top of that old coal chute north of the depot where the steamers used to coal. When he told me, I suddenly remembered when I used to make trips down on the old Orange Blossom Limited and there was a coaling stop right in the middle of the piney woods. I hung over the edge of the open observation platform and looked ahead to a rail crossing and beyond it a depot and now I know it must have been your coaling station.

I'm sorry I couldn't help your son with his religious country songs. I am around one part of the song business but, unfortunately, it has no connection with religious music and I can't find anyone who knows anyone who works in it.

One more thing: I addressed you as "uncle." I hope you don't mind as I don't know you that well. The only reason I did it was I've heard other people call you that and I meant it as a term of affection.

All my best to you!

ALEC WILDER

Dear John:

I've found that no matter how I feel when I arrive in this town (Brunswick, Georgia), within a matter of hours I feel like composing and I thought you'd like to know that I've started that series of sonatas I told you I might write for every instrument in the orchestra. I take that back as I couldn't face the harp, the bass clarinet (not enough dynamic range) or, strangely enough, the violin. There have been too damn many magnificent pieces written for violin and unless I could write an undramatic sonata, I'd rather omit it.

And when I get to the French horn I'll write a second sonata for you and I'll do my damnedest to make it better than the first.

Christ! Have you got me flying?! Five years ago I would have flatly stated that such a purpose as I now have could never happen. I only pray that I don't fall into a dry spell! In commercial music you work straight through dry spells; the results reveal the sand in the salad. But with as personal music as I now need to write, there must be a virtual euphoria of hope and faith and conviction. All cynicism must be erased from your being. At least *my* being. For I'm not interested in reflecting the world I live in; my concern is to transmute the very best of myself into disciplined, loving and if possible witty and civilized sound!

Excuse me, John; I have to get back to work!

ALEC

Dear Mabel:

Have I ever written to you of what you have meant to me through the years?

I've written about you on the backs of albums, I've talked about you in interviews, I've written songs for you and about you, but I've never written *to* you.

Suddenly I remember that I *have* written to you but only letters of gratitude after spending days of spiritual transfusion up at Red Rock.

What I want to write to you about now is something much more difficult: what you did for me during the war years on 52nd Street. (I was always taught to write out the words for numbers. Should I have done that here or could 52nd Street never be Fifty-second Street?)

I was very embarrassed to be a civilian during those years even though I had made all kinds of unpatriotic gestures in order to remain one. Most of my good friends were in outlandish islands (what else could an island be but outlandish?) or in England, Africa, Germany and here was I, trying to make a living in New York City writing songs!

I did have a few friends who either had not been called up or who had dependents, but I have never been inclined to "get together." My courage came in hundred-proof bottles, so by the time you were about to start singing at Tony's, I'd be brave enough to come up from the Algonquin. Not that the Street, so called, was a scary place; on the contrary, it was one of the friendliest areas I've ever known. There was every level of human society on it, from John Hammond, who had snuck out of a side door in his Vanderbilt relative's house on the Fifth Avenue end of the block ("snuck" for fear of being seen doing so by, let's say, Lester Young) to Lester Young who may have taken the reverse of the A train from Harlem.

You were the exception to the Street rule which was jazz. You never pretended to do anything but impeccably sing great standard songs in your own fashion which always respected the writer of both music and lyric.

Whenever I acted up (laughed too loudly, behaved unbecomingly) you had a way of letting me know. I hope this wasn't too often. The night I was sitting at the front table with Thelma Carpenter, that exquisite child, and "turned on," blowing the smoke in your direction, I have never seen such a magnificent meeting on a human face of dignity and bewilderment. It was very naughty, but Thelma was irresistible and I was very proud to be with such a beautiful *enfant terrible*.

I remember evenings when I was so obviously depressed but not drunk, that you would sing a whole set of my songs, many of them now lost, unknown, and I don't mind a bit. I have the memory of your great compassion.

I think the words to "Night Talk" very well expressed those evenings in the life of a maverick like me. Strangely that song *is* published due to the goodness of Howie Richmond, though never sung by anyone but yourself. I can't remember any but a few lines from it:

> *Night talk, that's when the ghosts walk*
> *That's when the past comes up and hits you*
> *And the something hour permits you to relax*
> *With all your crazy facts and fancies.*

You sang "The Olive Tree," that almost Elizabethan song I wrote to the lovely, untypical verse of Edmund Anderson. Nothing, by the way, in this man's personality or later life gives a clue as to how he came to write such an untwentieth-century sentiment.

There were lots of other songs like "Goodbye John," "Who Can I Turn To?" (the original one), "Did You Ever Cross Over to Snedens?" (which is listed on your record as "Snedon's Landing") and "While We're Young."

I wrote the Sneden's song after spending a drunken night at a house rented by Ginger Johnson, who had asked me to come out from New York to discuss reharmonizing the hymnbook in modern jazz altered chords. Not unnaturally, no discussion took place. I had heard that a shad fisherman would transport people across the Hudson to catch a train on the east side of the river.

I rode across with him in the dawn which was more than normally pink from the state of my eyes and, while waiting for a train, I began to think of one of my aunts whom I remembered having gone to boarding school at Dobbs Ferry. I wrote the lyric there and then (though, ironically, I later learned that she had gone to Farmington School, nowhere near Dobbs Ferry).

You remember Frank Baker? He heard the finished song and wisely suggested I write different music for the two middle verses to avoid the sin of monotony. I did. How I came to play it for you I can't remember, except that I always played everything but strictly "art" songs for you.

I was astounded and perplexed when you decided to perform

it. I couldn't see how you could make it work in even the most polite "saloon." The verse was long, the story was sad, the music unlike that of even show tunes. Yet you *did* perform it and it has remained one of your most requested songs.

There was a lot of sitting about and laughing in those days. People were more communicative and prepared to listen as well as talk. Tony's was an asylum for me, like a church to a criminal. I somehow felt I couldn't be arrested for whatever mysterious crime I had committed as long as I remained. I felt that even those I would suspect and fear anyplace else would behave pleasantly toward me there.

And that was all because of you, dear Maybelle, as I called you in those days! And still do!

ALEC

Dear Mr. Carpenter:

There's no reason why you should remember me. I was just one more among thousands of passengers whom you have served in your travels.

I was riding east on Number 4 last Wednesday, the 27th, from L.A. to Chicago. I had Bedroom E. You just may remember me as the man who kept asking for a table. I was playing a solitaire someone had just taught me. And you were kind enough to bring me pots of coffee from time to time. We found we had a friend in common, that wonderful old faker, Bradshaw, who used to ride old Number 25 and con all his customers into buying him whiskey. He had been the dresser for an English actor and Lord knows he had the broad A down to a science.

The reason I'm writing you is to thank you for a word I was sure, until I met you, had been taken out of the dictionary: Service. You seemed to enjoy giving it: you didn't act as if you were being insulted when I asked you for a few extra favors. And God knows I never felt as if you were a servant. On the contrary, I felt as if your job was making my ride more comfortable and the way you made that happen was to provide me with service. And I'm positive you didn't provide it just to be sure of getting a bigger than average tip. You did it because you knew how to, it was a job you had accepted, and I'll even go so far as to say I think you liked me.

This kind of attitude is practically extinct. Nowadays, everyone wants to be the person getting the service. Everyone thinks that serving others means that they're at the bottom of the ladder.

I'm a music writer as I think I told you. When I bring a new arrangement into a recording studio and a player or a singer wants a change I make the change, if it's not idiotic, and I don't feel as if I'm some kind of slave just because I'm providing someone with something they want and need. Besides which I'm being paid for it.

No one's insulting me, making me lose my self-respect. I think that anyone who wants to do a respectable job and is proud if he does it well, is a jackass if he's ashamed because the job is being done for someone else.

So, Mr. Carpenter, I'm writing to thank you for doing a job and a service well, for making me happy on a long train trip, and for doing a professional piece of work.

ALEC WILDER

Dear Bill:

I have suffered just as deeply as you have from the Rock takeover, and I can't honestly blame you for refusing to write any more lyrics.

Of course the irony is that those few you *have* written in the past few years happen to be almost without exception the best you have ever written. It fascinates me that you wrote them, since your position has been that you wouldn't write another lyric unless there was a reasonable probability that someone would record the song.

Well, those last lyrics you wrote to those film cues have less chance of being sung or played than any songs we've ever written together. In the first place I wrote the film music in a kind of song form but so far-out and so loosely constructed as to make the most chance-taking singer back away.

Yet they're your finest lyrics.

Do you realize that the best luck we've had with songs was with those we wrote only for fun and with no recording artist or publisher in mind. And everything we wrote deliberately to make money never made a dime?!

Are you so depressed and bitter that you no longer can conceive of having any fun simply writing a song and playing it for a few faithful friends?

I know you seriously call your long stay here in the East your "thirty-year insult." But has it occurred to you that songwriting entails a degree of selling as well as writing? I admit I'm lousy at it but at least I don't throw a conniption fit every time one of those schlocky slobs turns down a song with a cheap insult.

I figure there must be other more civilized people around like Howie, for example, who you must admit produced a tribute to our talent in that songbook he put out. Yet because you don't hear from him you've concluded he's another bad guy. How about your calling him? He is, you must admit, considerably busier than you are!

But the hell with all that! How about the fun we used to have? Don't you want to have any more? Are you so "insulted" that all the verve and joy has fled? Are there to be no more golden moments, no more laughter and happy tears when it all comes right?

ALEC

Dear Dr. Watson:

At last I did find someone to decipher those verses of mine and thank you for acknowledging the receipt of them. You say you will file them and alphabetize them by first lines, but won't that be a lot of work and very boring? It's a lovely notion but I'd assume you would want to spend your leisure hours more entertainingly than by filing the raves and rants of an unpolished poet.

May I congratulate you for your remarkable contribution to medical science — your x-ray *movie* camera. Those who know about these matters and don't know you are my friend, tell me it is one of the greatest discoveries of our age. But, knowing you as well as I believe I do, I imagine you give most of the credit to Sid Weinberg.

Since 1952 I've written the best score for a musical I've ever written. Unfortunately it was for a movie which never was made. I also wrote two full-length operas, one of which never got performed due to lack of financing, and the other which was performed mostly by amateur singers in a high school auditorium under the producership of your nephew-in-law, Frank Baker.

Unfortunately his anger over my overzealous concern for the production of the opera has caused a rift in the lute (whatever that may be) which can never, I fear, be mended.

It was a lovely opera, too. Very sentimental and witty, bittersweet and almost tactile. I'm very nearly proud of its music. The libretto, by Bill Engvick, is a masterpiece, unless you believe masterpieces must be large and pontifical, gothic and grim.

There's a new youth emerging which is not only shutting itself off from its elders but believes it has been traduced and given a sickly, corrupt and evil world. It blames all of us and, I believe to a great extent, it is precise in its accusations.

I think they are going to close ranks and stand their ground. I think they are flowers in a field of nettles. I think they will be abused and also pampered, I think they will be reviled, misunderstood and that, in their early stages of revolt, will employ childish tactics and strategy.

But it will spread. It will reach over the face of the earth. It will almost totally isolate youth from age and show this rift most dramatically in places of education. Naturally the home will be shattered except in those instances in which the parents are eager to learn how to help rebuild and reform the corrupt, materialistic mess society has been sinking into as far back as the end of the First World War.

Already the young are creating their own music and it's fearful. It's amateurish, very loud, wholly illiterate and yet — it's theirs. They listen to it and they write it. Almost all the poorly written lyrics are some form of protest or else boisterous encouragement to do what you damn well want to because there's nothing left to live for or look forward to.

Among the angry are the pretentious imitators and leeches, the militant ones seeking power more than redress, and all those who have closed their ears to reason or debate.

I don't think I ever risked my shaky theories in your presence when I was their age. I had less to be angry about but I certainly distrusted what I could comprehend of the System. But I never joined any groups and was very leery of those smooth young men who approached me during the thirties to attend Communist cell meetings. Nor have I been anything but contemptuous of all those who called me a "red baiter" on the grounds that I questioned the validity of their Party fanaticism. It is of interest to me that without exception all those who were the most violent against the powerful blocks of wealth are now tacky status seekers and sleekly wealthy people themselves.

I still drink but at least I've managed to rid myself of the most destructive emasculatrix I've ever known and now am comparatively free. I spend more time than ever writing "concert" music.

Due to the growing market for young amateur music coming to be termed Rock, my level of popular song is rapidly going out of fashion. The spending money given the very young is causing the "pop" record-buying market to be controlled by musically illiterate and hysterical children. Oh, my!

ALEC

Dear Dan:

I wrote you a couple of years ago a letter so personal it might have been an embarrassment. As you remember, it was a letter of gratitude, affection and praise. Gratitude for your great hospitality and concern for my well-being, affection because you are one of the most warmhearted people I've ever met and praise for your being cheerful in adversity, dauntless in hard times; and valiant in loss and loneliness.

I'm pretty damned fed up with the still prevalent tension that occurs every time the subject of a homosexual is introduced in a heterosexual group. As a dear, nutty friend once told some curious friends who had seen him leave the theater one night with a girl, another night with a boy, "Don't worry, fellows! You have nothing to worry about! All I'm looking for is a nice warm place!"

You're so damned healthy about it as well as sidesplittingly witty that I am constantly forgetting that in spite of all the Gay Lib and the alleged emancipation of our age, you're still a member of a frowned-on minority group. And you have to bear its constant crosses and indignities.

If you weren't living in Key West, I think I'd have stopped coming down there years ago. Of course it has its advantages for me: no interruptions in my work, no commitments to fruitless projects, such as loom up in the North, very attractive in its racketty-packetty fashion but no! I'd go to Savannah or one of the upper keys if it weren't for you.

And I'm highly complimented that you so totally accept me whenever the gathering is exclusively homosexual.

Even when life is at its lowest ebb for you, you manage to be witty and more than that, you listen. When you drink, you become reiterative and even pontifical; you even, for moments, forget to laugh at yourself. But what's all that compared to the despicable way I behave in my cups?

I'm coming back just as soon as I can and in the meantime I'm praying every good piece of fortune will come to you including a cartload of doubloons.

I can't think of anyone I'd rather see rich and rude to everyone who deserves being put down.

ALEC

Dear June:

I know I'll never be able to tell you how I feel about what you did for me all those years ago. I'm sure Bill wrote a beautiful letter telling you how respectfully and lovingly you treated his words.

I can't write that Addison-and-Steele way he can. So I'll have to stumble on, aiming and missing most of the time.

You prepared the role in an astoundingly short time. You caused no problems in rehearsal. You didn't get panicky when you got laryngitis two nights before we opened.

You commuted from New York; you adjusted to a cast largely of amateur actors and singers, and you gave two absolutely perfect performances.

And you, a twenty-eight-year-old woman, played the role of a thirteen-year-old girl! How I'll never know.

I truly tried. Every note was important to me partly because every word Bill wrote was so apt and singing.

But more than that; I was completely captivated by the bittersweet premise of the romantic young girl having to learn that the dream doesn't work, seldom lasts, and so she has to settle for, in this instance, the grocery boy.

Were you to sing such a role today, nearly twenty years later, you would still be a thirteen-year-old, even if you have gout by this time; the only trouble is you'd be arrested for sense and sensibility, for loving heroes and dreams, joy and sentimental sadness. You'd be arrested for style and simplicity, for spunk and valiance.

But before they clamped the irons on you (and Bill and me) they'd jeer, they'd howl their current "primal howl" as Jim Maher calls it, they'd punish you mercilessly for "remembering," for *not* letting it all hang out, for keeping a magic wall between the proscenium arch and the stalls, for weeping for yourself instead of for some faceless horde of needy strangers.

Oh, no, very dangerous! Looking back, I guess we got in just under the wire and even then I doubt if we could have had the use of any more elegant a display case than a high school auditorium.

You noticed, didn't you, that never was a word said in the Great City about our little suburban production. And there were plenty of ferret-eyed scouts there just in case. But of course nothing was said or done! Remember that Gogarty said that "life is an arena without a culture."

We're in it now, dear heart, the arena where your fate is decided by the position of a thumb, where the art is a bloodbath and the audience a crazed, irrational horde of sensation seekers and hot-dog gourmets, sheep to baa on cue at baa cards, and hearts open only to the stimuli that send fresh supplies of blood to the erogenous zones and that cage of the brain where lie all the thumbscrews hidden under an altar cloth of emancipation.

"But," as your last line and *the* last line of the opera said, "I'll remember."

ALEC WILDER

Dear Lou:

When we rode around the countryside yesterday and I made that impassioned speech about small groups of players, chamber music to be exact, I had the feeling that I lost you along the way.

And I don't blame you; I know I sputter and repeat myself when I try to describe matters near my heart. It may seem absurd that I am writing you when I'll be seeing you constantly while I'm here in Rochester, yet I'm sure I can disperse with the sputtering if I write it down.

As you know, I prefer to write music for friends. After all, it adds a dimension to friendship if I respect a man's playing and he in turn respects my composing sufficiently to ask for a piece. And then when he has performed it, revealing his awareness of all the secrets I reserve for music, then the friendship is almost Damonian and Pythian.

There's a solo piece, a sonata, let's say, for French horn and piano. But then there are the chamber groups, trios, quartets, quintets. They remain for me the truest expression of music, not only because they demand that every note be the right one, but because they are musical expressions of what I might dare to term "overt individuals." What I mean is that while every player in an orchestra may be superb, the very presence of so many players may well reduce the personal intensity of the music. As well, I'm certain that a composer can skate over thin ice in an orchestra piece simply by substituting clever color or massed sound for true content.

In chamber music there can be no deception or sleight of hand. And more than that, there must be a willingness, even more, a desire to cooperate, to assist, to interlock, to sacrifice, and to check substantial amounts of ego at the door of the rehearsal hall.

I'm not a player but I can tell with little effort that the co-operation and interdependence essential to superior ensemble playing by a chamber music group is a clear, invaluable lesson in responsible social behavior without which (he said sententiously) civilized living would be impossible.

Furthermore, since I'm a nut on loving (as opposed to "stroking") I can love a woodwind quintet, but it's damned difficult to love an orchestra.

Maybe this need is greater than it would be otherwise if I had a family; maybe it's substitutional. I'm not too concerned about that because I prefer intensely loving and respecting for a few Catherine-wheel hours among musicians than having to love a family under the same roof twenty-four hours a day. Maybe I'm cynical but the latter would be like spending a lifetime writing for the kazoo!

ALEC

p.s. See you for lunch on Wednesday.

Dear Mr. De Vries:

I seem to pester you, don't I, for each new book. It's only because I need your irresistible, wry and resigned wit, your precise and explosive commentary on suburban society and the general malaise of the middle class.

You answer my letters, you appear at the Algonquin simply because I wish to present you with a wild notion to film "The Mackerel Plaza," you cheer me at lunch when I'm hung-over and lost and you even send me advance copies because you know how eager I am for your latest distinguished diatribe. For all of which I'm extremely grateful!

How you ever understood the terror of losing teeth as you did in *Reuben, Reuben* is extraordinary. When I phoned to ask you, you were as considerate as usual, but uninformative about the teeth. How did you know?

ALEC WILDER

Dear Cuzzin:

I am highly complimented to be privileged to call you by such an intimate name!

Do you remember how we happened to meet? Harry Segrue, the bar waiter at the Algonquin, never a man to hesitate about foolishly rushing in, approached you one evening to say that he had a great idea for a musical. It was that it be written by three Wilders: yourself, Billy Wilder and myself. He added that I was already available and could be found in the rear of the Rose Room.

You, being always the good, kind man you are, went to the Rose Room. I was with two friends discussing the demerits of *The Visit* we had just walked out of — also Miss Fontaine's desperate attempts to hold her head so that her extra chins be less apparent.

I looked up, saw you standing hesitantly a discreet distance away, went into a state of near shock and inquired if we could do, be, supply, arrange, contribute anything. You told the Segrue story, sat down, and we all had a splendid evening.

I had read every one of your published words, had even written to ask permission to make an opera of *Our Town* to which you had politely replied (in longhand) that you preferred not to allow it to be used in any but its original form.

Since that time, some twelve years ago (when was that abortive *Visit?*), we have met many times, and even though almost always by chance, every meeting has been a delight for me. Sometimes, due to the great range of your voice levels, I have lost some of your wise words, but fortunately only a few.

There was one glorious late evening when I, fortified by alcohol, persuaded you to visit a famous jazz musicians' bar, Jim and Benny's. We arrived just as they were closing (we were no pikers: it was four AM!) but I noticed lights in a bar down the block. It, too, was closed, but my dear friend Sunny Carson was at the bar and spotted me. He persuaded the bartender to let us in and after I had introduced you, informed you in his Damon Runyon fashion, gravel voice and all, that you had better treat me right because I was his good friend. You took all this with your usual unflustered equanimity.

What you didn't know (and which I'm sure Sunny wouldn't mind my telling you) was that he was, to put it politely, a "pur-loiner," that Jim of the musicians' bar liked and trusted him and often put him behind the bar, which meant in charge of the cash register — he was a wholly reliable employee. Also Sunny was extremely sentimental and was deeply touched when I sent him a Christmas telegram from San Francisco. When Jim sent him to Scribner's to buy a book of lullabies I had produced with Maurice Sendak drawings, he felt compelled to warn Sunny not to "purloin" any extra copies.

When I saw you recently I was delighted to note that your effervescence had returned, that you said your new book was progressing happily, and that you were less given to lowering your voice to a whisper so that your words would become unintelligible.

You spoke very warmly of my music to the gentleman who had come to the hotel to have lunch with you.

The books and plays you have written constitute, for me, a spiritual and moral constitution and testament. Your words have had a profound influence on my conclusions about my responsibilities as a human being, the immorality of total isolation (and impossibility), the necessity for a microcosmic as well as a macrocosmic view of all life, a respect for learning, language, history and all aspects of man's rise from the brute.

Thank you for your gentleness, your modesty and your love.

The best of good fortune to you and to your dear sister.

ALEC WILDER

Dear Eric Hoffer:

I hesitate to write to you because of, simply, awe. I have read all your published works, but unfortunately missed your broadcasts. It is typical of our tawdry era that you are not as widely acclaimed as you should be. Obviously your wisdom does not meet with the intellectual approval of the dogmatic, academic, scientific mind, nor with the attention and concentrated consideration required by the average reader to absorb your wisdom and incisive intelligence.

Your clarity, directness, essential simplicity, your wisdom, your constant quest for truth, your quotableness, profound respect for Montaigne, all serve to make you one of the few great and passionate minds I have ever encountered.

I keep an eye out always for any new book of yours but have

failed to find one in the past few years. I sincerely trust that this doesn't mean you are too ill or too despondent to write. Perhaps, on the other hand, you have said all you wish or need to say. It has been a great, truly great, contribution and I humbly thank you.

ALEC WILDER

Dear Miss Sharp:

When I was seventeen, deeply disturbed, unable to think clearly or act sensibly, I went, as a dog to grass, for a visit to a seldom-seen but long-respected relative down in the State of Maine.

She helped clarify a lot of my muddle and you helped me to laugh and dream and to start thinking of the lively side of life. For on a table in my Aunt Clara's dear little Orchard House I found a copy of *The Flowering Thorn*.

I've read every book you've written since, including the Miss Bianca series and that masterpiece *The Innocents*.

When I was recently being interviewed by a very young, obviously new-at-the-game girl reporter, she asked me what I liked to read. I reeled off a list from Gerald (not Lawrence!) Durrell to Robert Ardrey. Among the list, naturally, was yourself. I saw the edges of a sneer when I mentioned your name.

I'm old enough now to speak more bluntly than I used to. So I instantly backed her into the Algonquin paneling by giving her an acerbic lecture on what constituted merit in literature and wound up advising her to remove herself if she must limit herself to the fashionable "relevance" of Kafka, Kierkegaard and Hesse.

You have made me very happy all these years. You make me believe that life can be truly less ominous than it seems to be most of the time and as a result I try harder to add some of your sunniness to it. Thank you.

ALEC WILDER

Dear Mr. Cheever:

It was a delight to meet you and not just because I had read and admired your short stories and novels. Your acerbic wit, your acid-etched anecdotes, your cynical asides and your almost imperceptible reaching out damned near broke my heart.

You kindly answered all the notes I wrote you except for the one I wrote about the wrong character name I found in *The Wapshot Scandal*. Was that because I was wrong or because you are too cynical to believe the publishers could consider altering a single word? Or because the very thought of writing, present or past, was anathema?

I was extremely pleased to hear that you were teaching at Sing Sing. And why not, for God's sake? I also asked the copy editor of *Playboy* to send me the stories you wrote for them. Does it matter a damn that I was very fond of two but not of the third? That I felt that one was written cynically for the pseudointellectual masturbator market?

I have reread all your other published work as I think I wrote you before, and am even more impressed than the first time. This fact pleases me as I find that those who, by accident or perseverance, hear my music more than once, only then begin to see what I'm after and also to discover that it's not quite as Chaminadish as they had at first believed.

Thank you very, very much for those permanent people in my life and memory, the Wapshots. Their slam-bang eccentricity, their devil-take-the-hindmost insistence on *their* way reminds me of the Wilder side of my family, though Aunt Emma's collecting and then gold-painting olive pits isn't on a par with Honoria's sitting there drinking and waiting for death.

One of those *Playboy* stories intimated another Wapshot book. Is such a happy occurrence likely?

Thanks for all the rest!

ALEC WILDER

Dear Monsieur Simenon:

How can anyone risk thanking you, knowing that your mail flows in from the four quarters of the globe in special mail planes?

Nevertheless, if my friend Harry Bouras can do it, so can I. I believe you have even received a collage from him as well as correspondence.

It was a happy day when he and I discovered our mutual obsession with your work.

He may have established a correspondence friendship with you but at least he doesn't know Carvel Collins and I do. Carvel told me of the many-thousand-voice howl of *SIMENON!* that went up when your boat docked in Cherbourg. What an extraordinary sensation that must have been! The obverse of a Hitler rally! He also told me of your refusal to accept free restaurant dinners wherever you went, obviously recognized. Parenthetically, I don't believe Thornton Wilder or Auden would be recognized in any public place in America except perhaps an art museum or a theater lobby. I remember so well, so many times, seeing Mr. Faulkner waiting patiently at the desk of the Algonquin, quietly puffing his pipe, until the clerk got around to handing him his room key. No one else was any the wiser as to who he was.

Yet perhaps there are countless times when you pray for anonymity.

I've read all your books which have been translated or written in English and am completely rewarded each time. I admit to being unable to finish two of them due only to my incapacity to stand the strain. Your statement to Mr. Collins that you always took your protagonist to his breaking point to see if he would break or not takes a strong stomach on the part of a timid reader like myself.

My life is other than it would have been had I not read your books. You have forced me to accept the monstrous tricks of fate, poverty, ignorance and death. Besides which you have taught me the strength and beauty of the simple, unadorned, unqualified line.

Thank you, Monsieur Simenon!

ALEC WILDER

Dear Mr. Ardrey:

I have recommended your books more than those of any man I have ever read.

I'm certain the dogmatic academicians despise you and more so since your convictions have become incontrovertible truths.

How ignorance manages to thrive so surrounded and interwoven as it is with the patently true findings of open-minded men is a commentary on the desperate plight of our Dark Age.

But you are one of those pinpricks of light Mr. Forster spoke of in one of his essays in *Two Cheers for Democracy*.

ALEC WILDER

Dear Mr. Greene:

It was most kind of you to invite me to your Algonquin suite for a drink. I am a great admirer of all your books and, had I not been slightly tight, I wouldn't have dared accept your invitation.

The reason I'm writing is not just to thank you for having given me so much pleasure as a writer but to apologize to you for what may have seemed a sly commentary on a phone conversation you had shortly after we reached your quarters.

You said approximately, "Oh, my darling, I'm sorry that I struck you! But let's hope we meet in Venice, Rome, Paris, London . . ."

And when you returned to your chair I asked you if you had ever heard of a famous American wit, S. J. Perelman. You said you hadn't. I then told you one of his more marvelous puns.

I'm apologizing for fear you might have assumed that my quoting the pun was due to your end of the phone conversation I couldn't help but overhear. This wasn't so unless my unconscious mind is more vicious than I ever realized.

The pun was "A greater love hath Onan."

ALEC WILDER

Dear Bruce:

As you know I've read every printed word you've written and even set to music some of them. You remember that lovely prose poem you wrote for Carl Haverlin, "Names from the War"? Well, I was very proud to have had the privilege of setting those beautiful sentiments.

In your last book you spoke of the Michigan Indians. I don't have a copy here so I can't quote, but you noted that their confused behavior might well have been induced by being caught between two cultures, their own and the white man's.

Then you wrote of the hollow nature of our own times, without any discernible culture, moving on into no conceivable culture, but more likely, chaos. And you added something like "We're the Indians."

I see you sitting at your special table in the Algonquin at lunchtime and more often than not I don't disturb you, much as I'd love to shake your hand and see you smile. For I feel that you are trying to work up in your being a state of euphoria which will permit you to see, even if for only an hour, the world in a more attractive light.

You have the features of an emperor and you're looking out at a Rome of shanties and tattered tents. Where are the elegant, heroic edifices, the noble faces and the wise words? Where are the respected laws and the high styles, the virtuous critics and the heroic poets?

Please at least know that you have a friend as sad as yourself who, like you, knows that in spite of the rubble one must move, as the jazz musicians say when one's spirits are low, "Straight ahead."

My very best to you, dear, dear, sir!

ALEC WILDER

Dear American Heritage Dictionary:

I wrote you some time ago how impressed I was by your loving and healthy dictionary. You kindly acknowledged my note and admitted that putting it together *had* been a labor of love.

Your printing of most of the taboo words came as a great surprise and a delight. If only your dictionary had been on that stand in the corner of the study hall when I was young, I would have become bored making that long trek to it from where I sat in the back. For I would have found that every four-letter word was there with no bell of guilt ringing because I had looked it up.

Your board of a hundred writers and educators to consider the fitness of certain new usages and your printing the percentage of pros and cons next to the word was an inspired notion. I haven't dared look up all my pet peeves but I have to say I was shocked to find that only 43 percent of your judges were against the use of the verb "identify" without its essential object. How can any civilized person suffer the sound of such a phrase as "Do you identify with the Rolling Stones"? Identify *what???!*

Don't tell me, for God's sake, that your judges condone such monstrosities as "I don't relate to the Rolling Stones." Relate *what???!*

What's their opinion of "high-type" salesmen? Has "of" been sent to limbo along with the true meaning of "disinterested"? Damn it, don't we need a few synonyms for "unprejudiced"? Evidently not!

I believe "imply" and "infer" are still kept in well-separated enclosures as opposed to the efforts of those linguistic capons up at Merriam's!

"Flammable" is a perfect instance of the rest of the equality culture: adjust language and education to the stupidest!

That fellow who wrote *The Treasure of Our Tongue*, a Mr. Barnett, wrote two-thirds of his book brilliantly tracing the painfully long development of the English language, a period of at least four hundred years. The last third was given to a lamentation over the apathetic and tasteless corruption of that same lovely language over a period of not more than thirty years!

So thank you for your loving efforts to preserve what's left of it!

ALEC WILDER

Dear Mike:

When your mother plopped your infant self into a large arm-chair out in the Stony Point house, I said automatically, "He looks like a Chinese emperor."

You don't any longer and oh, so much time has passed, so much sad and tragic time. I've had my miseries but you barely survived yours.

I'm not one for reminiscing so never fear! I shan't start beating dead horses except to say that I'm very happy if I was of any use to you during those dreary, frightening times.

You're out of the gloomy landscape now, you're living a life very much your own. You love Bach, thank heaven, and you are even reading fiction, which, you may recall, you said you never would.

You love to laugh, but I'm still on my guard as I never know when you'll start spitting like a civet cat.

The drawings in the books you've illustrated I've examined with extreme care and oftentimes astonishment. I suppose every good artist creates a world of his own. I even knew a beautiful boy once with whom I used to pick wildflowers, who had created an entire country and a language to go with it, not, thank God, one of those humorless Tolkien worlds!

After Maurice Sendak did those loving drawings for the lulla-bies I harmonized and composed a few of, I was impressed by the world he had created. I wanted a passport and a password to it. And there's your much more mysterious world! Sometimes witty as in *The Monkey's Uncle* (I know that's the wrong title but you know which book I mean), but mostly a world of people and creatures who (which) wouldn't survive an hour if you deserted them, that is, let them escape from the pages.

I understood that frieze of bearded gargoyles you drew in your bedroom on Central Park West, but now that some sunlight has stolen past the jalousies, I look for a few more signs of joy.

On the other hand, you're a most complex, snobbish, autocratic, trigger-tempered man, and I should watch my language very carefully.

It's all unpredictable as, when I expect a violent diatribe, I get a village-pump guffaw. When I expect an excoriation of my old-age moralities, I get a plea for help.

All I want to ask, and I know you will never answer, is this: do you believe that anyone shall be allowed into that most special and highly mysterious landscape and population you have created? Will you ever tell the secret? To a girl? An old lady? A stranger?

ALEC

Dear Lavinia:

I'm considering having this letter Xeroxed a hundred times and sending it to all those long-suffering friends who have tolerated my miserable behavior for many too many years due to my drinking.

I'VE STOPPED!!!

I know many cynics and world-weary ones will refuse to believe that I'll stay stopped. They'll assume I've quit because of an especially ghastly hangover and that within a month or two I'll be back at it with all its accompanying insults and monstrous behavior.

All I can say is that I've stopped before and have been terrified of the thousand temptations I knew would present themselves. This time I'm no longer terrified. For hard as it may be for you to believe, I'm absolutely certain I've had my last drink.

Since I stopped there have been several disastrous situations which would have sent every Carrie Nation to a bar not for smashing it but to get smashed. I could smell juniper in the air. A thousand demons screamed "DRINK" and I didn't.

I'm certain that the forty-year indulgence is done with. And, while I'll never be able to redeem myself for all my dreadful diatribes, I sure as hell will do what I can to be a generous, loyal, civilized friend!

ALEC

Dear Jackass:

Now what do you think of your self-pity, your moaning in all the patient friends' parlors, the grinding away at them over the parlous state of the world, the boring accounts of your creative deficiencies? *Now* what do you think?!

You've not only made an Ancient Mariner of yourself, you've boasted of your willpower in not catapulting back into the gin bottle, indeed, you've made a fool of yourself! Do you think all those bright, loving people don't know how rotten the world has become, don't you know that they're trying to make it a little less bleak? Do you think they've never known creative slumps, suffered pain, fought the urge to stay drunk for the rest of their lives?

Just who in hell do you assume yourself to be? Some rara avis? Or to leap to its predator, some special breed of cat?

Certainly you're miserable and terrified of old age! Who isn't (who's old)? But, you poor pathetic phallusy, you're alive, aren't you? You're pissing, shitting, belching, scrubbing your dentures, laughing at Woodstock (the secretary bird). You wrote a fan letter to Woody Allen, didn't you? Are you going to perpetrate the ultimate act of bad manners and kill yourself? If so, why did you sob over the scent of honeysuckle?

So read this, don't tear it up, put it in your overloaded pocket, pick up your music manuscript notebook and GO TO WORK!!!

Dear Lou:

I have no doubt that you're not just being polite when you ask me questions about writing music and all the peripheral experiences that go with it.

I also know that though your photography has brought a lot of music to you that otherwise you might never have heard, what with your music school and concert pictures, you still have no knowledge of the creating and putting together of it. So since you're always asking questions, I'll put down some simple answers. Don't, for God's sake, mistake their simplicity for condescension!

We have one creative process in common: we know only minimally what we're doing and we distrust too much knowledge about our arts. I know the ranges of the instruments and how best to group them just as you know what lenses to use and how to mix developer and all the darkroom techniques. But neither of us wishes to delve too deeply into the academic thoroughness of how to do what we do.

You've told me often that your best pictures have been due to a keen eye, a hunch and little else. I've told you that intuition, good taste, and blind luck have been responsible for my best pieces. I'm sure that if either of us were cross-examined by experts concerning our methods of work, you would come off the more knowledgeable.

In all areas but the creative I am obsessed with the need for knowledge. But all my life I have shied away from knowing more than an essential minimum about the creative process. It is possible that had I studied more my music would be better; on the other hand, it's also possible that too much knowledge would have put my creative muscles into a permanent charley horse.

What astounds me—and I must say it twice: astounds me—is that those kind souls who have written analytical studies of my music seem to have found it shapely, disciplined and somehow well within the stringent demands of the academic mind.

Let me give you a strange instance of this paradox. I once asked the most superb musician I know, John Barrows, what a passacaglia was. (I won't bother you with what he told me, frankly because the memory is fuzzy.) He told me somewhat startledly, "But you've written one!" He recalled a woodwind piece I had written and, when he realized I was unaware of what I had done, explained that a recurring chromatic line I had kept repeating throughout the piece simply to keep it from flying off in all directions was, in fact, enough to have made it a passacaglia.

I keep telling other musicians that I'm an ignoramus and I probably shouldn't because someday soon one of them is going to agree. When I say I don't know what I'm doing, they look suspiciously at me as if I were either putting them on or fishing for a compliment.

You remember that dissertation Glenn Bowen wrote? Some two-hundred-odd pages of analysis of my music, bar by bar? Well, I don't understand more than a few pages of it and that's the absolute truth.

All I can say is that if any of my music is good, its sources are almost solely intuitive.

If you'd like me to natter on about music in another letter, let me know!

ALEC

Dear Peggy:

I was up at the apartment of a very courteous but alarming man who fancied himself a "free spirit" by removing his socks and shoes, by blowing a police whistle when he considered a subject closed.

He played a long tape he had made of what music he could track down of mine. I'm sure he thinks he likes pop and other light music but he really likes only the memories they evoke. So musically his collection left quite a lot to be desired.

However, he did have one record I haven't heard in a long time. (As you know, I don't own a single record of any of my music. I'm not boasting; it's just one of the losses I have to sustain if I wish to live my two-suitcase life.)

It was yours and Dave's record of "Goodbye John." Dear

Peggy, how absolutely dear and loving that record was! Every word you uttered I believed and every note you sang was definitive. Dave's section was a model of distillation and choice! Really a very special record for anyone, let alone the writer of the music.

And just where, can you tell me, has the belief and sweet sadness, the genuine love and the gentle touch gone? Into the bitterness or loneliness of age? Into the desperate fear of turning to salt if you look back? Remember, what you'd see burning would be only the light in a young girl's eyes, not a deserved holocaust.

So you aren't young? So a great deal has happened to make a person crouch in the shadows? So an age of innocence, of joy and wonderment is at an end? So we must survive and somehow come to grips with today's goblin society?

All granted. But must we allow the best of ourselves, still breathing and living a lonely life in the secure world of our memory, die because the face in the mirror has changed or because little brown spots begin to sprinkle the backs of our hands?

You remember the lecture I gave you the day we took the walk and I told you to sit down on the curbstone to listen? I think you do remember, as many years later when you were behaving cruelly to one of your vast entourage I said simply "curbstone" and you shut up and smiled at me.

And I know you remember the song I wrote for you when you were with Benny at the New Yorker. Some young air force guy you'd fallen for had to go overseas. So I wrote a song to console you.

It was called "Is It Always Like This?" and you've never referred to it from the day I gave it to you (words and music) to this. Too sacred?

I suppose it's all too late now, isn't it, to sit you down on a curbstone?

ALEC

Dear Sir:

The stewardess (excuse *me!*) flight attendant was kind enough to give me your name from her list. I looked you up in three or four phone books in the New York area and found only one Roderick Hasseltine. So I'm assuming you are the same person who sat next to me in the plane from Memphis yesterday.

As you may recall we never exchanged a word. You opened a book of Philip Roth, *Letting Go,* but I noticed your eyes never moved. You must have stared at that page for a half hour.

Clearly you were profoundly disturbed. It doesn't help matters, but most people I meet are either hysterical, depressed, irrational, bewildered or in a word, wholly unable to cope.

I presume you are a businessman even though your face suggests work much more creative in-and-out trays than business ones.

Could that be the cause of your disturbance? (Please realize that I am writing this only because your sadness impelled me to find out who you were so that I could let you know that someone with nothing to gain was concerned for your welfare.)

Did you have a dream once long ago and have you found that there is no more room for dreams in this poetry-less society?

I, for some reason least understood by myself, don't believe the source of your woes is physical illness of your own or anyone dear to you.

I believe that you have ceased to search. I believe that you have become so lost in the miasma of the alien society you are forced to live in that you don't know how to begin to search for other worlds, other areas where people laugh and love, read and listen to music, take long walks in the woods, sit by waterfalls (not with a group of red-faced noisy autumn-hunters), sit in parks and watch children play games and sail boats. I think you've forgotten or have become too tired to fight for your dignity, your inalienable rights and the kind of love that seeks to share and understand your confusion and loneliness.

If you haven't lost the blessed characteristic of taking chances, why don't you phone me and make a date for dinner?

I'm not a religious fanatic, I'm not a member of an esoteric cult. I don't sell self-improvement tracts. To put your mind at ease, all I do is write music, read books, travel, watch my bobble birds, listen to the sound of fountains, laugh at the absurdity of humanity, and weep over its confusion.

ALEC WILDER

Dear Doctor Stirt:

It's a long time since I lay on that couch day after day. Almost thirty years.

I must have been a very difficult patient with my devious mind, my stubborn refusal to adjust to the goblin culture, and my neither fish-nor-fowlishness.

You were extremely considerate of my financial straits and for a long time charged me only eight dollars an hour.

When I left my first payment of five dollar bills in the shape of a body on the couch, it didn't get the laugh I had hoped for. I was so naive as to fail to see the symbolism of my body being outlined in dollar bills.

After all those years and all those days, you wanted me to taper off by coming two days a week. I wouldn't, and worried for years that I'd start frothing at the mouth unexpectedly in the middle of playing a new song for a publisher or in the middle of a dalliance with a lady.

I never did adjust, as you know. I've managed to survive rowing against the current, but I take little of the credit. I really believe much of it has been luck and something in the mystical world of the miracle.

It hasn't been easy to live my way and still make a living, but I've managed. It will not surprise you that my relationships with the ladies have been far from fulfilling. There again I think luck played a part and the other part was suspicion.

Sex has always been a deterrent and an intrusion. I do very nicely without it in my older years.

I told you lies, not all of which I think you were unaware of. You were, as far as I'm concerned, extraordinarily trusting for a doctor who deals with congenital liars.

My profoundest need when I came to you was to avoid induction in the army. I suppose my terror of being bottled up exclusively with men stemmed from my bad times as a child with brutal boys.

Besides which I had the problem of a small penis which I'm certain women are not that concerned about, but men find an object of derision. I'm not ashamed that you helped me stay out of the army.

I was delighted when you accepted the invitation to the reception given for my book on American Popular Song.

I don't know what I said when I met you there but it was something like, "Well, Dr. Stirt, I must have done something right," and it made me happy to see you laugh.

I go on living pretty much as I always did, though I see fewer people. I continue to compose and to make diatribes against ignorance and injustice. I move from town to town, room to room, read lots of books, and play a beautiful, hitherto unfamiliar form of solitaire.

As you might expect, I've not indulged in more than minimal publicity for the book.

I'll call you for a date for dinner sometime soon.

ALEC WILDER

Dear Marvin Bellis:

Your sign demanding that I refrain from smoking while riding in your ramshackle taxi I'll accept, as you just might have wrecked lungs from breathing worse than nicotine and tar, that is, New York air.

But I'm damned if I haven't the right to make a demand of my own, your silence. I could see you seeing me reading. Are you so frightened of the threat to the status of the common man implicit

in books that you feel impelled to interrupt the reading of one?
Or am I moving too fast for you? Am I failing to avoid the
potholes of the three-syllable words as capably as you are failing
to avoid all the potholes you can manage to steer into on every
block?

Well, I'm pretty fucking bored with your blabbermouth city
politics, your arrogance about the riding public (your meal
ticket), and your presumption that you constitute a great substitute for the book I've been trying to read.

You're a slob, you respect no one except your hard-hat brother,
and you're a lousy driver.

In case you feel you've won another victory over printed
learning by seeing me reading and grunting response to your
grotesque opinions, perhaps when I hand you this little mash note
with the fare and a substantial tip, you may become somewhat
irritated.

As a clarification of my bad temper, I suggest you rent a
cassette machine and tape a few hours of your monologues and
then when you play them back, you may decide to replace your
no smoking sign with one that reads SILENCE!

ALEC WILDER

Dear Mr. Dry Cleaner:

Of course it was stupid of me to leave all that stuff in my
pocket before sending it off to you.

Of course it was kind of you to send back the unused airplane
tickets!

But how about that envelope with the $300.00 in it? I suppose
the temptation was too much for you, wasn't it? And you knew
(furtively grinning) that I couldn't prove a thing!

Okay. So you're in 300 and I'm out 300. I suppose it will make
a great story at your local bar. Are you going to be a Big
Spender or put down a payment on a Continental? Now don't

give me that shit about your paralyzed mother! (It would be just my luck if you had one!)

The thing that bothers me is that probably you've been sleeping like a baby. No conscience at all. Well, if it makes you any happier, you're right in with all the best people. It's very fashionable nowadays to get away with anything you can and laugh loudly about it. After all, Mr. Dry Cleaner, who are our heroes?

So go right ahead and keep checking all the pockets! A lot of superstars stay here. I take that back. You'll never check their pockets. They're dressed like field hands and dockworkers and a jacket would bust up their image. So just check my pockets and Thornton's. We're both pretty forgetful gentlemen. And who knows, you might come across the second payment on your Continental!

Happy Filching!

ALEC WILDER

Dear Harry:

I've been reading Josephine Johnson's book, *Seven Houses*. She's a damned fine writer, one who can evoke all manner of things I certainly assumed I'd forgotten. I write of her because of the shock her words have given me. For she writes not only of houses but of furniture and barns and steps, of glass-covered bookcases and flowers, of diaries and how it felt being a child.

But most of all she writes of memory triggers, "things." As you know, I've run from "things" all my life. I've kept nothing, not a single memory trigger, not a letter, a photograph, not even a book.

I'm not afraid of memory, I simply have no use for it. I've never even known what hour of the day or night I was born.

Yesterday I met a man whose choral conducting I've heard and which I very much respect. He is a splendid fellow, vivid, cheery, direct. He told me that the reason he is in music is due to me. I gaped at him.

It seems that in the forties he had sung in the CIO chorus in New York. Simon Rady, a friend of mine, conducted it. This fellow went on to say that Rady once brought him to the Algonquin where, as you know, I lived for years. He said the purpose of the visit was for me to advise him whether or not to take up music as a profession. He said that due to my impassioned speech he went to Juilliard and studied.

I remember nothing, not his face, his name or the occasion. The past and I are a standoff.

Sure, I remember picking out with one finger "Little Alice Blue Gown" on my uncle's piano in Geneva. I remember it took a long time for me to master it.

I remember a cardboard record which must have been one of the very first of its kind. It had a very thin surface of, I suppose, wax. On it was a tune which so enraptured me that I played it continuously until it wore down to the cardboard.

I've always wanted to remember the tune.

I remember a letter—oh, the hell with it! I remember isolated incidents, random remarks, thousands of views, gardens, houses—but practically no faces. I read *The Possessed* over and over, possessed. I remember nothing about it, nothing.

As you know, I remember none of my own music. So you see why I'm so shocked by Mrs. Johnson—or is it Miss?

ALEC

Dear George:

You can't possibly imagine what almost tearful delight it gives me to be able to write to you and know that you can read my words.

Heaven knows it has to have been a long and unspeakable torture for you so how dare I in the same breath mention my own deep sadness?

My sadness I must talk about to this extent: not only your

failing vision was a constant worry, but even worse was that I couldn't persuade you to let me help you.

When there are only two left and one gets into serious trouble and can't bring himself, for whatever reason, to let the other one help him, life has lost all meaning.

So when you finally did let me help you it was like letting a wild bird out of a cage. There wasn't enough I could do to try to make your anguish less and to see to it that your vision was returned to you.

The Irish maid at the Algonquin has had cataract operations within the past year and that, coupled with the fact that she's fond of me, caused her to pray to Saint Anthony for your vision to be restored.

As you know, I am not a formally religious man, but I can promise you I wasn't being casually polite when I thanked her for her prayers.

This whole situation has made me aware, as only a crisis can, that I have not kept in touch with you nearly as much as I should have, for which I humbly apologize.

All I want is for there to be a degree of well-being and good cheer in your life and I'll do whatever I can to ensure it. I only wish I had been more of an aggressor throughout my life. For then I'd have the money to make you more comfortable.

As it is, I've had to face up to a smaller income due to that rotten rock music and this is the reason, as you know, for my being in New York as little as possible during recent years. Obviously I can live much more reasonably in almost any other community.

But simply because I'm not here all the time is no reason for us not to stay in closer touch and I promise you whenever I can afford to I'll send you what I can.

From now on please try to let me help you whenever you are in a spot. I promise you it's a very empty and lost feeling to think that your brother has a hesitation about asking help from the one person who owes it to him, and furthermore is delighted to offer it.

I wish you nothing but the best!

ALEC

Dear Almost Poet:

What else can I call a man as far removed from the machinations which most of the competitive, driven strivers all about you spend their adult lives manipulating and contriving?

For two days, for many hours in each, you listened to a man describe in detail the devices and attitudes adopted by the ambitious. Now you know that the man doing the describing has not been able to achieve his success without having deviated from the chalk line of morality. Yet of all the successful men you have met whose careers have been achieved in as crude and harsh a world as that of popular music publishing, he is the only one you love and trust.

He tried, these last days, to make you realize that he wasn't deserving of your high praise; your trust, yes, because you represent a species of man he has seldom known or dealt with, one who demands that he live up to what you believe him to be. And he is that man and always was that man, but probably during his stormy competitive years, less so than you would have had him.

The point of this really is that his long accounts of the chicanery and expectable, customary dishonesty of ambitious people is as far from the reality of your own life as the farthest-out of science fiction.

How, then, comes the question, how have you managed to live all these long, unsafe, precipice-walking years without having been more aware of the perfidious character of business and without becoming infected by it?

I think I have the answer: you were never ambitious, you had no master plan, you wanted to prove nothing materialistically, *you had no one you were devoted to who wanted you to be a success*!

When you open this in Boston you may writhe with shame over such a Kathleen Norris conclusion (oh, she was a backstairs writer, children).

I'm sure, however, in the hands of a scholar that hypothesis could be put into highly significant language.

Cliché or no, think about this: besides the primal drive to be the alpha fish, wouldn't any ambitious person be desolated if he couldn't show off his success to someone else, whether it be a loved one or a crowd (certainly a love object to a vain man).

You have wanted to please your trusted friends, granted. But whom, except yourself, are you most eager to be accepted by? Grove's Dictionary? Leonard Bernstein? Gunther Schuller? Jay Harrison? John Cage? Milton Babbitt? Alvin Ettler? No, you idiot! *Yourself*—and, perhaps tragically, only yourself.

Take, for example, this new trio for Bernie Garfield. You'd like him to like it, right? If he wants changes, you'll make them, right? But does your willingness to make those changes mean that you're more eager to please him than yourself? No, it means that you respect his judgment, wish to please him, indeed, you know he is much more musically intelligent than yourself. Still, in all your bewilderment and ignorance, you wish more for your own acceptance of yourself than that of a man even as informed and superior as John Barrows.

It's a little like that last sentence of that dreary novel of Isherwood's of which I remember only a paraphrase: "I forgive myself. I really, truly do forgive myself." Except in your case it's: "I really, truly do respect myself."

Dear Lavinia:

You're, let's see now, er, um, 69, and I'm a mere 66, what I might vulgarly call Medicarrion.

There's a reason for such an unsavory pun. This afternoon, after I had reported Rogers's plight to a very kind and considerate man, he asked if he was a heavy smoker. I allowed that this was true and he allowed that he'd been meaning to show me a two-page report from the *Reader's Digest* (which he admitted he disliked generally, but which revealed all about tobacco).

Well, you know what? If he sends it to me, I'm not going to read it. And if I have to beg a blast-off from a friendly medico I shall do so. But kind as this gentleman's intentions are, I find myself reacting as I did to the water-pick aficionados who virtually took me to the drugstore to buy them at the precise time when I was waiting for the word from my dentist that all my teeth would have to be removed.

I feel as might a collector of dimes for Muscatel if, instead of the final necessary dime, he got a lecture from a WCTU lady on the probability of his dropping dead if he drank another drop. Or like an insomniac being told he'd become a drug addict if he took one more sedative, even though he hadn't slept for seventy-two hours!

I suppose all this make me a megalomaniac. For I see now that it's MY music, MY extravagance, MY traveling, MY never unpacking a suitcase, MY sleeping in tomorrow's otherwise fresh shirt, MY shouting at poorly boiled eggs, MY sleeping pills, MY smoking and MY DEATH!

Of course some of life is still fun and much more has been. Of course something always seems more desirable than nothing. Appetite for life and laughter but damn it, not greed! Looking both ways at a street crossing—but not standing on the curb until nothing is in sight for as far as one can see before taking a step. Not deliberately reading in a dim light, but not refusing to read a love letter even if there's only a candle a mile away!

You'll hear from me later on many other ghastly subjects!

ALEC

Dear Mrs. Rutledge:

My Aunt Clara was, I believe, your dearest friend. I visited her when she spent winters with you down in that lovely house on West Avenue.

One afternoon, after she had gone to take a nap, you stopped halfway up the stairs and talked to me for at least a half an hour. You were extraordinarily beautiful as well as utterly understanding. My mind darts and leaps about and most people justifiably find it alarming. But you didn't. You found it all quite acceptable and even enjoyable.

You must have been in your seventies then. Now you are farther along in your nineties. So it may seem intrusive and inept of me to be writing you a love letter. Age is only an embarrassment I find, but changes none of the dreams and romantic concepts of the mind and heart.

So, late as the hour is, I tell you now that I love you profoundly.

ALEXANDER WILDER

Dear Mr. Durrell:

I believe we've corresponded about some of your friends who were going to stay at the Algonquin last year and for whom I was planning to lay down the reddest carpet I could find.

I think you also know that I have contributed not nearly adequate sums of money to your noble cause but as much and as often as I could.

I've read with immense pleasure all of your books and have given many sets of them to those I felt should know about your work and would possibly become enthusiastic to the extent of contributing to it.

I've always had a demon sitting on my shoulder whispering malevolently in my ear that I haven't done enough in my life to make me worthy of the miracle of life itself. God knows, I've tried to write as good music as I could, I've often done kindnesses which were truly close to unselfish, and not just to avoid feeling guilty if I didn't.

I've tried to learn to understand and, on occasion, even to forgive what very well might have been something too shabby to be forgivable.

I'm sad, and always have been, that I'm temperamentally unfit for public life, as I believe the world is in dire need of honorable, courageous, farsighted men and women to function in public affairs, if not to bring some degree of enlightenment, then at the very least to counterbalance some of the evil being perpetrated by the greedy, the ruthless and the immoral in high places.

Had I known what you were trying to do, at an age in which I could have been useful to you, I would have offered you my services for no more reward than food and lodging. The great reward would have come from contributing in any fashion to your battle to keep unique species of life from extinction.

Nor would I have regretted giving up music composition since, after all, art, while it may brighten the dull shades of life, cannot truly be said to create life. Parenthetically, out of respect for my craft, I cannot deny that good art is a form of creation, but never as miraculous as heart-beating life itself.

But alas, I am too old to be anything but a profound enthusiast. Physically I wouldn't have the staying power to be of any more use than a bird feeder. And I'm sure you have plenty of those.

So let me do the next best thing and send you money whenever I can and try to proselytize for your monumental cause.

ALEC WILDER

Dear Al:

As a matter of record I should encapsulate some of my background.

When I was about six, my mother found me kissing Sarah, our Negro cook. She took me aside and explained carefully that "us white folks" (though God knows she'd never have said "folks") just didn't kiss "those people."

Next and paradoxically, I was told not to tell an American

Indian who came to wax the dining room table (is this possible?!) that his skin was the same color as the dining room table.

Next. All my white contemporaries (coevals?) in the summer resort my family went to were bullies. I didn't fight back and besides, was beginning to get interested in music. I had a three-string banjo (lazy bastard! It was built for *five* strings!) and somehow the brown-skinned band that played for brown-skinned dances got wind of it. So I was the only sallow-skinned person at the dances I played banjo at.

One night coming back from the next town in a rickety bus, one of the band hollered "Ku Klux!" and everyone dropped to the floor of the bus howling with laughter. I swear I don't remember what I did, but I do remember that there were no sidelong, jeery glances at me from anyone.

Next, I met a group of young men (about fourteen years old) who cared about popular music and probably had more talent at playing it than I did. I dimly recall trying to put some notes together for the instruments we had among us. All were brown-skinned but me. The others were sons of the men who worked at the summer hotels. They weren't bullies and they and I had music and laughter in common.

How it happened I don't know, but one night we all played at a dance given in the ballroom of the hotel my family stayed at. I wouldn't say that all hell broke loose but my mother wasn't exactly joyous to see me (now at the piano and playing none but the wrong bass notes) seated in the midst of a group of the kind of people "we" didn't kiss.

That's the early background.

Later I came to work with a great many of the great jazz musicians and to become a friend of even more. Many were brown-skinned.

I read a great deal and was fairly well-informed. I traveled a lot, in the South as much as other parts of the country, maybe more because it was so damned beautiful, but knew nothing of the conditions of the poor whites or brown-skinned. I saw out-sides of it from train windows—Pullman car windows, to boot.

I read that study by the Swedish man, I read novels and met Walter White. I heard the muttering and comfortable complaints of the chic American Communists of the thirties.

Then Mr. Ellison smacked me over the head with his book. I was aware of being permitted to look inside the windows of the houses I had seen only from my plate-glass windows.

But you really did it with *South to a Very Old Place.* You opened not a window, but the front door and you invited me in.

I had once visited the home of a family in Brunswick, Georgia. I had known the father, had sent presents, Christmas checks, and when I came out on the front stoop of his home, a police car was parked out at the curb. It followed me (I was walking) back to my hotel, calling out appropriate epithets.

I put the oldest son (there were seven children) through two years of college. The father's health failed and he was so ashamed to be unable to contribute to the support of his family that he left them, very ill, and went to live with an undertaker. I have never heard from or of him since.

The last I heard from Mrs. Williams was that she was trying to work at three jobs, that her second oldest son was going in the army and that she was at the end of her strength. The last I heard from Ernest, Junior, the boy I had helped with his education, was that his mother could no longer go from place to place on her bicycle and needed a car.

I told him I couldn't afford one. I have never heard another word from the Williams family.

I sound perhaps as if I were digressing but I was trying to describe a situation in which I was allowed to be a white Santa Claus but not a white friend.

You don't make me feel as if it were my obligation to accept the white man's guilt and therefore be ashamed and uneasy in your presence.

I can't believe that Joe Wilder baked me an angel food cake instead of a chocolate cake, to warn me not to become too intimate!

You make me believe that when we're together it's not an

armed truce. I'm convinced that I'm your friend and you are mine.

ALEC WILDER

P.S. Very recently one of the Williams kids tracked me down in Rochester. He seems very eager to see me. He told me he'd love to have me stay at his home whenever I'm in Rochester. He's now working in a bank there and two of his brothers have jobs in Rochester. He was a baby back then when I was trying to help out. It was twenty years ago. I, cynical jackass, presumed they'd all forgotten.

I don't mean to imply I was some kind of beneficent Santa Claus, merely that I loved a whole family and was sad that they had forgotten me. But, you see, they never did. They never lost me; just lost my address!

Dear Bradley:

As you know, Vicki died last week. And as you also know, she was one of the loveliest and dearest girls ever.

When she was a little girl she called me Mr. Wizard. I wish I could remember why. Can I possibly have performed some act that she considered magic?

The last time I saw her was about eight years ago. Her mother and father brought her in on a Sunday afternoon to a rehearsal of a piece I'd written for George Barnes and Carl Kress. It was a surprise as I had never known George knew Jackie and Roy.

Just before they started playing Vicki walked up to me with a marvelous blend of pride and shyness, her child hands delicately smoothing down her dress.

She stood before me smiling and then she said, "I'm all in pink."

And so she was and God knows I've never forgotten the moment.

I thought you'd be the person to tell this small story to.

ALEC

Dear Young Men:

I note that you live on Bucyrus Street. I also note that the train I'm in is backing down a spur track in Crestline, Ohio.

You, I'm sure, are puzzled by the sight of a train you usually hear about four in the morning rumbling toward the crumbling platform of the torn-down Crestline depot.

In case no one explains it to you, there was another freight wreck, this time in Mansfield, Ohio. So our train, the old Broadway Limited, was rerouted to Cleveland, probably up the old P. and L.E. Then, instead of continuing on the old New York Central right of way, we were routed back to Crestline. Why? To pick up the eight passengers waiting there? To drop off the dozen passengers ticketed for Fort Wayne? Why does it really matter? It's all the Penn Central or Amtrak or Disneyland! Would they really run an extra two hours late just for these few discommoded passengers or is this simply one more illustration of the psychotic state of America?

You're both much too young to care about *that* part of it. All you've gotten out of it is the unprecedented backing up of the Broadway Limited from a spur track you haven't seen used in your entire life. (I could hear the crackles of the rust from the rails.)

I don't know your names, so I'm going to address this to The Stocky Ten-Year-Old Boy and add the number I just saw when the train moved forward, Number 17 Bucyrus Street, Crestline, Ohio. I suppose we'll never meet but here's wishing you and your younger brother (now sprawled out on the front steps) a very happy life.

ALEC WILDER

Dear Lou:

I don't remember anyone ever being so interested in my musical opinions. So I'll risk boring you silly with some more.

I suppose I'd have quit composing a long time ago if John Barrows hadn't introduced me to so many glorious players. It was a godsend to meet and get to know those who truly loved the same kind of music I did, who played marvelously and, best of all, who liked the way I wrote. For on such splendid occasions as those when one of them would ask me to compose a piece I already felt safe since the person asking wasn't a stranger and wanted music such as I knew I would be able to turn out.

As a result of meeting all these talented musicians I have found myself for the past twenty-five years composing almost exclusively for friends. My not asking for commission money has been for two reasons. The first is my fear of not writing music worthy of the player or the commission. The second is a conviction that money has a way of infecting the relationship between composer and performer.

I have a great respect for great performers. I believe they do much more than interpret music: they re-create it. And in so doing they add a dimension to it. After all, the best marked music in the world is only a guide and it takes the awareness and sensitiveness of a conductor, a group or a soloist to put the breath of life into it.

Many composers treat players as necessary evils, much as playwrights treat actors. This may be true of run-of-the-mill actors and players, but the superior ones are godsends and I defer to them always. Indeed, great players have kept me composing.

I know that you, as a nonmusician and honest listener, like consonant, melodic, warm and loving music. But I promise you that the avant-garde, made up of experimenters, fakers, humorless lecture-hall "significators," has now become the musical Establishment. As a result, such traditional, unaggressive writers as myself are considered absurdities by both critics and audiences.

Yet — and I can't figure out why — the young, who you'd assume would be the champions of the New, seem to like what I write. Not, I'm sure, the young composers, but certainly, if I'm to judge by the letters I receive, the players.

Maybe all these disordered comments can serve to tell you why my musical behavior is what it is.

ALEC

Dear Mr. Hargrave:

It was possibly presumptuous of me to write asking that you consider changing the plaque in your Geneva branch bank. As I mentioned, the framed set of old dollar bills was a gift of my grandfather, whose bank it once was.

I never knew him or much about him except that he was a very formal, stiff gentleman of the old school. He never kissed his daughters; he shook hands with them. He was probably a dreadful stick. And yet, out of respect for the form and style of his day I wished to contribute to it by having that plaque changed from "Alex Lafayette Chew" to his full name "Alexander Lafayette Chew." It seemed only fitting.

In these days when the person to whom I have just been introduced replies by saying "Glad to meet you, Al," I am aware that everyone is a buddy, from Ike to Dick. All this is a concomitant of rummage-sale garments, no neckties, soulless sex, McDonald's, and carnival-midway manners.

I don't claim to be a worthy representative of gentility and personal dignity but I most assuredly respect them. And trivial though the corrected plaque may seem in this world of corruption, atomic weapons, shallow art and motel architecture, I am nevertheless pleased and rewarded by the knowledge that a gentleman's name exists for any or all to see as he would have wanted it and even gruffly demanded it.

For this I have you to thank.

I wonder if I now would be expressing my gratitude were your first name not Alexander.

ALEXANDER LAFAYETTE CHEW WILDER

Dear Dr. Watson:

As I expected, the madness is now in almost total control. I truly believe this. Except for very special areas, sanity is no longer in charge of American society. I believe this so strongly I don't even bother to qualify my statement by adding "I think."

I'm appalled and almost unsad at the shortness of life left to me. I weep for the young, I weep for the Sequoias, I weep for the extinction of species of animal and bird life, I weep for the overwhelming threat to the survival of all life on earth.

I cannot do much. I do try to help to a greater degree than I ever thought I could. I'll try harder. Perhaps in the verse I send you I can speak more clearly about all the terrifying awarenesses crashing into my consciousness hourly.

I refuse to stop laughing.

I refuse to stop writing.

I refuse to stop trying to help.

And all the while I see a boat filled with glowing-eyed children moving inexorably toward its doom, and another boatload of howling revelers in masks and hats made from thousand-dollar bills moving even more swiftly down into Mr. Poe's maelstrom.

And I have three teeth left (but that's a measly aside, I promise).

Follows an unlikely poem for these damned and damning days:

On the weathered gray shingle wall
I saw a raceme of barely budding wisteria.
I knew it instantly was a vision never to be forgotten.
I returned to it many times a day
Seeking, nearly feverishly, the opened buds.
The village was a joyous burst of Spring;
No glance could rest on less than color,
Some shy and modest and others passionate
With celebration of their return to sun and air.
The apple tree opulent with blossom,
The lacquered ornamental cherries,
The proud and elegant daffodils
And the tattered robes of wind-torn tulips,
Gnarled old lilacs heavy with scented bloom,
Elms and chestnuts showing tips of virgin green.
All about me, on every side,
Down every lane and winding cobbled street
All of Spring's triumphs bursting out together;
No subtle suspense this year,
But all saved up for one glorious celebration.
Yet back and back again I went
To the weathered gray shingle wall
To see if there were any sign of an unfurled bud
Of the only blue fit to grow against that gray.

The day I left that haunting place
The long raceme was almost all revealed.
I stood and stared till curtains moved
In neighboring windows.

Then in the autumn I returned
And found what might have been a ghost town:
All the lovely streets and cozy houses,
The white and delicate spires,
The elms and chestnuts,
The winding streets
And warning toll of midnight,
All were there.
But my needed magic had disappeared.
Only streets and buildings, people and the midnight tolling bell
Were left behind to mock me.

I never saw that shingled wall again.
But shall I, can I, could I
See that blue emerge against that gray
Another Spring?
If so, I ask for nothing more
Except the eyes to see them.

ALEC

Dear Sirs:

In 1968 I had a hunch that Nantucket would be pretty beautiful in the spring. I was so right that I hesitated about ever returning in that season. Lightning just may strike twice in the same place but miracles, I assumed, never. I dampened my compulsion to come back by reminding myself that I had that 1968 spring carefully tucked away in my best-guarded memory vault and besides, nothing could equal it.

But this year, 1972, I was swinging around the landscape listening to first and second performances of music I had written and in the course of setting up the itinerary, I added a flight from Boston to Nantucket. Then I called you at the Coffin House and reserved a room, postponed it after I saw how late spring was running, and finally arrived very disturbed lest I had missed the glorious blooming.

God be praised! I could scarcely take the time to register and look at my room for the absolutely storybook blooming in the gardens, massed in the flowering fruit trees along the streets.

I was in a trance for as long as I was there. I must have walked fifty miles. I know I went into every alley, lane, dead-end street in the village.

You even let me use the piano in the basement bar in the mornings. I believe I wrote a few loving passages down there, right beside the open doorway through which wafted the scent of lilacs, apple blossoms, sea air. Indeed, it's a wonder I wrote a note.

Sometimes, because its perfection touched me so deeply, I'd have to go back to my room. I'd calm down by playing my newly discovered solitaire called Cornerstones, but still through the open window would steal the reminders of the ineffable world outside.

I know I've never been so happy. I even made a point of avoiding conversations for fear one of them might break the spell.

I wished for nothing. I had what I wanted and needed. I regretted nothing; I slept like a child.

So miracles not only repeat, they improve.

Thank you for all your kindness and cordiality.

ALEC WILDER

P.S. I may even try it again next spring. My memory tells me I don't really need another time but I have a hunch . . .

Dear Harry:

Thanks very much for your long, loving letter. I hate to get frosty and petulant but I am impelled to toward those like yourself whom I'm afraid of losing. And now to more head scratching . . .

You know all about dry spells and you've always impressed me with your not having become victimized by them. Part of your successful handling of this, to me, traumatic experience is your youth, but even more than that you learned early on how to use that blocked creative flow in other ways.

For many years I was convinced that my only contribution to the miracle of life was the notes I wrote, inadequate though they might be. I assumed that my character and even my very being was so warped and weak, immature and confused, that only creations could help compensate for my countless personal lacunae.

And alcohol, while it gave me daily courage, also, I knew, turned me into a dreadful person and I knew that many people, as a result, found me intolerable. God bless my friends, including you and your family, for your patience and particularly yourself for your almost uncanny understanding.

Is it my sobriety for the past five years which has made it possible for me to deal with the inevitable dry spells? Has my increased self-respect caused me to find devices for surviving those sterile times? Formerly, when they would hit, often without a hint of warning, I would make a wholly negative adjustment to them by concluding that my music was of too little consequence and merit for me to be so concerned about its nonfunctioning.

Today I am no more impressed by my abilities than I ever was, unless your enthusiasm and linking my music with Poulenc's has made me more self-respectful. Yet I'm finally able to face the barrens without panic. I don't even sweat over the possibility that I'll never have another worthy creative idea again.

Were I a man of ego I would be complacent from recalling all I have written. But, as you know, I'm not such a man and I can recall very few, not even whole pieces but small sections of pieces which I'm happy to have put to paper.

The acceptance and enthusiasm of musicians whom I respect certainly help preserve my sanity and alleviate my loneliness. But, oh, how I wish I had grown into a tree rather than simply a series of loving blooms! Still, I must accept that I am not a tree-man and I must be protective and conscientious about my garden, make no comparisons, seek no public victories, and try as best I can to celebrate in the most civilized, orderly, sensitive way I know the ineffable miracle of life.

Forgive the sententious sentiments! They truly aren't that; but when I become excited about this miracle I tend to splatter purple ink all over the page.

Thank you for hearing, truly hearing what I'm trying to say in sound.

ALEC

Dear Sheldon:

I've told you for how many years I wanted to write a book about the great professional songs of the pre-rock era.

I never dreamed that I'd be able to raise the money necessary for such a project and when I dared to dream so far as to wonder what publishing firm would consider it, I drew a total blank.

So you can imagine what it's like for me to have received a grant and, miracle of miracles, to have signed a contract with Oxford University Press!

That may be the official name but I'm positive that there never would have been a contract if you hadn't been an Oxford editor.

Your gentle manner, your enthusiasm for the project as well as for the songs themselves, have given me a surge of confidence I'm sure I never would have had otherwise.

So thank you for having treated me with such graciousness; for clarifying so many aspects of the book which I have been uncertain of and for having given me (you and James Maher, of course), the directional sense that kept the writing of the book from becoming a nightmare.

My every good wish to you!

ALEC WILDER

Dear Harvey:

That final list you've sent me is staggering. I find it hard to believe that it comprises only the music I've written in the last twenty years. It's so long you'd think I had done nothing but compose seven days a week without interruption for all that time. Whereas the truth is that until five and a half years ago I spent most evenings drinking and most mornings unable to get out of bed because of monumental hangovers. And what of those seemingly endless months when I couldn't write a note?

I must have written like a madman when I did write. But again I almost never have worked more than four hours a day except when orchestrating.

What of those jammed files which used to be in Bill Engvick's attic? You had them put in storage, you said. I've no idea where, and I've avoided asking because I can't face all that mass of music manuscript. Film scores, songs, whole scores for musicals, piano pieces, God knows what.

I'm literally shocked when I look over this list. But frankly, it's not an unpleasant shock. For even if most of the music is in-adequate, at least the length of the list proves that I have done a hell of a lot of work!

That's really what the shock is: all these years I've felt guilty for not having done enough. But the list denies that. Of course don't let's speak of my forgetting what I've done or why I forget. I really don't want to know the answer or the source of *that* psychological block.

It would certainly be great to make more of this music avail-able to those who write me for it. That old monster money, of course. At the rate these letters come in I might even make a little loot out of it if it were in print. But no one except you and the letter writers care!

Sometimes I find myself a little bitter when I hear of only fair-to-middlin' composers getting their total output printed — and sometimes even promoted. You expect the big boys to be published, Sam Barber, Copland, Bernstein, Schuller, but Christ! Look at the names on some of the Peters covers! They simply aren't that talented or even that capable of hack appeal!

Is it all hustling? Oh, I'll shut up. After all, it's undoubtedly my own fault for having stayed in the shade for so long, for having avoided publicity, not "getting with" the power boys in the publishing world, failing to ask for help from the big names I know.

It's my fault and yet it still pisses me off!

Thank God for your efforts, though. At least you're managing to get the onionskins run off and you have gotten some pieces into print! Bless you, Mr. Tuba!

ALEC

Dear Lavinia:

Every time I return to New York which is, to begin with, much too expensive for my dwindling checkbook, I fall into these dreadful traps. Why, oh why don't I simply tell the operator to say I'm not in if the name she says is calling is unfamiliar to me?

Today, for example, I accepted a call from some strange name. His voice, at least over the phone, hadn't any quality of false cheer or pretension, so I stupidly told him to come to the hotel this afternoon.

He had, it seems, a synopsis for a ballet. I had been recommended to him by a rather blowhardy man from Rochester. Well, right off the bat he did the wrong thing. I'm sorry if I seem stuffy, but he didn't call up from the lobby, simply arrived at my room.

He was one of those young executives who you know plans to retire at thirty-two. He wasn't garishly dressed and his hair wasn't a cloche hat. But his voice was orotund and humorless and his words seemed to emerge wrapped in cellophane. Had all the new Watergate vocabulary with a dash of the ad business to give it, I'm sure he assumed, color.

Well, the goddamned ballet not only wasn't a ballet, since it had songs, but it had to be for television and the purpose was to run it every goddamned year at Thanksgiving time like *Amahl and the Night Visitors* runs at Christmas.

I'll save the synopsis for you. At first I thought the idea might be something I could handle since it's about a small-town boy who wants to be a ballet dancer. Oh, I know all of them are supposed to be queens, but it pleased me that any New York producer would be interested in such an unconventional subject, certainly unconventional for television audiences. I'd have preferred a poet but, I thought, maybe —

What does it turn out to be? A story of a boy persecuted by the other boys because of his interest in ballet, who gains their respect by dancing across a white-water river on projecting rocks and thereby making it possible for the football coach, who up till then has loathed him, to be brought back across the river and do the final coaching of the team which as a result wins the Big Game.

Think about it! Okay, you *have* thought about it. Does this skipping stone deed assure the poor little bastard of a standing ovation when he performs his first *pas seul* in the local high school auditorium? Do his persecuting enemies take up a kitty to send him to Russia to study how to leap through stage windows? Is there any likelihood that their loathing of art will shift because he has made it possible for their goddamned football team to win the Big Game?

Why, why, why don't I turn a deaf ear to all names of strangers? Why am I such a dunderhead? Guilt? Guilt about *what?*

ALEC

Dear Harry:

I'm entertained by the signs of acceptance I've been shown by those who are familiar faces in the Establishment Pentagon.

For thirty years I have stayed quite deliberately outside of groups, away from publicity, and done my work as best I could. Then, due not so much, in fact not at all, to ambition as to coincidence and curious encounter, I wound up with a spate of publicity. Maybe it all started with that book I wrote. In any event I've had overtures from otherwise good and kind people who have always kept me within talking distance but never close and never for more than a formal few minutes.

Ahh! — but not now! I won't sniggle over naming names except to say that I wouldn't be surprised to receive an invitation to dinner from Truman Capote! You see, "it's all right now." They all feel that I carry a genuine passport to their hierarchal hanging gardens, that it won't offend the gardeners if I'm found photographing the ha-ha!

I'm grateful to them, rather than offended. For they have given me the needed warning that it's time to step back into the wainscoting.

You have a way with you, Mr. B., by means of which you may be found on either side of it and only rarely have I worried about the influence of the floodlights on you. Nor do I believe I need worry ever again.

I suppose they wouldn't seem so comical if I needed them. If I believed that their acceptance was a sign of growth, of achievement, I would undoubtedly hang on their every "stroking" remark. But knowing their pathetic concept of "position," their disdain for anyone who hasn't demonstrated their right to belong to their "aristocratic" society, I find myself highly entertained and more than ever convinced that my instinct to avoid them, my refusal to move out of my privacy, was right.

I believe it was Gertrude Stein who eliminated all potential readers from her mind when she wrote and finally realized she must not write even for *herself*. Sounds so typical of her, yet I quite agree with her. Whatever is created must *come from* whatever self-discipline, intuition and taste you may be blessed with but it shouldn't *go* even to *you*. It should simply be created. You find out if it works by listening to a reading of it, not a public performance. Then you dismiss it. If you don't, it may wind up something not to have *come from* you but whose unconscious purpose is to *go to you*.

No good.

And so it makes me considerably more cheerful to note that I never wish to hear anything I write more than to find out if it works. I never knew why this indifference was so constant, now I see quite possibly it's because, after all my rejection of audiences, I don't want *me* to wind up as one.

ALEC

Dear Lavinia:

I know I'm guilty of many too many end-of-civilization speeches and I apologize. My views are scarcely news. All people who have observed, read, listened, are aware of the appalling corruption and coarsening of society.

But I became irritated by your insistence on reporting all the sunny experiences you've had and the occasional encouraging attitudes and beliefs you encounter. This was very stupid of me because I, too, go out of my way to find those of the young who move, no matter what obstacles may block them, into the sunlit places, who do their work, get excited about it, and who refuse to allow the moral squalor all around them to deter them from fulfilling their dreams. Most of these are the music students and young chamber music groups.

Right after you told me of the cheery young men who were touring the Village in a pickup truck selling pumpkins in which they had carved absurd faces and how uplifted you were by their rollicking spirits and genial calls to the passing public — the same day I visited a group on the Upper West Side which was about to perform a trio I had written for clarinet, bassoon and piano.

I only went because one of the players had called me and, knowing I couldn't get to the performance, I felt I owed them the courtesy of attending a rehearsal.

The small apartment house was run-down, the halls looked as if the building had once been used for some unmentionable purposes, so much so that when I had trouble finding the right door I sensed the echoes of evil. Then I found the door, pressed the bell and it was opened by a young, innocent-looking boy, followed by an affectionate gray cat.

As I passed down the gloomy hall I happened to look up and the high ceiling was a mass of large curls of flaking paint. Then I was in a room, equally gloomy, where two more young people sat in front of music stands, one a bearded boy and the other a thin, intense girl. They were the bassoonist and clarinetist.

We exchanged those words which can never, nor should, be remembered whenever unaggressive strangers meet. I realized immediately that they were nervous at the prospect of playing a piece with the composer in the room whom they'd never seen before.

Well, as you know, I don't think of myself as a composer. (Thank God!) I think of myself as a person who has, among other things, tried to write some pieces of music.

They played.

They played exquisitely. They played not only musically but with conscience. They played as if that was the whole point of living.

I nearly wept.

Fortunately the piece happens to be one of the few of all the hundreds I've written of which I'm unashamed. So, not being embarrassed, I was able to tell them lucidly and passionately how I felt about their playing.

There were a lot more treasures in the toe of the stocking, but it's enough to say that I was wholly fulfilled by their individual and mutual spirits, by their mastery of their instruments, by their extraordinary comprehension of the atypical statement the piece wished to make. And I walked out of that gloomy flat, that hallway exorcised of its smell of evil, into the daylight as if I had been informed by God that he was going to give humanity one more chance and that these three children were his messengers.

"Signifying nothing," my foot! If Shakespeare had been there, he'd have blushed were he reminded of that line.

Sure, they'll be dust, all three of those inspired children. Sure, there'll be no pyramid built in memory of them!

But not even the devil could deny what took place in that room though the belief, the faith, the conviction permeating it would have driven him back to hell!

Forgive the melodrama, but, Lavinia, I was in a Presence. Such ineffable moments defy and shout with glorious laughter at mortality and the waiting worm.

I remember once in a book written by a self-elected voice for the California hippie there was a remark made by a bearded young man who had been asked what he supposed he'd be doing when the Bomb dropped. He replied, "Oh, I'll be right here, painting."

Skin of our teeth, yes, but the miracle is still all around us.

ALEC

Dear Father Atwell:

You're a very concerned and self-giving "Father," but my impulse is to write "Dear Henry."

Whenever I am depressed, lonely, confused, I think of you moving cheerily and busily about that gentle-looking (but probably rife with ungentleness) community of Avon. I think of your constant invitation to stay as long as I choose in that extra bedroom. I think of Louise Coyne, that marvelous, doughty lady who serves you so faithfully and bakes such great honest-to-goodness apple pies.

And I think of your goodness, your courage and your open mind, your valiance and dignity.

I'm very happy that I composed the Children's Plea for Peace for you. Granted that it was for your church, it truly was for you.

Lavinia Russ, whom I'm sure you remember, walked down the block after that performance because she was crying. And that about summed it all up.

It was no great musical work. But everything surrounding it *was* great: the beautiful, beautiful children crocodiling across to the church from the school, the perfect spring day, the tender green of the budding leaves, the spring flowers, the friendly spirit of the congregation, Warren Benson's loving narration, you and I up in that little choir loft looking down at it all!

But little of that would have shone through had it not been for your spirit, not your devotion to God, your devotion to all of life. Well, I'm not religious, but maybe devotion to and reverence for life is close to a religious person's concept of God.

So be it.

But every time Louis and I drive down to the rectory for dinner, no matter what weather or season, that same hope enters my being as it did on that precious spring day. It must be you.

ALEC

Dear Harry:

You asked me to write you my sentiments and convictions regarding the new fashions in music and morality.

I believe we are living in an age of the Emperor's clothes. Very few dare to state the obvious fact that the poor old gentleman is stark naked and instead praise his beautiful ermine robes. He is not even wearing the fig-leaf of imagination.

I believe we are living in an age without style, virtue, dignity or honor. And worse than that, one in which the new is equated with the excellent. Indeed, for those whose obsession is the new a valid word has been coined: Neophiliac.

I believe that a creator's obligation is to filter and reflect and present in an orderly, disciplined fashion his own being. I do not believe he should attempt to reflect his time, which, by the way, may be better reflected aurally by opening a window in any large city.

I believe in human imperfection as opposed to mechanical perfection. I do not enjoy, in any way, synthetic "musical" sounds.

I do not believe that art should parrot science and I do not believe that one art should attempt to rationalize itself by means of another. The literary flimflam which is employed to explain and justify much of the grotesque sonal experiments is instantly suspect, in as much as the work should be its own explanation.

I believe that the extreme experiments in contemporary so-called music should be renamed generically. Should a well-founded word be devised meaning "experiment in sound" and concerts of this new art(?) be given in its name my irritation would subside.

I am not against experiment. I am against moving out of the sacred grove of art into the anarchistic playpen of newness and nowness for their own sakes.

I believe in direction, continuity, shape, communication, wit, sophistication, simplicity, order, honesty and taste.

At least the Dadaists laughed at themselves.

An age which has the extremely bad manners and infantile judgment to dismiss as remnants of the past such giants as Hindemith and Prokofief, to name just two, is really not worth the anger of a civilized person.

I have listened recently to a considerable amount of contemporary music. I listened as I always do, for ideas, shape, inter-relationships, direction, strength, passion, joy, wit, wonderment, pulse, decisiveness, breathing, searching, balance, development.

In all of what I heard I could detect no direction, shape, balance or development. I admit that the complexity of the music may have made me incapable of finding the shape or the development.

I occasionally heard pulse and decisiveness, more anger than passion. I heard no breathing, few interrelationships. I heard ideas but I'm damned if I know what happened to them. I suppose what I did hear was searching, but of a sort which causes me to have preferred finding.

Naturally I heard nothing resembling harmony or euphony. I heard no counterpoint. I heard melodic fragments. More than anything I heard violence: violent rhythms and unresolved, violent dissonance.

I heard great restlessness; I heard dark thoughts; I heard aural frowns and no aural smiles. No gaiety, no elegance, no charm, little lucidity, no calm, no simplicity, no longing, no memory and no analogies to nature (outside of tidal waves and elm blight).

I heard the city, the laboratory, the computer, the textbook, the city street.

I heard little of man as I have known him for half a century. I heard the machine, I heard the pronouncement, the document, didacticism.

I heard no doubt. I heard no questioning. I heard no poetry or allusion to childhood. I heard no derivation.

I heard granite rigidity, little sinew, no looseness. I heard no sounds which suggested life as it is lived in a sane mind hour by hour, day by day.

I heard alien, unhuman, deeply disturbed sounds written not by hands but by clenched fists.

It is awkward at my age, sixty-six, to make claims as to how I would have evaluated the music of today were I much younger, for how could I possibly know?

Well, strangely enough, it is not entirely impossible to know. For music, an expression of living man, is a reflection and affirmation of life. And so if a man is noncompetitive, unaggressive, undisturbed, unangry, if he is serene, passive, more respectful of nature than of man, involved with simplification, resolution, distillation, gentleness, wisdom, poetry, butterflies and flowers, children and small animals, then all these elements are bound to be revealed in whatever art form he expresses himself.

This, of course, depends on the artist's honesty. If he is only a faddist, he is beneath consideration.

So, after all, perhaps I can know how I would have reacted to today's experimentation had I heard it at an earlier age. For I still believe as I did then, and the music of today contains most of the characteristics of man I least respect or admire.

ALEC

Dear Whitney:

I suppose you're aware that the profile you wrote of me in *The New Yorker* has been a breach of the defenses against publicity I set up thirty years ago. You have no notion how strange it feels to be "outside" as a result of it. I thought it would scare me silly but the compensation cancels the fear.

And that compensation is being treated less like a freak. Of course those who have treated me so are all people I have no use for, but often they are those who can make the mechanics of daily living more of a trial than they tend to be under any circumstances.

I'm not even mentioning the affection and warmth of your writing. I'm restricting myself to the unforeseeable results. And they are, in a word, oil poured in the rusty joints of daily living.

When I suggested you use another name than mine for the title of your book collection of profiles on the grounds that I wasn't well enough known, you gave me one of your gentle but mysterious smiles and suggested that I was better known than I might think.

This literally astounds me. I'm not set for such a possibility. I'm not trying to act out an "aw, shucks!" "jes folks" attitude; I simply find it spooky and bizarre and too far from my long-assumed and accepted state of virtual anonymity.

ALEC

p.s. Your loving exposure has me spinning like a top!

Dear Marian:

You know I truly love you. You know, or God knows, should, that I'm aware of and grateful for your thousand kindnesses and considerations. You know that your going to all that expense of a lovely album cover, your renting that glorious piano and your especially endearing and personal playing of my pieces, all of it you must know touches me very deeply.

But do you know that you inadvertently depressed the hell out of me by conning me to do that television show? For Christ's sake! When I looked at the playback of that videotape I damn near threw up and fainted, in that order. I look as if I were on loan from Mount Hope Cemetery! If that's what people look at when they meet me, how can they possibly tell me I'm looking well? I look as if I were in the last stages of Bangheart's disease or jungle rot!

You asked me whom I went to in New York for a yearly checkup and I told you I didn't want to be told I had ten days to live. And I told you that *before* I saw the videotape!

For God's sake! I should tell the room clerk in every hotel and motel I check into that if I don't call down by nine o'clock the next morning he should call the morgue!

Why are you so determined to drag me into public life? You know, you must believe me, that privacy is what I must have in order to maintain any semblance of balance and peace of mind. I hate to sound so damned snobbish, but who in God's name wants to be notorious in this schlock society? What possible distinction can there be in being accepted by a public you have no respect for?

I'm not denying the existence of multifarious talents all about the landscape, talents far superior to my own. But those talents aren't the ones who accept and reject. They mind their own business and ignore the shallow world most squalidly exemplified by the so-called talk shows.

I'm aware that you, as a performer, must have publicity, that it is an integral part of any performing career. But I'm a writer and

I'm quite willing to forgo any rewards which would accrue from being a more public figure.

To you, of course, adept as you are at it, it's fun. To me, no matter how relaxed I may seem, it is total anathema. So if in the future I balk at more of these scenes, please understand, even if you find it hard to forgive!

ALEC

Dear Cuzzin:

Seeing you last night after such a long time was a great delight and a special kind of reassurance.

I've loved your writing ever since I read your first book, *The Cabala*. I've read every word since and known I was in the presence not only of a masterly craftsman but of a profound lover of mankind.

You asked me two things which added still more to my well-being. One had to do with the possibility of my working with you (musically, naturally) on a new adventure of your current hero, Theophilus North, in an ideal community such as Brook Farm. That you would consider me I find most complimentary and heady. We even shook hands on the project.

The other question had to do with the progress of my five-year abstinence. With anyone of less acuity and wisdom I might have proffered a flippant response. But I tried to give you a considered answer. What I believed for forty years to be a necessity in any crisis I find isn't one. How I managed to create substitutions for the enormous reassurance alcohol gave me all those years I'll never know. But I do know that those substitutions may all be lumped under one term. It's self-respect. God knows, not vanity! But I no longer presume that I'm inadequate, inept, absurd, unwanted and whatever other negative adjectives I thought I was for all those years.

It's not because the reviews of the book I wrote were good or that *The New Yorker* considered me fit for a profile.

It is partly because I believe I compose a little better than I used to and it's also because I find that people whom I respect, in turn respect me much more than I've ever known them to. Is this because I have become a better person?

You, kind sir, have never before been so open and communicative as you were the other evening. I can describe my feeling only by saying that "you let me in." Friendly and jolly though you've always been with me, I always had the slight uneasiness one had when talking to someone through a Judas window. Their faces, eyes and voices are as close as in any intimate conversation, but the door happens to be locked.

Am I imagining all this?

If it's true, I in no way blame you for I realize I wasn't worthy of your trust. Even my oldest friends I find more open than ever before.

It's rather sad that this should occur so late in life. But because it is so late I have no time to dig about in the garrets of the past to discover why it didn't happen sooner, this unfamiliar self-respect.

I do hope you remain enthusiastic about our project. My very best to you.

ALEC WILDER

Dear Arnold:

But for Jerome Hill I should never have more than met you. But through his good offices I dared to ask for your legal aid.

You have given of it unstintingly and have even, on more than one occasion, refused remuneration. I know that your position in the world of the theater is one of high repute and that a list of your clients reads like Debrett's. That you should have taken time and effort to help me is a lovely memory for me and a sunny thought in these gray and greedy times.

I am even more grateful for your having helped my friends, not only because you liked and respected them, but because I sent them to you. And finally that you should have gone to all the trouble you did for the talented man (who shall remain nameless) who could have but would not pay the reasonable bill you sent him puts me further in your debt. And again you did this because I suggested you to him.

I hope when I see you for lunch on Monday that you will be able to tell me that he finally paid you, if only to ease my guilt.

You once told me of your deep respect for creative talent and that it was a pleasure for you to help those with it over tough legal hurdles. I'm not certain if I deserve a place among the talented but you certainly deserve a place among the compassionate and warmhearted in this human ice age.

Thank you, dear sir!

ALEC WILDER

Dear Frank:

I must have written you just a few less than fifty letters without replies. Of course I mind; after all, for many years you were my good friend and fellow laugher.

I know, as my letters have indicated, how complex, how mercurial, how trigger-tempered you are. I know that your sights have been set on birds far beyond my vision. (Feathered birds, that is.) I realize that you live in a rarefied atmosphere, a pitilessly lit arena where public figures posture and strut and move in what they presume to be a stately formal dance. But I continue to believe that despite your political capitulation, your strange bedfellows, your often unfortunate choice of songs, and, saddest of all, your silence, that you would be, given a sane society and time for a deep breath, once again my active friend and once again we could sit in a room locked against the intrusion of the leeches, the court jesters, the presidents of vice, the dreary little girls, and we could talk about beliefs and longings and wonderments. To boot, and praise be, we might even laugh.

I'll never forget or stop being grateful for your many kindnesses and constant faith in me. And I'm touched deeply by your almost small-boy gesture of friendship in sending me Christmas presents, even though you may have done no more than add my name to a list.

Frank, we're growing old.

Do you suppose awareness of mortality is what caused you to start spinning, to choose shallow companions, to desert former convictions, to cynically (or desperately?) decide to "get with it" by singing fashionable but unsuitable songs?

No matter what has happened inside your head, I wish I could be close enough to help you resolve whatever haunts or warps you. I'll admit I have countless times decided that that was *that*. I admit that your new persona and accounts of your tastes and concerns of the past decade have depressed and even disgusted me.

In a perverse way I'm glad my life and yours are existing in such a tragic vacuum that I need fear no longer that you might mistake a protestation of friendship as a circuitous bid for a seat on your bandwagon. Tragic though life has become, at least it has made it possible for you to believe that no matter how rude and seemingly hostile my words may be, all I want is to see you alone, to find out if the man I knew is still there hiding behind the garish, the violent, the reactionary and the lost.

Believe it or not, I'm still available if you ever need me. All it needs is your request and my survival.

ALEC

Dear Harry:

I told you about all those letters I wrote but I never sent them to you. I must have had my eye on some kind of sparrow since I paid two hundred bucks to have them typed.

But you also know me very well, sometimes infuriatingly so, and you know I'm not after the bright lights or the accolades. You also know I would take, were it a choice, the assurance that I could go on writing music than that my letters be published.

I've told you of the "I-shall-be-vindicated-when-my-diaries-are-published" gentleman in Rochester. Well, I want none of that shit, particularly since I believe I don't need vindication with? from? by? the only audience I care about, my friends.

You also know that I always do the best I know how. So, now that a very forthright man from a reputable publishing house *is* interested in the letters, I'm in a kind of daze. For I'm truly more concerned with how in hell I'm going to finish this wind ensemble piece for a man who has the band at Yale in time for his December concert than I am with how I'll get these letters and others into such shape that the editor will give me a contract.

There's supposed to be an advance for a book, I realize, and God knows I could use the money. (I'm sick to death of "bread"!) But I'm not so concerned that whipping it into shape takes precedence over the Yale piece or over the trio I promised Bernie Garfield, the bassoonist.

That trio, by the way, if it's good enough, will get one perfect performance at the Library of Congress next spring and maybe a few more which I'll never hear or know about. So why is it or the band piece of so much consequence?

As you know, much of my music gets played once or twice and never again. Why doesn't that make me quit and jump for joy that another area of creativity has opened up for me?

Do I like only edited, controlled creations? Does the absence of a master plan — any plan — in my life make me inattentive, less than absorbed because the holes in the target are so scattered? I really believe I'm much less interested in my life than I am in the small dishes set out on the long table such as spring in Nantucket, a railroad ride, sights, sounds, smells. Not *a life*. That's wrong; an orderly, planned, shaped life but not this day-to-day passage of mine which you know quite well is uncharted, rudderless, directionless.

Mind you, that's okay with me. It's just that when I have to buckle down and, by means of carefully chosen words, make it charted and pointed, even though by so doing I give it editing and shape, it still doesn't interest me as much as trying to write one more, two more, a dozen more pieces of music which may very easily turn out to be poorly constructed and an embarrassment when tried out!

Yet I'm so damned fond of Mr. Sions and grateful to him for his belief that I'm capable of putting some letters together that I am morally bound to do the job.

Of course if it is published I run the same old risk of being clobbered by the reviewers who, I'm certain, will find it too this and too that and altogether more childish than they can stand. And, damn it! I can easily resist the temptation to read music reviews but it's much harder to pass up book reviews. Fuck it! If it's published and I get the word from friends that it's considered a dog, I will resist and jump, with all my clothes on, into one more hit-or-miss piece of music!

Alec

Dear Percy:

It shocks me that so often love fails to get a fair shake. Love, after all, is an agreeable creature, willing to roll with a lot of nasty bruises and rabbit punches. But outside of ESP it has no way to combat separation.

The moment I met you (through Goddard, of all people!) I loved you. And while life was reasonably simple we saw one another constantly. But slowly all those city mosquito bites began to interrupt and before I knew it we weren't seeing each other at all.

In those early days I was politically very naive. I knew there were endless abuses and injustices but I never gave the time I should have to finding out more. Fortunately I had friends who were informed and therefore I wasn't a complete ignoramus.

But I knew that certain people had at their fingertips all manner of facts and figures, dates, names, were informed politically and sociologically as well as were most political scientists.

My leanings have always been toward the so-called "lower" forms of life: birds, beasts, trees, fish, flowers, more than toward man. Obviously since I was a human being I had to be concerned with other humans in order to survive and in order to share pleasures and intimacies which I couldn't with the other forms.

I also was disturbed by corruption, injustice, poverty, unequal opportunity, prejudice and all the rest. But I could never quite accept the Russian experiment, much as I had heard of its raising enslaved millions to a level of subsistence and a trace of dignity. I knew there was ferment and great anger in America against many of the capitalistic abuses and little regard for the exploited members of its society. But I wouldn't join any group, nor have I to this day.

I mention this as background to my realization that in the days when I first knew you there were many others whom I knew were members of all sorts of "left-wing" organizations and even the American Communist party.

Many of them I was suspicious of for the reason that they refused to consider the plight of the individual — their concern (and how deep did it really go?) was for an amorphous mass of strangers. Whenever I asked questions, evidently the very asking made me in their estimation a "red-baiter." I most certainly was not; I was seeking information.

Out of all those liberal, sometimes violently outspoken people, there were, as I said, only a few I trusted and believed were profoundly concerned. I sensed in the others fashion and fad. I noticed that none of them sacrificed (those who had money) anything but time. And few of them sacrificed much of that. But communism at that time was as "in" as "camp" thirty years later.

You were one person who made me wonder if perhaps I wouldn't be a better person if I were to give up time and money and even consider a total dedication to what you made me believe was a most worthy cause. You never proselytized, you never "approached" me. You never jeered at me for my ignorance. You simply stood fast, read everything in sight and, best of all, never fed me party line pap.

You were essentially, throughout all this era, a good, good man. You may even have been a member of the party. It didn't matter, for you never made a social device of it. Your heart went out to all those who were victims of an implacable, cruel system. You wanted to help. You didn't castigate those like myself who were good persons but who didn't see their way clear to move among the iron machinery of groups, slogans, manifestos and consideration only for mankind in the mass.

So it's great that we've begun to correspond again, to see each other, and it was a lovely gesture on your part to put me so sweetly into that marvelous, however financially unsuccessful, book *Is Anything All Right?*

I hope we meet soon!

ALEC

Dear Clark:

For a great many years you have been recording my chamber music. God knows it hasn't been for profit! I'm certain there hasn't been a single record which has paid for its initial costs.

Since that fortuitous evening when Arnold Sundgaard introduced us you have recorded practically everything I've suggested and, as well, two pieces for large complements of musicians. Even those failed to sell and must have cost you a packet.

All the musicians I've brought out to your studio have in turn been treated with the same patience and consideration as I have.

The fact that your distribution is not like the big recording companies sometimes makes it frustrating trying to get records for friends. But I shouldn't even bring that up, especially when I think of the hundreds of joyous hours I've spent in the control room with you through backbreaking retakes and splices and inserts by such perfectionists as Harvey Phillips.

You've never become angry or impatient. You've done astounding editing, you've sent dozens of records to friends who couldn't get them from retail dealers and you've never charged them.

Clearly you have been everything the word "friend" implies. It's wonderful to have believing musical friends like John Barrows, Harvey Phillips, Bernie Garfield, John Swallow, Dave Soyer and all the other beautiful players, but there's something extraspecial knowing someone who is willing and eager to take the time and go through all the technical trouble to produce recordings. They're like permanent concerts and affirmations that *I exist as a composer*.

I know my music is far from current fashion and that even if the records you've made were easier to find in record stores, they still wouldn't sell. But when I become depressed and without respect for or confidence in what I write, it's a very reassuring sensation to pick up a Schwann catalogue and find so many records listed under my name. I know it's against every principle I've clung to for me to grin over finding a longer list than those with more prominent names, but it does make me feel a little less isolated and less like the child with his nose pressed against the window behind which a party's going on.

And finally when I need to give my spirits a boost, what a lovely reassurance it is to know that I can always call some loyal friend like Jim Maher and go to his apartment and hear those records! In almost every instance they're recorded by the people I wrote them for and they're all the best musicians ever. I don't need to ask them to perform the piece in some indifferent hall. They've already chiseled the piece out of granite. And though the granite in truth is vinyl, like granite I don't have to worry about its breaking.

All in all, I am deeply in your debt. Thank you, thank you, thank you!

ALEC WILDER

Dear Bernie:

You, God knows, are a responsible man, so I'm sending this strange communication to you first. If you cast your eye down the page you'll notice that it's addressed to many people. I'm not certain that all of them will accept words written to them being read by all the others. I'm not being stingy by saving all the stamps. I really do want everyone to read about everyone else.

Some of you know some of the others, some know none, and none know all.

What I have to say to you is that at the precise time in my life when I needed musical reassurance, you gave it to me. Since I know your total probity, I didn't have to worry about your buttering me up.

No one else but John Barrows ever truly convinced me that I was a composer. God knows, had it not been for him, I'd have quit trying to write music a very long time ago.

But now John's gone and in my practically catastrophic loss, it has been a godsend to hear that you, for whom I have such very high respect, also consider me a composer of merit.

I'm forever in your debt for your encouragement and enthusiasm.

Will you please mail this to:

Mrs. Charlotte Allen
46 Croyden Road
Rochester, N.Y.

Dear Charlotte:

It may have taken you a few minutes to realize that part of this letter was written to you. You don't know Mr. Garfield to whom I wrote the first portion. He is, in my opinion, the best bassoonist in the world and my friend, to boot.

You know only a few of my friends — Dr. Watson, Louis Ouzer and dear Warren Fox. You do know that my life is scattered about in many communities, among many levels of people and professions. You have seen me, however, in only the most proper circumstances, in your home, at the old Corner Club, in your bookstore.

We are good friends with lives as unalike as possibly could be imagined. You are a lady and have lived as ladies once insisted upon living: with dignity, privacy, propriety and elegance. I, on the other hand, though I was born of "polite" parents, have lived a most ungentlemanly existence. Much of it has been spent in rough-and-tumble bars where I would have refused to take you, in streets I would have never promenaded with you and among people to whom I would never have introduced you.

Yet we are good and even special friends. I admit I edit my language in your presence because I know you would find much of it vulgar and inimical. Yet I do not present a false front to you; I simply offer that aspect of myself which I believe you will find the most tolerable and enjoyable.

Your wit and warmth, your stoicism, your insistence on a way of living far from middle-class pretension, your elegance, these I find superior and not, in their adamantine absolutism, wholly unlike my own refusal to accept the new world's carnival, tawdry, Laundromat ways.

I'm proud that I may consider myself your friend and I'm asking a special favor of you because of that friendship: that you not be irritated by my including your portion in this long letter. I even ask that you read the other pages as I believe you may thereby know me better and also possibly be amused.

Thank you for your steadfast affection.

Will you be kind enough to mail this on to:

> Miss Ana Roth
> Ross
> California

Dear Ana:

I've written you other letters. But now that you're a young woman I want you to know more about the man to whom you once sent a heart. You know how I feel about you, you may be so involved with all the discoveries that come with womanliness that you may well be embarrassed that once in your innocence you sent a heart to a man so very much older than yourself. I hope not.

When you take your first deep breath after the breakneck ride of young love and young revelations, please give a moment's thought to me, someone who loves you very, very dearly.

And also read the rest of this!

Will you mail it on, before you lose it, to:

> Charles Bourgeois
> 330 West 55th Street
> New York City

Dear Charlie:

Did it take you long to find yourself in this odd round robin? Do you find it too grotesque to give it more than a passing glance? Would you prefer a private communication instead?

I believe it when I'm told that you refused to read the passage about yourself in the piece Whitney Balliett wrote about George Wein. Yet surely you don't claim that knowing you are deeply loved and respected is entirely distasteful to you?

I find your loyalty and concern a rare and lovely thing. Your constant communication with Mabel Mercer, Jackie and Roy, Teddi King, Marian McPartland, and God knows how many others is evidence of love the way it used to be. For a man who becomes wrathful over the failings of small towns, you manage nevertheless to be the ultimate Scattergood Baines. Or were he and the *Saturday Evening Post* before your time?

You're a good man, Charlie B! So there!

Would you be kind enough to mail this on to:

> Howard Richmond
> TRO
> 10 Columbus Circle
> New York City

Dear Howie:

You may find this a strange kind of letter what with all the other addresses. Yet I know you're always curious and even fascinated by men's endless patterns. So here are a few of them.

I'm writing you to make certain that you know how constantly I am aware of your concern for me and your almost embarrassing financial help. You are a very good and rare friend. I think of you often and only with love.

I know how easily embarrassed you are by intimate confessions, so I'll stop right here except to ask you to send this preposterous letter on to:

> Sunny Carson
> c/o Jim & Benny's
> 10 West 86th Street
> New York City

Dear Sunny:

You may think I'm a real nut to be writing you this way. I can say only that I miss you and I think of you with great affection. I know that your way of making a living has sometimes been illegal, but I also know that you are the most honest bartender Jim Koulavaris ever had.

Your fondness for me is something I'm grateful for, especially as our worlds are so far apart, on the outside at least.

Since I stopped drinking I have had little desire to go to the places I used to. I'm not afraid of being tempted into drinking, so why don't I at least drop in and say hello to a few old drinking buddies?

I hope your eye trouble has cleared up and that life isn't too bad. I'm sure you miss Jim, but not any more than I do. He was a glorious guy!

All the best to you, Sunny!

Will you please mail this to:

> Grace Williams
> Manhattan Restaurant
> East Avenue
> Rochester, N.Y.

Dear Mrs. Williams:

You've probably never seen anything quite like this before and probably, if you read all the letters before this one, you've decided it was mailed to the wrong Mrs. Williams.

Well, it isn't the wrong Mrs. Williams, if you're the cheerful lady to whom I keep giving orders for dishes which they've run out of and who finally brings me rare chopped beef.

I've sat in that alcove a great many times, written a great many letters, read a great many books, and except for your night off, have had all my dinners served by your sunny self.

You can't imagine how relaxing it is to go to a restaurant knowing that you won't have to face road-company Mafia captains and insolent, agate-eyed waiters. You made an entire Rochester winter that much more bearable by being so cheerful and kind.

This note is to thank you for all that was far beyond the call of duty! Would you be kind enough to mail these pages to:

> Loonis McGlohon
> 222 Wonderwood Drive
> Charlotte, N. C.

Dear Loonis:

I know I don't ever have to explain anything to you. Why this is I'm not sure, and yet I know I can't surprise or dismay you with odd behavior. Your devotion to people is inspiring to one as suspicious as I am. I mention it because it is probably this unqualified acceptance of people's aberrations, fantasies, peculiarities, whims, viciousness, perversities which only increases in intensity (the acceptance, not the perversities) the closer you get to a person.

I remember the time you phoned, out of the blue, a total stranger, and wanted me to participate in a telephone interview. I think if you hadn't sounded so warm and undevious that I would have wriggled out of it.

As a result of that I started dropping in on you in Charlotte, we began writing songs together, and although nothing has ever come of them, thanks to this lovely era of squalor, we've had a splendid time. Furthermore, your stubborn insistence on writing the kind of song you believed in, in spite of total rejection in the marketplace, has sharply reminded me that true fulfillment is achieved only by contenting one's spirit and doing one's best regardless of profit and fashion.

So my profound thanks for your friendship, lovely lyrics and tunes, and for keeping the lamp lit in a darkening landscape.

Will you forward this odd document to:

> Suzan Kenyon
> Aurora
> New York

Dear Tudy:

If ever there were a person who would unreservedly accept this oddity, it is you. God knows you've moved against the current ever since I met you at Wells College all those years ago. You've stuck to your beliefs to the extent of becoming the town character. And you couldn't care less. You live your happiest hours with your animals, you maintain a marvelous amalgam of cynicism and naiveté. And in a crisis (*I* should know!) you provide such profound reassurance and generosity of spirit that you lift people out of pits of depression and set them on their feet with their faces toward the sun.

All these years you've lived what must be a lonely life, a somewhat lost life. Yet you never complain, you never ask for sympathy or help. In fact you still draw circle faces with smiles in your letters.

I don't pull my own weight in our friendship. I don't write often enough, I don't come to Aurora to visit. But even my failure doesn't bring down your wrath on my head. You're still, after more than twenty-five years, as loving, as young in spirit and wit and effervescence as you were when you were the best athlete and most popular senior Wells College ever had.

You've come through the fire, dodged the stones, stared back, shaken your fist and survived, smiling! I guess you notice that this is what all the people I've written to in this multiple letter have done. I'm a very fortunate man to be their friend. It sure as hell has kept me afloat through the years to know that all around me there were a few other stalwart souls also insisting on maintaining those principles and convictions in which they believed and which not even the grand march of the goblins could destroy. Bless you, dear Tudy!

You know Lou Ouzer, certainly? After all, if he hadn't been taking the yearbook pictures that year at Wells I'd never have met you. He's another holdout against the Monster Machine so I think he should read about you other holdouts. In case you don't know where to write, his address is 14 Gibbs Street, Rochester 14604.

Dear Lou:

You are the last on this list of beautiful souls who have kept their own counsel, followed their own star, stuck to their own vision. But you're certainly not the least as I'm sure you know. Good God! It's been over forty years that we've been friends!

You'll never know how many of my trips to Rochester were solely to reassure myself that humanity hadn't totally failed. But in the course of all those trips, our hundreds of country rides together, I'm afraid I may have influenced you to your possible loss. I knew you felt as I did about selling out, joining, hustling, kowtowing, being victimized. But I could indulge myself in these holdouts and barricades because I always and mysteriously managed to make enough money to thumb my nose while you not only were always scuffling for more but as well had a wife and two children.

How in hell you've gotten away with your independence, your refusal to knuckle under, how you've managed to give away so many thousands of photographs, I shall never know. But you have!

Furthermore, you've made all the sacrifices with style and wry wit, with great love and absolute honor. And I should add that Helen, as much as she may disagree with many of your attitudes, has adjusted to the less-than-comfortable income by managing to clothe and feed all of you with great skill and no complaints.

I go on at such length partly because I would feel shattered if I felt that my violent convictions have influenced you to the extent of causing you to suffer unduly.

I have infinitely more respect for your victory than for mine. But, by God, I can tell you one thing: it's beautiful to be around you, to be your friend and to know that literally nothing can touch what we have and what we are.

Keep this strange document. It should belong to you! Full circle!

ALEC

Dear Wally:

Some years ago I was complaining to a young friend that I lacked reassurance, that I needed to be told I had a trace of talent, a dollop of merit.

He, a hyperbolist if ever there were one, immediately suggested I hire a "throng." It would be made up of a group of young friends, generations removed from me but very affectionate, who would follow me everywhere and on a signal, cheer me loudly and throw their hats in the air.

Wild as was the notion, it made me speculate as to whom I would like to have in that throng. Before I tell you, you must understand that these friends in no way would serve as sycophants. They were and are people two generations younger than myself whom I love, respect and trust and who feel similarly toward me.

You and Lorraine Bouras are in the forefront. *You* give the signals. *You* know when I'm so unsure of myself that I need some cheering and hat-tossing. Then there is the man who conceived the "throng," Mike Miller, then a half dozen young people whom you don't know but to whom I would introduce you with no fear that you would be anything but fond of them.

How damned fortunate I am that I was sitting on the upper deck of the Atlantic Shores Motel that morning all these years ago when you happened to come charging around the corner in your cowboy suit (aged three?).

You could barely speak but you instantly understood me when I told you I never wanted anyone to point even a toy gun at me. You had two.

Bless you, dear, dear Wally!

ALEC

Dear Judy:

One day in Brunswick, Georgia, I was sitting on a baggage truck watching freight cars being shunted. Having a writing pad with me, as I almost always do, and stamped envelopes — for who knows when the impulse to write to a friend might come upon you? — I wrote you a note.

Whatever I said I'll never know but it caused you to write back to the effect that you were really and truly a very simple person and that any notions I had to the effect that you were complex or even able to comprehend the complex was a figment of my imagination.

Of course you were simple!

And of course you were complex!

But more than both you were all the strong and gentle, clear and understanding things I've ever dreamed as being part of the personality of a sometime, someplace woman, girl, female. I've never met her since.

I had become cynical about American women long before I met you. You reversed that. I loved you a great deal. I laughed a lot with you and if we both hadn't been so complex I think you would have cleared up my virtual impotence. But I never dared suggest sex to you! As it was, our relationship had all the elements of two people who knew each other as they knew themselves.

I think you loved me lots more than you ever let on, that is, physically. It's of no consequence except for the security we might have provided for each other.

The only time I didn't like you was when you used that goddamned analyst term "hostile" just because I was trying to keep that queen from disturbing Dick Hyman while he was playing the piano. You made me even angrier because you wore high-heeled shoes with blue jeans! You certainly had too much taste for that!

But there were lots of lovely moments: the afternoon we drove aimlessly about the countryside in the springtime and I told you it would be a great day to drop in at roadside taverns and drink, of all things, gin. I never expected you to see the lunatic fitness of such a notion. But you did and I knew you did.

The flute pieces I wrote for you and which you were too embarrassed to play for me; the audition I did for that goblin producer from Hollywood, his dreadful rudeness to me and your turning on him out of loyalty to me even though he was to sign you for a new film. The night that man got locked in the bathroom and panicked while your then husband tried to break the door down while you and I laughed immoderately at the dementia of it all — slightly stoned on pot, as I recall. That marvelous lyric you wrote to a tune of mine. You called it "Welcome Home."

The Scrabble games we used to play when you weren't working and your constantly knowing what was going on in my head!
My first experience with ESP.

I failed you toward the end, didn't I? Oh, how cowardly of me!
I should have been there by your side all those final days and
nights! I wasn't, was I?

ALEC

P.S. You never failed me unless it was that time you were charmingly loaded and could have let — no, I take that back. For *I* was
supposed to take over that moment and play the part of Lochinvar
or at least the Golden Prince. I should have hushed you and loved
you.

You knew the measures I most loved in every concert piece I
ever played for you. I don't know about other composers but
I have secret places which are complete expressions of myself.
They may last for no more than a few measures but they're
quivery spots. They more often than not are quiet places. Nothing to attract attention, simply special tenderness, special self-
revelation.

You always knew them the instant you heard them. No one,
not even John Barrows, knows those secret places. And you're no
longer here or anywhere at all except in my mind and memory.

Dear Lorraine:

Any time a man my age writes to a girl as young as you with
words of praise and deep affection, the girl is likely to wonder if
perhaps a few creaky goat steps are being danced in the old fool's
bedroom!

I've known you since you were a small child, and I've never
failed to be impressed by you. I'm sure you know of my great
fondness for you but what you may not be aware of is that I trust
you *as a woman.*

This is unprecedented, with maybe one exception. Oh, sure, I like and am fond of many women but only by keeping at a distance their femaleness. They may and do behave femininely and that's no threat. But the moment they become *women* as opposed to *persons*, then I take for the hills or get rotten rude. But I don't get into my track shoes when I consider that you *are a female*.

You make me feel safe.

You *know* me.

You *accept* me.

You like me and I hope you love me.

I would like to have you at my side if I were conscious while dying.

Thank you.

ALEC (UNCLE AL?)

P.S. I've been reading about the sentience of plants. This further widens the area outside the mind and the conscious being. It's part of the extraordinary interrelationship of *all* living creatures (flora and fauna) speculated about by Mesmer.

I believe that our relationship, yours and mine, exists as does that between a flower and a flower lover. Except that this flower speaks.

Dear Harold:

It made me very, very happy to hear you say, after all these dark and forboding years, that you are not only well but writing songs once again!

You certainly know how much I admire your very special talent. After all, there are pages of printed words in my book which attest to that. So I'll resist the temptation to tell you all over again.

But one thing I didn't say. And that is why we create. I believe the acceptance, the applause, the financial rewards are only a part of it. I believe that even in this age which, for the most part, rejects your style of song, you should continue to write.

And I know your immediate question, "But what will I do with them? Who will play them, sing them?" Well, my answer is that even if no one plays or sings them, you have known the marvelous experience of creating them. That initial tingle is so quickly forgotten but it is the moment of awe and wonderment, the moment of birth.

I think we fashioners of song should always be aware that birth and rearing are two distinct experiences. Obviously, the former comes first and no number of reasons why the creation should never have occurred can gainsay the miracle. "But I can't afford to send him to school! I can't afford baby-sitters! I'm terrified he will be corrupted by his lawless friends!"

No. First bear the child! Second, bemoan its fate!

ALEC WILDER

Dear Harry Sions:

You know what you said to me fifteen minutes after we first met? "I wouldn't be here if I didn't like you." This directness relaxed me as if I had been an infant being rocked in a cradle. Remarkable, considering I usually flee from forthrightness.

We don't live in an honest age or one given to revelation of self. So to hear words of unequivocal affection from a total stranger flattered any (and there were plenty) defenses I may have erected. Since you've read these sometimes embarrassingly honest letters, you can understand that my guard is more often up than down.

Now that we've met a couple of times and discussed the book, now that there are more letters filling the unfulfilled years, now that you have shown further your lucid candor and undevious affection, I feel more relaxed and safer than I have for a great many years.

Here I am, an elderly eccentric (nut, if you prefer) who has lived a life almost totally against current fashions and mores. Nothing in our backgrounds or adult lives has a common ground except our obsession with art and truth. You had no clue to my personality except the letters and yet you knew the intensity of my search and when you met me you accepted me. More than that, you trusted me and, in your own firecracker fashion, loved me.

I'm speaking of more than the book, about the miracle of two strangers late in life, from widely divergent backgrounds, finding themselves immediate friends. And for me it's the miracle of being understood and accepted by a man I'd have assumed would have dismissed me curtly as a remnant of a dead world.

In your acceptance you have given me a greater degree of self-respect than I've ever known. John Barrows has kept me musically sane and productive for forty years and Dr. Watson has patiently heard me out in my endless panics for even longer. But you, a stranger, have read a very vulnerable account of a maverick life and found it worthy.

So of course this book should contain a letter of gratitude to you, dear, dear Harry Sions!

But God damn it! It's too late to mail this now! For, monstrously, you're gone! Yet you're here, sacrosanct, in my mind and heart and in the minds and hearts of all those who were fortunate enough to have known and loved you.

ALEC

Dear Mitch:

And now after over forty years of friendship, alienation, tentative reaching to reestablish some sort of rapprochement, you have come full circle — or should I say "we"?

You still yell and holler and make high-school remarks but you've come back, not to me, but back to yourself.

For the first time in twenty-five years I have had a completely relaxed time with you. Have you noticed the old man honing his scythe? Or have you been away from the hard-sell publicists long enough to see the strawman-life for what it is?

You listened when I spoke.

You laughed genuinely.

You looked at me when I looked at you.

You know what I think? I think you have found that being vulnerable is not only not a dire threat but that it's essential when your hunger requires nourishment only others can supply.

ALEC

Dear Mrs. Longworth:

I read recently of your amusement over those "silly things" that dangle about men's crotches, or, as you succinctly added, "penises."

I happen to be a man to whom is appended such a "silly thing." It prompts me to ask you for your sentiments concerning that other not so silly, perhaps, but certainly grotesque "thing," the "wound that never heals," "the vertical smile," "the little man in the boat," Shakespeare's "bearded clam."

ALEXANDER LAFAYETTE CHEW WILDER

Dear Dead Friend:

I'm positive you are the only one who would be interested in this small discovery of mine. Women obviously would be irritated and/or embarrassed by it; irritated, I think, as they simply cannot believe that any sexual malaise can't be set right by either themselves or some other female. Most American women, by the way, are ludicrous in their presumptions that their judgment once given on any subject concerning day-to-day living would be far superior to a man's. They indulge him his philosophy, poetry, music, politics, but they know all that stuff is really the equivalent of children's toys. When it comes to the truly big stuff they, the women, have all the right answers. To which I reply, "bullshit!"

But what I'm writing you about is my long-term impotence and my sudden understanding of it. *I've never been able to share anything as intrusive as sex.* Of course I've dallied about through the years but almost always it was like the answer the man gives in response to the question about the girl's adequacy in bed: "Oh, it's like jerking off, only you have someone to talk to."

Consequently, in unpredictable moments of lust I'm more inclined to masturbate than to call a woman. I admit that the fantasies which arise simultaneously with my pathetic little erections are less fantasies than memories of moments with women. But those moments, I sorely fear, were perhaps unconsciously set up for future masturbatory images.

Here comes what is possibly a sad realization. I remember a great many locales where I have masturbated and, since I've done more of that than cut notches in my gun, I just may recall more of the former than of the latter conquests.

The lounge of the old Alexandra apartment house in Rochester, behind a huge old elm at eight in the evening on Barrington Street, on the shore of the Sheepscot River in Maine, in a roomette on the Old Crescent Limited coming (coming, indeed!) up from New Orleans, oh, countless places.

Note, however: never in planes.

You see, that little fifteen-year-old girl who used to come to the Plaza Theatre balcony fifty years ago and who daringly cut a slit in her bloomers so that I could get my hand on her silken little box was setting up a masturbatory image. She used to fondle my cock and I swear I can't recall if she brought about the eruption or not. The terrible fact is that I never even asked her for her name, let alone her address! It's possible that we never even spoke. We were mutual masturbating agents.

I meant it when an old friend recently was complaining of having no way to rid himself of unprecedented horniness. I said, "Well, sex just isn't for me." He asked, "For God's sake, why not?" And I said, perfectly seriously, "It's too personal."

All this may account for my never having married, for my being content to be alone and, obviously, for my impotence. Oh, I know I'm old now and *should* be impotent, but it's been going on for some time.

And another small passing thought: I've never known intimately but *one* sexually aggressive female. And I must admit that with her I had no trouble with instant erections.

But all this is of secondary importance, not because I'm old, but because so much else is completely fulfilling.

Another memory just surfaced. Only one person knows about it. I guess I was ashamed of it. All during my youth I used to ride Fifth Avenue buses for hours for the sole purpose of sitting next to a girl to whom I would never speak but against whose leg I would try to press mine and against whose breast I would try to press my arm. Whenever it worked of course I would have an orgasm. Once in twenty times or more I'd be this lucky. Sometimes there were storms of protest, very, very embarrassing. Yet I was never arrested. An old friend, Paul Turner, was the one person I told about it. He called it "bussing," and so today when I read about it in another context and misspelled ("busing"), I am almost glad for the absence of the extra "s" as BUSING looks like some odd practice of the human race of which I don't know the significance.

You, dear Walton, have been dead for over forty-seven years. You were my friend. We were too young for any awareness of sex or if we weren't, we somehow or other were never sufficiently concerned to discuss it or even to show off our "things."

I can't imagine what you would have thought of me had you survived. Perhaps you'd have found me too old, too cowardly, too freaky. But my memory of you is the best and you made my early Rochester years more than bearable! Thank you, dear friend!

ALEXANDER WILDER

Dear Tony:

As you know, we had a nodding acquaintance for many years. I don't believe I ever even wrote you, let alone called up, to thank you for recording "While We're Young," "It's So Peaceful," "I'll

Be Around" and whatever else. But this wasn't rudeness, I swear. I assumed in those days that stars never received even mail marked PERSONAL. And besides, all you ladies and gentlemen who were "up there," as far as I was concerned, lived on another planet.

How or why we came to see so much of each other I couldn't figure out for a while. Then I realized that it was because you were, of the big-money singers, the only one who refused almost without exception to be budged from your belief in music as you knew and loved it. Nor would you settle for any but the best players and arrangers.

Even Frank had put on his musical hippie clothes and gone slumming into the world of the amateur writers.

But you stuck it out! Naturally I was impressed. And I remember writing you a very long letter when you were working at the Copa and worrying about the pressure you were getting from that bum at the recording company who wears ties of the same material as his shirts.

We don't mention it but you knew that my great awe was for Sinatra. How could it have been otherwise? I was fond of your singing but I was in awe of his.

Then one night I watched you perform in a Chicago club. I'd never seen you work before. I was astounded and very impressed. Since then we have seen each other often and talked at length over the phone.

You *do* have the reputation for being slow to make up your mind! It's practically a legend. So I was prepared for the long wait when you suggested an album to be called "All About Children." It's a great idea and I am very eager to have "The Children's Plea for Peace" reach a larger audience. As well I'd like to hear that English boy recite his poems to my music backgrounds. I'd like to hear "Love Among the Young," "Lullaby Land," "While We're Young," "Listen to Your Heart" and any other songs of innocence and wide-eyed, childlike simplicity and wonderment.

I'm still waiting.

It may never come to be, but I still love you and highly respect your sticking to your beliefs, doing without record hits and keeping the unpolluted stream of melody flowing.

ALEC

Dear Room 105:

You were just what I needed. Thank you! If anyone were to read this they would jeer at gratitude to an inanimate object. Well, screw them! They haven't the slightest notion of the calm that settled over me after a few hours puttering around your four walls, lying on your bed, playing solitaire at your table, making tea with the electric coil in your shipwright's bathroom. And the white, hinged-inside shutters! Jalousies? Whatever they are, it was very cozy shutting and hooking them every night, better than drawing shades.

I orchestrated Marian McPartland's piece at that long mirrored desk; I worked on those perverse *London Times* puzzles; I even slept without resorting to sedatives, which 1 assumed had hooked me.

And, as you know, there were no giddy girls, no one at all, not even Father Atwell. It was the best of aloneness. And *I* should know! I've been in a thousand impersonal transient rooms and only a very few have given me that marvelous sense of peace and safety. I'll grant that your being in a quiet village helped, a place where walking at night is as safe as it was twenty years ago.

But it was you, good ole one-aught-five, that I wanted to return to every night and drop in on during the day. Those fathers and husbands and snowmobiles could never know about you!

ALEC WILDER

Dear Carl:

When you were the head man at BMI I came to know you well

and to admire you greatly. When we first met I was thrown off by your less than poetic mannerisms and almost corny speech patterns.

Of course the opposite always hides behind the mask: for you were obsessed with poetry and its creators and you were as gentle as *Charlotte's Web.*

As I hope you recall, I wrote at your suggestion "The Sandburg Suite" and music to those inspired words of Bruce Catton.

What you may not remember is the panic call I made one afternoon when I could no longer cope with my problems. I can never forget or cease to be grateful for your response. Instead of suggesting I come up to an impersonal office, go through the switchboard announcement, pass down the long passage filled with typewriters and treadmill work, you immediately told me to go to the bar across from your building.

And there you calmed me, soothed me, brought me back to some sort of operable sanity. Who, of all the busy men I knew, would have considered such an interruption? I can think of none.

Then you put me in touch with Mr. Vaughan who, I'm told, is now up at Doubleday's in the catbird's seat. More power to him! Then you suggested that I try my hand at an autobiography. At least an account of my nutty life in the popular music world. As you know, I tried but I simply couldn't find a way to say it that met with Mr. Vaughan's needs. I remember I called it *No Tuxedo.* That was because I concluded that all useful business got done at parties, formal gatherings, and that my lack of appropriate clothes had stunted any pretensions to a career I might have had.

After you left BMI I tried a second time for Atheneum. But their man concluded I had written too casually, with not enough fever. (Little did he know how exhausting had been that soul-searching!)

And now I've tried a third time. It's comprised of all the letters I never mailed. So, much as I wish to mail this letter of gratitude to you this very minute, I shan't. For if it's among the letters I never mailed, then a few (many?) can know how I feel about you!

ALEC WILDER

Dear Z:

I remember the first night you came out on the floor of Café Society Downtown and improvised an act. It was funny and anarchic and sloppy. I've forgotten how we came to know each other but we did and became as close as a mouse can be to a rhinoceros.

I don't mean your physical size, but your manic compulsions. Remember how you'd use me as your stooge, how one night you decided to be a barber, put a napkin around my neck, picked my vanilla ice cream from its dish, smeared it on my face and shaved me with a butter knife—all the time babbling barber chatter?

Or the evening you made me lie on a couch and became a Viennese psychoanalyst? I guess I stopped seeing you partly because you were too strenuous and partly because you became a star.

But you are a very dear and loving man. Katie would never have stuck it if you weren't. I have to admit (parenthetically) that your improvised oratorio based on Millard Fillmore in all the forms I ever heard it, was a masterpiece. And the evenings of your manic portrayals of all manner of types were exhaustingly funny. Not Jonathan Winters, for he, I felt, literally couldn't pull out of his characterizations and therefore became somewhat frightening, hilarious as he was. You, on the other hand, always had a political point behind your madness.

And now, twenty-five years later, I've been called to write background music for your revival of *Ulysses in Night Town*. Should I do it? Are you less anarchical? Will you turn the rehearsals into a shambles? Should we make the full circle?

Or should I stick to my semiisolation and continue to write the kind of music I've started to become fairly adept at? Should I mess up once more with show folk and show biz? Will it make me too nervous? Or have I reached the point of control where I can function in a mature, self-protecting fashion and still turn out adequate music?

One thing I can tell you: no more shall a nonmusician inform me about my craft! Either I shall be hired with respect and faith, allowed fairly free rein, or not at all.

I'll phone when I get back to New York and check this project with you.

ALEC

Dear Bill:

I don't see you nearly enough. Your spirit, forthrightness, irreverent wit — and naturally your great medical and surgical talents, along with an open mind.

I wrote you a few letters which had to do with how I felt about your immense concern for the despondent as well as for the ailing. In one letter I told you that you were the only doctor I had ever known who could tell me I was about to die without my going to pieces. You would make death something you would walk me to the door of, as a strong, loving friend. It's hard to explain what it's like having a "death" friend in the same person as a "life" friend.

I know other kind, gentle, knowledgeable doctors — but no one who can make the inevitable endurable.

I'm not certain what you'll do if I get the news of the Big Toboggan and call you or, if banged up, have someone else call you. Will you ship up a big fat quick-exit pill, will you fly up from Florida and suffocate me when no one's in the hospital room?

I know one thing: you'll see that I get through that black doorway in the liveliest fashion. And with you around I'll do it with dignity and possibly a hoot of laughter.

Of course I'd also like to see you under less final circumstances. If I come down to Gainesville next month will it be convenient?

ALEC

Dear Sibley:

Now, after all these years, I have the courage to address you without formality. I kept saying and writing "Dr. Watson" partly from deep respect and partly because you continued to call me "Mr. Wilder."

As you gather by now, I'm impelled to write you progress or deterioration reports. I dislike embarrassing you, yet you are the only person I've ever known to whom I wish to tell everything (not always spewed out, I hope, but made at least more palatable than an early Sunday morning confession by a hung-over Catholic).

It's not the need to confess but rather to clarify. When I write you I cannot lie or distort or gloss. So, in making clear to you, I make clear to myself. God knows how you view my life as you know it! As encouraging, as complimentary as your letters often are, I would not be hurt to learn that you considered me an amusing, somewhat talented but essentially gormless, mindless bhoyo. At least, however, I've managed to achieve, I trust, a degree more of dignity since I stopped drinking.

One hears extraordinary tales of elderly men's prowess with the ladies. But I, though in terms of these legendary men a mere sixty-six, consider myself permanently beyond desire. Even the occasional sexual fantasy fails to bring me to the pathetic travesty of masturbation.

I was deeply (interruptedly) involved with, let's see now . . . about four females. Sorry, six. The first one I truly loved. The third one less so, but still I was very fond of her and have deep respect for her, though I don't even know if she's still alive.

The others were sex objects. Naturally there had to be something in the relationships besides sex, but in all truth, had that been forbidden, I'd have shot up into space.

My psychoanalyst gave me to believe that my close relationships with men implied homosexuality. Well, I've never known but one very innocent childhood evening in which another boy fondled my penis. I remember I made him stop because I was beginning to feel sick. It took several years for me to realize that the sickness was really the first rumble of an orgasm.

Frankly, it's a great relief to be rid of the whole mess. (I think I'd have cut myself off sooner had I stopped drinking sooner.) The somewhat horrid speculation has occurred to me to the effect that my entire sexual life might never have existed had it not been for the warped stimulation of alcohol.

The first girl I truly loved is still alive. She managed to get the message conveyed to me through a mutual friend that she wished me never to see her old. So I haven't seen her for over thirty years. I believe she is five years older than I so she must be seventy-one. And damned attractive, I'll bet.

With her the sole purpose was not to get her into bed, and I only did that once. I remember little about it, having been, as usual, drunk. Somehow I'm certain that there was only frantic groping, moaning, kissing, clutching, but no straightforward fulfilling sexual act of whatever sort.

Has this shallow-rooted libido been the reason for my never having sought for long orgasm-simulating musical climaxes? Why I found solitary train trips wholly rewarding? Why I always managed to find excuses for not literally "sleeping" with whatever girl I had been fussing about with? Am I, in other words, masturbatory by nature? Surely not narcissistic? No, I'm much too unsure of myself to do better than get along with myself without too many arguments. In the alcohol days the battles were dreadful, I must admit.

I suppose cowardice, that determining element in my character, has made it impossible for me to share anything with anyone, even sex. The terror of being trapped, inextricably involved, dependent, victimized.

Has music been the substitute? Did I turn to it because I sensed that intimacy would never work? I suppose I'll never know — unless you tell me.

I am quite aware of the inconvenience and discomfort any excessive movement causes you. You've told me your limp is less painful but I'm certain you're much too stoical and considerate of others to complain. I also know that at the best of times you have found gatherings and public places uncomfortable and irritating. So your appearance in Kilbourn Hall last Sunday at the performance of *The Truth about Windmills* was a profound compliment for which I am very, very grateful.

I've known you for over forty years. I've loved and respected you, even depended on you, for all that time. The only occasion when you showed the slightest ill-feeling toward me was when Mitchell Miller had to appear in a skit in that musical I wrote long ago and you needed him for the recording of the music Louis Segal wrote for the Sodom film.

You've never shown any impatience with my endless carping, confessive, complaining letters, you've been kind to and protective of all the verse I've sent you, you've sent me money when you mysteriously sensed I needed it. You've done everything one dreams that a friend, a father, a brother would do.

My hysterical behavior when I come to dinner may once have been due to alcohol; now that I've given it up I'm certain that the hysteria is due to the constant knowledge that I can never meet you as an equal. Literarily I'm a dud; I remember no quotations, I speak little French, I have absolutely no intellect. That's why I endlessly make foolish remarks: I know what kind of nonsense makes you laugh so when you do, for a moment I feel I'm on the same level.

The mileposts of this book have been my letters to you and at least they're less self-pitying than all the letters I *did* mail to you. I'm sixty-seven, and have the constant conviction every day is my last one. You are what? Eighty? Eighty-one? Yet you behave as you always have. You show no sign of awareness of the Big Toboggan, your interests and awareness are those of a person who sees years ahead of him.

The actuarial tables say they will take you away from me, and yet I could drop my pen before this letter is done. But I can't allow my own end until I have written it. For when this letter is finished it will be the end of the book. The reason I'm glad is not only because it is always a great relief to finish any long creative effort, but because I want to be able to hand you a copy of it and, no matter how maudlin it may sound, say to you if only by giving you the book: "Here is my life. I hope you give it a passing grade."

It's dedicated to you, obviously. There are those whom I've known even longer than I've known you who may be hurt because they have been loyal and steadfast for these many years. But much as I love them, they didn't *make* me live. They didn't silently demand, as I feel certain you have, that I be and do the very best I knew how. If this is not true, the effect is the same, for I've always believed that you were watching and listening and asking in your inimitable fashion, that I grow and bloom and fulfill myself.

I haven't, as these letters only too clearly show. But goddamn it, I've tried. And I know I'd never have tried as hard as I have if it hadn't been for your existence, to say nothing of your love and patience and understanding.

I can die much easier since seeing you in that aisle seat. Much as I loved John Barrows, who kept me musically alive for thirty-odd years, I was more joyous knowing that you had made such a gesture, not to the opera, not to music, not to my having a performance, but simply to me.

The days, my most dear mentor, guide, friend and father, "dwindle down." And if you can handle those "precious few" moments with wit, calm, curiosity and style, I guess I damned well better try to handle them too!

So thank you for giving me enough strength and self-discipline to be able to look back and say to myself, "Pretty nutty looking bunch of circles and squares and colors and smears and splotches but, nevertheless, I do believe it just might look like an honest-to-goodness life."

Thank you for it!

ALEC

Annotations by David Demsey

Annotated Addressee List

Numbers in brackets refer to the page(s) on which the person is mentioned.

Dear . . .

Aaron [113]   Composer Aaron Copland (1900–1990) [also "Mr. Copland"]. Copland created what could be called the quintessential American classical vocabulary with such works as *Fanfare for the Common Man*, the Pulitzer Prize–winning *Appalachian Spring*, *Rodeo*, and *Lincoln Portrait*. His 1939 book *What to Listen for in Music* is still widely read.

Abby [161]   Unidentified woman with whom Wilder had an early relationship.

Al [206]   Author Albert Murray (b. 1916), widely read African-American writer who is known for his early essays "The Omni-Americans," such books as *The Blue Devils of Nada* and *South to a Very Old Place*, and numerous books and articles on jazz and jazz musicians.

Allen [60]   Allen Kelly, childhood neighbor on Westminster Road in Rochester whom Wilder met again, along with his sister Jane, upon his return to his hometown. Wilder credits Kelly with starting his return to drinking. "Skineatalis" is a phonetic spelling of the town of Skaneateles, NY, near Syracuse.

Allen, Charlotte W.	*See* "Charlotte [II]"
Almost Poet [202]	Wilder to himself.
American Heritage Dictionary [187]	Letter to the publisher.
Ana [147, 242]	Ana Roth, whose relationship to Wilder is not known.
Ardrey, Mr. [185]	Anthropologist, author, and screenwriter Robert Ardrey (1908–80), whose best-selling books include *The Territorial Imperative*, *The Hunting Hypothesis*, and other works involved with the origins of human violence and confrontation. Before turning to these studies, he spent twenty years in Hollywood, writing the screenplays for such movies as *Khartoum* and *The Green Years*.
Arlen, Harold	*See* "Harold"
Arnold [232]	Lyricist Arnold Sundgaard (b. 1911), longtime Wilder collaborator with whom he wrote a number of well-known songs and who did the libretti for several Wilder operas. Sundgaard also collaborated with Kurt Weill and others, and is well known for his children's book *The Lamb and the Butterfly*, illustrated by Eric Carle.
Atwell, Father [225]	Henry Atwell (d. 1980), a Catholic priest from Rochester who was transferred by the Church from Rochester to a St. Agnes parish in Avon, where Alec and Atwell are both buried. Alec and Father Atwell became very close late in Wilder's life; they collaborated on Wilder's *Children's Plea for Peace*.
Bailey, Mildred	*See* "Mildred"
Balliett, Whitney	*See* "Whitney"
Baron, Samuel	*See* "Sam [II]"
Barrows, John	*See* "John"

Bennett, Tony	*See* "Tony"
Bernie [240]	Bernard Garfield, bassoonist who performed on the original Wilder Octet recordings, premiered several solo works for bassoon, and recorded many Wilder chamber works as a member of the New York Woodwind Quintet.
Bill [I] [171]	William Engvick, lyricist and collaborator with Wilder on numerous songs, including the standards "While We're Young" and "Moon and Sand," several stage productions, and edited the *Lullabies and Night Songs* book. Engvick is also well known as the lyricist of the song "Moulin Rouge."
Bill [II] [261]	William Ploss, Alec's longtime doctor, who cared for him in his final illness in Gainesville, Florida.
Bouras, Harry	*See* "Harry"
Bouras, Lorraine [Bowen]	*See* "Lorraine"
Bourgeois, Charles	*See* "Charlie"
Bowen, Lorraine Bouras	*See* "Lorraine"
Brackett, Rogers	*See* "Rogers"
Bradley [210]	Bradley Cunningham, owner of Bradley's, then the premiere piano room in Greenwich Village, New York City. "Vicki," who is described in the letter, was Nicoli (Niki), the late daughter of singers Jackie Cain and Roy Kral.
Brandt, Eddie	*See* "Eddie [I]"
Brown, Henry	*See* "Brownie"
Brownie [141]	Henry Brown, Algonquin Hotel superintendent of services, a Wilder friend who often

	helped him to book his complicated long-distance train itineraries.
Bruce [186]	Author/historian Bruce Catton (1899–1978), whose books about the Civil War Alec particularly admired. One of the most notable Civil War historians, he is best known for his two trilogies on the subject, *The Army of the Potomac* and *The Centennial History of the Civil War.*
Bundison, Mr. [136]	Stranger who spoke with Wilder at a dinner party during his Eastman days.
Campon, Phil	*See* "Phil"
Canfield, Mr. [133]	Unidentified stonemason in the area of Lisbon Falls, Maine, whose craftsmanship Alec admired.
Carl [258]	Carl Haverlin, President of Broadcast Music, Inc. (BMI), from 1947 to 1968.
Carpenter, Mr. [170]	Unidentified waiter on a Los Angeles to Chicago train trip.
Carroll [69, 76, 78, 82, 87]	Carroll Dunn, Wilder's close friend during the period after he finished high school and before he returned to Rochester. Older than Alec, Dunn was Alec's confidant and an early influence on him as a composer. "Aunt Clara" on p. 76 is Clara Wilder Haushalter, sister of Alec's father.
Carson, Sunny	*See* "Sunny"
Catton, Bruce	*See* "Bruce"
Charlie [242]	Charles Bourgeois is a music promoter long active in the promotion of what was originally the Newport (now the JVC) Jazz Festival and its progeny after moving to New York City.
Charlotte [I] [152]	Charlotte Drum, object of Alec's boyhood affections. She is called Charlotte Benson

when this same tale is told in a "Search" narrative insert piece entitled "The Twig is Bent," but there was a Drum family living in Bay Head while Alec was staying there, so this is likely the correct name.

Charlotte [II] [241] Charlotte Whitney Allen (1891–1978), one of the *grandes dames* of Rochester society. Her family was associated with Wilder's through society circles, and her family was among the small number of prominent Rochester residents who attended the Valentine Day 1900 wedding of Alec's parents in Geneva.

Cheever, Mr. [183] Alec admired the work of author John Cheever (1912–82), whose award-winning major works include *The Wapshot Scandal*, which won the Howell's Medal from the National Academy of Arts and Letters, and the Pulitzer Prize–winning collection *The Stories of John Cheever*. "Aunt Emma" mentioned is the sister of Wilder's father.

Chew, Mrs. [63] Madelaine Chew (d. 1927), first of three wives of Wilder's cousin Beverly Chew, an executive of the First National Bank of Geneva, NY. Chew family members were majority stockholders in the bank, and several of Alec's uncles were executives. Madelaine died when Wilder was twenty.

Chew, Thomas Hilhouse *See* "Uncle Hilly"

Clark [238] Clark Galehouse (d. 1984), founder and owner of Golden Crest Records who was greatly dedicated to Wilder's solo and chamber music. Golden Crest recorded a number of all-Wilder albums during the 1960s and 1970s; most recordings of Wilder's "classical" music from 1960 to 1985 are on this record label.

Clift, Montgomery *See* "David"

Collins, Mrs. [131] Unidentified chambermaid/ employee in a hotel where Wilder was a guest.

Cook, Walton	*See* "Walton" and "Dead Friend"
Copland, Mr. [100]	Aaron Copland (1900–1990), American composer. *See also* "Aaron"
Cunningham, Bradley	*See* "Bradley"
Cuzzin [179, 231]	Author/playwright Thornton Wilder (1897–1975), author of the legendary play *Our Town* and Pulitzer Prize winner for two works, *Skin of Our Teeth* and *Letters: Drama. Hello Dolly* was based on his play *The Matchmaker.* Alec often jokingly addressed Wilder and trumpeter Joe Wilder as "cuzzin," although he was not related to either.
Dan [175]	Dan Stirrup, Key West, FL, architect whom often hosted Wilder at his home in Wilder's later years.
David [149]	Actor Montgomery Clift (1922–66). Patricia Bosworth, author of *Montgomery Clift: A Biography*, claimed that there are several correlations to Clift's life in this letter, including his living in a hotel in Bel Air, endless listening to Sinatra records, and, most infamously, his car accident with facial injuries; however, she finds no clear reason why Wilder would use the name David. "F. S." in this letter is Frank Sinatra, "Libby" is singer and Wilder friend Libby Holman.
Dead Friend [254]	The late Walton Cook, who had been one of Wilder's earliest Rochester childhood friends and who was Alec's classmate at the Columbia School. *See also* "Dear Walton"
DeVries, Mr. [179]	Peter DeVries (1910–83), author known for his humor and satire, but who also wrote serious works. DeVries's well-known books include *Angels Can't Do Better, But Who Wakes the Bugler? Blood of the Lamb*, and *The Handsome Heart.*
DeWitt, Helen Wilder	*See* "Helen"

Drum, Charlotte	*See* "Charlotte [I]"
Dry Cleaner, Mr. [198]	Alec's unidentified cleaner, who sent back to him two unused plane tickets found in his pocket, but apparently kept $300 in cash that was with the tickets.
Dunn, Carroll	*See* "Carroll"
Durrell, Mr. [205]	Gerald Durrell (1925–95), wildlife writer of such books as *The Ark's Anniversary* and *My Family and Other Animals*, and founder of Jersey Wildlife Preservation Trust in the English Channel Islands. Wilder was very interested in wildlife preservation; this and several other preservation funds are the main beneficiaries of his will.
Eddie [I] [107]	Eddie Brandt, songwriter/lyricist who was an early Wilder collaborator.
Eddie [II] [123]	Eddie Finckel, a composer/arranger with whom Alec worked in his early days in New York City.
Engvick, William	*See* "Bill [I]"
Eric Hoffer [181]	Alec very much admired author and social philosopher Eric Hoffer (1902–83) who, like Alec, was self-educated, outspoken, and brooked no nonsense. Hoffer is best known for *The True Believer*, *The Ordeal of Change*, and *The Passionate State of Mind*. He won the Presidential Medal of Freedom.
Ericson, June	*See* "June"
Evelyn [92]	Unidentified fellow Eastman student while Wilder was there around 1930. There were five students by that name registered at that time, or Wilder could have created a fictitious name.
Finckel, Eddie	*See* "Eddie [II]"
Frank [119, 233]	Frank Sinatra (1915–98), arguably the quintessential American popular singer. After Sinatra rose to prominence in the forties, his classic

recordings (particularly those from the Capitol Records period, and involving Nelson Riddle arrangements) are often the best-known versions of numerous standards. Although he and Wilder had very little personal contact after Sinatra became a multi-media star in the fifties, Sinatra was always an admirer of Wilder and his music, and he offered financial assistance on several occasions as well.

Galehouse, Clark — *See* "Clark"

George [200] — Alec's older brother, George C. Wilder (1901–82). The two brothers had little contact throughout their adult lives.

Goodman, Mr. [106] — Clarinetist/bandleader Benny Goodman (1909–86). Wilder made his early reputation in New York writing a number of arrangements for Goodman's band, but is on a long list of musicians who did not get along well with him.

Goodwin, Rev. William — *See* "Rev. Goodwin"

Greene, Mr. [185] — British author Graham Greene (1904–91), worldwide traveler and creator of such works as *Heart of the Matter* and *Power and the Glory* and was a longtime writer for the London *Times*.

Gumm, Mrs. [55] — Unidentified mother of a childhood friend. There is no Gumm family in any Rochester census records from the time of Alec's boyhood. Although the story in this letter is likely true, the name is probably invented.

Hargrave, Mr. [212] — Alex Hargrave, President of Lincoln Rochester Trust Company, the bank to which Alec refers. The Geneva branch of this bank was formerly the First National Bank of Geneva, where Alec's mother's family, the Chews, were principal stockholders and executives.

Harlan, Mrs. [96]

Unidentified woman whom Alec had known when she was a small child, during the period when he had returned to Rochester as an Eastman student.

Harold [251]

Harold Arlen (1905–86), Alec's favorite songwriter, who was subject of a chapter in Wilder's *American Popular Song* book. One of America's great song composers, Arlen is best known for his classic tunes "Stormy Weather" and "Over the Rainbow" from *The Wizard of Oz*. He also composed other landmark songs such as "Blues in the Night," "My Shining Hour," and "I've Got the World on a String."

Harry [137, 151, 199, 216, 222, 226, 235]

Harry Bouras (d. 1990), Chicagoan and close Wilder confidant. Wilder met Bouras's future wife, Arlene, while they were Eastman students, and he stayed close to their daughter Lorraine. Many of Wilder's more philosophical statements are framed as letters to Bouras.

Harry Sions [252]

Editor of such publications as *Holiday* Magazine; was Wilder's editor at Little, Brown Publishers and worked with him on the production of the original 1975 edition of *Letters I Never Mailed*.

Harvey [219]

Harvey Phillips (b. 1930), renowned tuba player, close Wilder friend, and champion of Wilder's music. Phillips founded Wilder Music, first bringing Wilder's music to wide distribution. A large part of the current concert tuba repertoire consists of works written for Phillips by Wilder, many dedicated to members of the Phillips family.

Haverlin, Carl

See "Carl"

Helen [58]

Alec's sister Helen [Wilder] DeWitt (1903?–ca. 1935), the only member of the family with whom he got on. "Aunt Hattie" is Harriet Hillhouse Chew, sister of Wilder's

	mother and of "Uncle Hilly" (Thomas H. Chew).
Hoffer, Eric	*See* "Eric Hoffer"
Holliday, Judy	*See* "Judy"
Howie [243]	Howard Richmond, head of The Richmond Organization (TRO), publisher of Alec's popular music. His Columbus Circle offices often served as a base of operations for Alec in New York; Wilder composed there and would meet James Maher in an office space Richmond had set aside for them during their four years of work on the book *American Popular Song*.
Inch, Mr. [84]	Herbert Inch, Alec's counterpoint professor at the Eastman School of Music, was a member of the Eastman faculty from 1925 to 1928 and in 1930–31.
Income Tax Man, Mr. [153]	Unknown IRS representative who apparently questioned Wilder's tax statements.
Jackass [191]	Wilder's scolding letter to himself.
Jane [148]	Unidentified woman with whom Wilder had a relationship during the 1940s.
John [101, 102, 115, 135, 142, 145, 166]	John Barrows (1913–74), fellow student at Eastman and friend, a virtuoso horn player who had a long career as a New York performer and University of Wisconsin faculty member. Barrows, Mitch Miller, Goddard Lieberson, Sam Richlin, Jimmy Carroll, and Fran Miller formed Alec's circle of friends at Eastman, and his connection to them later launched his career in New York.
Judy [248]	Actress Judy Holliday (1921–65), whom Alec admired very much, and for whom he wrote several easy flute and recorder pieces. She is

	perhaps best known for her stage work in "Born Yesterday" and for her Oscar-winning film portrayal of that same role. She became one of the stars at Columbia Pictures and starred in numerous films, but her career was cut short by her premature death at age 43.
June [176]	June Ericson, singer/actress who appeared in a leading role in Wilder's Nyack-produced opera *Ellen*. Ericson appears on the recording *Melodies of Jerome Kern: The 1955 Walden Sessions*, now released on CD, with tenor David Daniels, and in the Cary Grant/Doris Day movie *That Touch of Mink*.
Katherine [54]	Katherine Knowlton, object of Wilder's boyhood affections.
Kelly, Allen	*See* "Allen"
Kenyon, Tudy	*See* "Tudy"
Kevin [147]	Unidentified son of a Wilder friend living in Laguna Beach, CA.
Lang, Paul Henry	*See* "Mr. Long"
Laura Perkins [68]	Childhood acquaintance of Wilder in Bay Head when he was twelve or thirteen years old. This could be an invented name, since Wilder relates this identical story in "The Search" but does not remember the girl's name. Paul Turner, mentioned in this letter, was one of the few boys at St. Paul's whom Wilder befriended. Turner had an interest in early music, became an organ designer, and at one point introduced Wilder to Maurice Ravel.
Lavinia [190, 203, 220, 223]	Lavinia (Faxon) Russ, early New York friend of Wilder's along with Carroll Dunn.
Lee, Peggy	*See* "Peggy"

Liza [164]   Woman whose likely real name will remain
                            unidentified, called by Wilder his "only true
                            love."

Long, Mr. [157]   Paul Henry Lang (1901–91), noted musicolo-
                            gist, editor of *Musical Quarterly* and chief
                            music critic for the New York *Herald Tribune*.
                            The misspelling could have simply been an
                            unedited typo (it also exists in the unedited
                            proofs of the book), or it could have been used
                            to avoid possible litigation. Wilder refers to
                            this same review in "Life Story," with Lang's
                            name spelled correctly.

Longworth, Mrs.   Likely Alice Roosevelt Longworth
[254]   (1884–1980), socialite, author, and daughter
                            of Franklin D. Roosevelt, often described as
                            "wild woman" given to writing, saying, and
                            doing outrageous things.

Loonis [245]   Composer, lyricist Loonis McGlohon
                            (1921–2002), Wilder's principal collaborator
                            in the later years of his life, including such
                            standards as "Blackberry Winter" and "Be A
                            Child."

Lorraine [250]   Lorraine Bouras Bowen, daughter of Wilder
                            friends Harry and Arlene Bouras.

Lou [177, 191,   Wilder's lifelong friend Louis Ouzer
211, 246]   (1913–2002). Ouzer was the official photogra-
                            pher of the Eastman School of Music for over
                            fifty years and had countless photos published
                            nationally and locally in newspaper and maga-
                            zine articles. A collection of his photos was
                            published in *Contemporary Musicians in
                            Photographs* (Dover, 1979).

Mabel [167]   Singer Mabel Mercer (1900–1984), one of the
                            great cabaret singers, winner of the
                            Presidential Medal of Freedom in 1985.
                            Mercer was as much storyteller as singer,
                            making her reputation as an intimate club
                            singer rather than with the big bands. She
                            sought out less well-known repertoire and

made it her own, and had a close relationship with many well-known songwriters, including Wilder.

Madelaine
[125, 126, 127]

Magdalen Daede, longtime household employee of the Mitch Miller family.

Margaret [129]

Wilder love interest whose name will remain unidentified.

Marian [230]

Jazz pianist Marian McPartland (b. 1918), who was a longtime champion of Wilder's songs, and who was one of the jazz musicians Wilder most admired, personally and musically. The television interview in question took place at WXXI-TV in Rochester, hosted by jazz radio host and Wilder estate executor Tom Hampson, later shown on PBS stations across the country.

Marvin Bellis [197]

New York City cabdriver.

McDermott,
Mrs. [66]

Unidentified Bay Head neighbor of Alec's. As a renter, albeit a year-round resident, neither she nor her son Jack appear in any Bay Head tax or census records.

McGlohon, Loonis

See "Loonis"

McPartland, Marian

See "Marian"

Mercer, Mabel

See "Mabel"

Meyer, Sheldon

See "Sheldon"

Mike [189]

Mike Miller, whose full name is Mitchell Miller, Jr., son of Mitch Miller.

Mildred [107]

Singer Mildred Bailey (1907–51), vocalist who was one of the first female big band singers when she was featured with Paul Whiteman beginning in 1929. She and husband Red Norvo collaborated often and, after recording "Rockin' Chair," the song that would be her trademark, she was often featured on Benny Goodman's radio programs.

Miller, Mitch

See "Mitch" and "Mitchell"

Miller, Mitchell, Jr.	*See* "Mike"
Milme, Mrs. [55]	Almost certainly either Caroline Milliman or Mary Pease Milliman, Principal and Associate Principal of Columbia School in Rochester at the time when Alec was a student until eighth grade (from 1912 to 1919). Mary Milliman Woodbury, as she was later known, was a co-founder of the school, which is still in existence today as the Allendale-Columbia School.
Mitch [118, 131, 144, 253]	Mitch Miller (b. 1911), oboist, longtime head of A&R at Columbia Records, but perhaps best known for his "Sing Along with Mitch" 1960s television show. Miller and Alec knew each other as students at Eastman and remained lifelong friends, though the relationship was not without the customary tensions that afflicted most of Alec's friendships.
Mitchell [124]	Mitch Miller. *See* "Mitch"
Mix Up [63]	Wilder to himself.
Morty [110]	Morty Palitz, music producer and arranger with whom Alec sometimes worked and who was responsible for the opening phrase of "While We're Young."
Mostel, Zero	*See* "Z"
Mother [56, 80]	Wilder's mother, Lillian Chew Wilder (1866–192?), a Geneva, NY native who married Alec's father, George Wilder, on Valentine's Day 1900. The family's cook, subject of a paragraph on p. 56, is Sarah Smith, employed by the Wilder family during the period around 1915.
Murray, Albert	*See* "Al"
Myron [70, 72, 74]	Fictitious classmate at Collegiate School, where Wilder attended beginning in February 1921, two weeks before he turned 14, and continued until he graduated, Class

of 1924. Although "Myron" was undoubtedly based on one or more of Wilder's classmates, there was no student enrolled by this name while Wilder was there. Similarly, there was no such student as Steve Rickert; there was a classmate named Irving Bunnell who is the likely basis for "Jack Bunnell."

Olds, Mr. [66] Head of summer camp on Lake Winnipesaukee, NH, where Wilder was a victim of hazing and abuse.

Ouzer, Louis *See* "Lou"

Palitz, Morty *See* "Morty"

Peggy [193] Singer Peggy Lee (1920–2002), who recorded several Wilder songs. Lee had great popular success for decades, appearing frequently on television variety shows hosted by Jack Paar, Frank Sinatra, Nat King Cole, and others. It is not as well known that she was also a songwriter who collaborated with the likes of Duke Ellington, Quincy Jones, and Johnny Mandel.

Percy [236] Percy Seitlin, author of *Is Anything All Right?* (Grossman Publishers, 1969). In this book, Seitlin uses a personality sketch of Wilder as a model for a character named Halsey Boudreau, who appears briefly on pp. 90–97 of Seitlin's book.

Perkins, Laura *See* "Laura Perkins"

Phil [116] Phil Campon, former Bay Head lifeguard who had saved Alec from drowning fifty years earlier.

Phillips, Harvey *See* "Harvey Phillips"

Ploss, Dr. William *See* "Bill [II]"

Poole, Mrs. [56] Mrs. Nanette Poole, who, with her husband Harry and their children Arthur and Alec's schoolmate Elizabeth, were the Wilder's next-door neighbors on Westminster Road.

Three-year-old Arthur was "kidnapped" by Alec, who was then nine. The ransom was a cake baked by the Poole family cook, who was either Cora Neddo or Eileen Rowley, both employed by the family at the time of the previous year's census.

Reilly, Mr. [155]

Unidentified New York City Postal worker whose poetry came to Wilder via Algonquin Hotel bellman and Wilder friend Harry Celentano.

Reverend Goodwin [53]

Rev. William Goodwin, Wilders' family pastor at St. Paul's Episcopal Church, still located on East Avenue in Rochester, around the corner from Wilder's boyhood home on Westminster Road.

Richlin, Sam

See "Sam [I]"

Richmond, Howard

See "Howie"

Rogers [162]

Rogers Brackett (1916–80), Hollywood movie and radio producer and advertising executive. Well connected in Hollywood circles, he collaborated as producer on several Wilder large-scale theater works. Brackett is perhaps equally well known for his association with actor James Dean.

Rogers, Mrs. [56]

Unidentified mother of a Wilder childhood friend Bobbie Rogers.

Room 105 [258]

Room in an unknown rural hotel where Wilder had spent enjoyable time. Likely locales for this hotel are in New England (Wilder loved Maine) and in Avon, NY.

Roth, Ana

See "Ana"

Royce, Mr. [86, 94]

Edward Royce was a professor with whom Alec studied composition at Eastman, also the son of the famous Harvard philosopher Josiah Royce. He was on the Eastman faculty from 1923 to 1947.

Russ, Lavinia
Faxon

See "Lavinia"

Rutledge, Mrs.
[204]

Unidentified friend of Wilder's
Aunt Clara Haushalter.

Sam [I] [89]

Sam Richlin, fellow Eastman School of Music
student. A valued friend and musical collaborator, he was a fellow rebel at Eastman who
was co-author with Wilder of *The Bird*, an
anti-faculty, anti-Howard Hanson document
that caused great administrative uproar.

Sam [II] [141]

Samuel Baron (1925–97), respected New
York flutist and longtime member of the New
York Woodwind Quintet, for whom Alec
wrote a number of solo and chamber works.

Saunders,
General [62]

Unidentified officer at Camp Mills,
a World War I–era military institution near
Wilder's boyhood home in Garden City,
Long Island, ca. 1917. This individual is
called "Capt. Saunders" in "The Search."

Seitlin, Percy

See "Percy"

Sharp, Miss [182]

Author Margery Sharp (1905–91), who is best
known for her children's book series *The
Rescuers*, and who also wrote novels for adults,
such as *Rhododendron Pie* and *Lise Lilywhite*.

Sheldon [218]

Sheldon Meyer, longtime editor at Oxford
University Press who provided the impetus
for Wilder's book *American Popular Song*.
Books published by Oxford under Meyer's
leadership include *The Duke Ellington Reader*
edited by Mark Tucker, Gene Lees' *Meet Me
at Jim and Andy's*, and Whitney Balliett's
American Musicians and American Singers.

Sibley [262]

Dr. James Sibley Watson (1894–1982), who is
addressed in numerous other letters as "Dr.
Watson."

Simenon,
Monsieur [184]

Wilder admired author Georges Simenon
(1903–89), the Belgian-born French novelist.
An unusually prolific writer, Simenon created

the eighty-four Maigret mysteries for which is perhaps best known, as well as 136 other novels.

Sinatra, Frank	*See* "Frank"
Sions, Harry	*See* "Harry Sions"
Sir [195]	Fellow plane passenger named Roderick Hasseltine.
Sirs [143]	Business letter to the Chicago Historical Society.
Sirs [215]	Unidentified owners of The Coffin House, a Nantucket Inn.
Smith, Mr. [93]	Rochester partygoer with business connections to Wilder's father. Fellow Eastman student Frank Baker, mentioned in the letter, went on to have a great career as a singer and had many later musical associations with Wilder.
Stirrup, Dan	*See* "Dan"
Stirt, Doctor [196]	Dr. Sonia Stirt, a psychoanalyst whom Wilder visited daily for about three years during his early adulthood.
Sundgaard, Arnold	*See* "Arnold"
Sunny [243]	Sunny Carson, bartender at Jim and Benny's, a well-known musicians' watering hole on New York City's Upper West Side.
Theodora [64]	Likely Wilder's cousin, Theodora Winship (later married name was Barstow), daughter of Alec's aunt, Kate Chew Winship. Wilder also had another cousin Theodora Chew Barstow; both lived in New Jersey near Wilder's home, although Miss Winship was the younger of the two and more likely to be living at home as described by Wilder.
Tomorrow [156]	Wilder, to himself.

Tony [256]

Singer Tony Bennett (b. 1926), whom Alec admired and who admired Alec as well, and recorded several Wilder songs. Bennett achieved early popular success with his signature hit "I Left My Heart in San Francisco," but went on to become an icon, one of today's most respected interpreters of American popular song and jazz.

Tudy [245]

Susan Kenyon, Wells College Class of 1953 (first name misspelled in this letter), whom Wilder met when he accompanied photographer Louis Ouzer on a trip to take senior pictures at this all-women's school on Cayuga Lake, north of Ithaca, NY. She is still today called by her nickname, Tudy.

Uncle Hilly [59]

Thomas Hillhouse Chew (1856–1932), brother of Wilder's mother Lillian Chew Wilder, and an executive with the First National Bank of Geneva, NY, a family business. Alec's grandfather, Alexander Lafayette Chew, was a former president of that bank and family members were majority stockholders.

Uncle Howland [165]

Chauffeur/driver who worked in the area of the railroad station in Brunswick, GA, a depot Wilder frequented on his train travels.

Victor [91]

Unidentified friend of Carroll Dunn's.

Wally [247]

Unknown individual who was presumably the son of one of Wilder's friends. Wilder knew him as a child at Atlantic Shores Hotel, Key West, where he often stayed.

Walton [52, 57, 65]

Walton Cook, Wilder boyhood friend, Westminster Road neighbor, Columbia School classmate, and early confidant. In the letter on p. 52, Geneva (NY) is Wilder's mother's family home; "Mr. McFarlin" is J. John McFarlin, an area druggist. [Wilder's much later letter to Cook is addressed to "Dead Friend" on p. 254.]

Watson, Dr.
[51, 90, 97,
99, 104, 112,
120, 133, 159,
173, 213]

Dr. James Sibley Watson (1894–1982)
was a life long mentor and something of a
surrogate father to Alec, whose own father
died when he was two years old. Dr. Watson
was trained as a medical doctor but did not
practice. He was born to wealth, to which he
added through various successful inventions.
He made two avant-garde films in the 1920s,
in which Alec had a hand. He also was the
owner and financial supporter of *The Dial*, a
significant avant-garde literary magazine of
the 1920s, which first published works of
T. S. Elliot, e. e. cummings, and Marianne
Moore, among others. Wilder's letters to
Dr. Watson serve as a narrative for the book,
opening chapters and commenting on
people, events and accomplishments in
Wilder's life.

Watson,
Dr. James Sibley

See "Sibley" and "Dr. Watson"

Whitney [229]

Whitney Balliett (b. 1926), veteran writer for
the *New Yorker*, whose July 1973 profile on
Wilder in that publication, "President of the
Derriere-Garde" is widely considered to be
the best written portrait of Wilder; the article
is contained in Balliett's book *Alec Wilder and
Friends*. Balliett is widely respected for his
numerous articles on musicians. The high-
lights have been collected in his books, which
include *Night Creature*, and *Such Sweet
Thunder*.

Wilder, George C.

See "George"

Wilder,
Lillian Chew

See "Mother"

Wilder, Thornton

See "Cuzzin"

Williams, Mrs.
[244]

Grace Williams was a waitress at
the Manhattan Restaurant who often served
Alec while he was in Rochester. Many in the

	Eastman community relate that Wilder would hold court for hours at the Manhattan.
Winship, Theodora	*See* "Theodora"
Worth, Mr. [132]	Unidentified local music critic who had angered Wilder with the tone and wording of his bad review.
Young Men [210]	Unknown Crestline, OH, boys watching Wilder's train as it passed.
Z [260]	Stage and screen star Zero Mostel (1915–77), the noted actor and comedian best known for his work in *A Funny Thing Happened on the Way to the Forum* and *Fiddler on the Roof*.

Selected Compositions
by Alec Wilder

Composition dates are listed in parentheses. Publishers are in brackets at the end of the entry.

Works for Large Ensemble

A Child's Introduction to the Orchestra (1954). Text by Marshall Barer. A musical primer. Eighteen movements featuring individual instruments of the orchestra. [Ludlow]

Children's Plea for Peace (1968). Children's SSAA chorus, narrator, and wind ensemble. Text by Wilder, adapted from writings of schoolchildren from Avon, NY. Dedicated to Rev. Henry Atwell. [Margun]

Eight Songs (1928). Voice and orchestra. Set to poems of James Stephens. Premiered in Eastman's Kilbourn Hall. [Unpublished ms. in the Alec Wilder Archive, Sibley Music Library, Eastman School of Music]

Entertainments: No. 1 (for wind ensemble, 1960). For Frederick Fennell and the Eastman Wind Ensemble [originally titled *An Entertainment*]; No. 2 (for orchestra, 1966). Commissioned by the Madison, WI, Chamber Orchestra; No. 3 (for wind ensemble, 1965). For Frank Battisti and the Ithaca, NY, High School Concert Band; No. 5 (for wind ensemble, ca. 1969); No. 6 (for orchestra, 1975). Commissioned by the New York State Arts Council; No. 7 (for wind ensemble, 1975). For Ronald Socciarelli and the Ohio University Wind Ensemble. [Margun]

Names from the War (1960). Narrator, chorus, chamber orchestra, including augmented brass quintet and augmented woodwind quintet. Text by Bruce Catton. [CFG]

Symphonic Piece for Orchestra (1929). Premiered Rochester, NY, Howard Hanson conducting. [Unpublished]

Works for Solo Instrument

For Woodwinds

Air for English Horn and String Orchestra (1945). For Mitch Miller. [Ludlow]

Air for Flute and Strings (1945). For Julius Baker. [Ludlow]

Air for Oboe and Strings (1945). For Mitch Miller. [Ludlow]

Concerto for Clarinet and Chamber Orchestra (Undated). For Glenn Bowen. [Margun]

Concerto for Tenor Saxophone and Chamber Orchestra (1968). For Stan Getz; premiered by Zoot Sims. [Margun]

Small Suite for Flute and Piano (ca. 1960) For Judy Holliday. [Margun]

Sonata for Alto Saxophone and Piano (1960). For Donald Sinta. [Margun]

Sonatas for Bassoon and Piano: No. 1 (1968); No. 2 (1968). Commissioned by the National Association of College Wind and Percussion Instructors; No. 3 (1974). For Bernard Garfield. [Margun]

Sonata for Clarinet and Piano (1963). For Glenn Bowen. [Margun]

Sonatas for Flute and Piano: No. 1 (1961). For Don Hammond; No. 2 (1965). For James Pellerite. [Margun]

Suite for Unaccompanied Flute (1975). For Virginia Nanzetta. [Margun]

Suite No. 2 for Tenor Saxophone and Strings (1966). For Zoot Sims. [Margun]

Three Ballads for Stan [also exists in Wilder's piano reduction as Suite No. 1 for Tenor Saxophone and Piano] (1963). For Stan Getz. [Margun]

For Brass

Concerto for Tuba and Wind Ensemble (1968). For Harvey Phillips. Piano reduction by Robert George Waddell. [Margun]

Concerto for Trumpet and Orchestra (1980). Commissioned by Frank Sinatra. [Unpublished manuscript]

Concerto No. 1 for Trumpet and Wind Ensemble (1967). For Doc Severinson. Arranged for wind ensemble by John Barrows. [Margun]

Concerto No. 2 for Trumpet/Flugelhorn and Wind Ensemble (1969). For Clark Terry. [Margun]

Little Detective Suites for Horn and Piano (No. 1, 1978; No. 2. 1980; No. 3, 1980). For Randi Levy. [Margun]

Sonata for Trumpet and Piano (1963). For Joe Wilder. [Margun]

Sonatas for Horn and Piano: No. 1 (1954). For John Barrows; No. 2 (1957). For John Barrows; No. 3 (1970). For John and Tait Sanford Barrows. [Margun]

Sonatas for Tuba and Piano: No. 1 (1959). For Harvey Phillips; No. 2 (1975). For Lottie Phillips. [Margun]

Suites for Tuba and Piano: Suite No. 1 (1960). For Harvey Phillips; Suite No. 2 (*Jesse Suite*), Suite No. 3 (*Suite for Little Harvey*). and Suite No. 4 (*Thomas Suite*). [Margun]

Suites for Unaccompanied Trumpet: No. 1 (1977); No. 2 (1978). Both for Robert Levy. [Margun]

Twenty-One Christmas Carols for Tuba Ensemble (1974). [TubaChristmas, Inc.]

For Strings

Small Suite for Bass and Piano (1968). For Gary Karr and Bernard Leighton. [Margun]

Sonatina for Violin and Piano (Undated). For Max Presberg. [Margun]

For Piano

Fantasy for Piano and Wind Ensemble (1974). For Marian McPartland. [Ambrose]

Pieces for Young Pianists (1969). Graded four-volume series, edited by Carol Baron. [Margun]

Small Fry Suite (Undated). For Vera Brodsky Lawrence. [Margun]

Chamber Works

Alice in Wonderland Suite (1963). For the New York Woodwind Quintet. [Margun]

Brass Quintets: No 1 (1959). For the New York Brass Quintet; No. 2 (1961); No. 3 (1970); No. 4 (1973). For Harvey Phillips; No. 5 (1975). For the Tidewater Brass Quintet; No. 6 (1977). For the Tidewater Brass Quintet; No. 7 (1978). For Frances Miller; No. 8 (1980). For Frances Miller. [Margun]

Brassininity (1972). For the Eastman Brass Quintet. [Margun]

Effie Suite (1960) for Tuba, Vibraphone, Piano, and Drums. For Harvey Phillips. Orchestrated as Suite No. 1 for Tuba and Orchestra (1966). [Margun]

Flute and Bongos (1958). Flute and improvised percussion. [Margun]

Four Duets for Oboe and English Horn (Undated). [Margun]

Jazz Suite for Four Horns (1951). Four horns with harpsichord, guitar, bass, and drums. [Ludlow; MJQ]

Octets (1939–41) Flute/Clarinet 2, oboe/English horn, clarinet 1, bass clarinet, bassoon, harpsichord, bass, drums: *Bull Fiddle in a China Shop*; *The Children Met the Train*; *Concerning Etchings*; *Dance Man Buys a Farm*; *A Debutante's Diary*; *Her Old Man Was Suspicious*; *His First Long Pants*; *House Detective Registers*; *It's Silk, Feel It!*; *Kindergarten Flower Pageant*; *Little Girl Grows Up*; *Neurotic Goldfish*; *She'll Be Seven In May*; *Such a Tender Night*; *Walking Home in Spring*. [TRO]

Octets (1947) [same instrumentation as earlier Octets]: *The Amorous Poltergeist*; *Footnote to a Summer Love*; *Jack, This Is My Husband*; *Little White Samba*; *Remember Me to Youth*; *They Needed No Words*. For Donald Sinta. [TRO]

Saxophone Quartet (1963). [Margun]. For Donald Sinta.

Six Duets for Flute and Violin (1980). For Virginia Nanzetta. [Margun]

Solo Suite for Horn and Improvisatory Percussion (1954). For John Barrows and David Kapp. [Margun]

Solo Suite for Woodwind Quintet (1956). For the New York Woodwind Quintet. [Unpublished]

Suite for Alto and Bass Flutes (1967). [Margun]

Suite For Baritone Saxophone, Woodwind Sextet, Bass, and Drums (1971). For Gerry Mulligan. [Margun]

Suite for Baritone Saxophone, Horn, and Wind Quintet (1966). For Gerry Mulligan. [Margun]

Suite for Flute and Marimba (1977). For Virginia Nanzetta and Gordon Stout. [Margun]

Suite for String Bass and Guitar (1968). For Gary Karr. [Margun]

Suite for Trumpet and Marimba (1978). For Robert Levy and Gordon Stout. [Margun]

Suites No. 1 (1963) and No. 2 (1971) for Horn, Tuba, and Piano. For John Barrows and Harvey Phillips. [Margun]

Woodwind Quintets: No. 1 (1954). For the New York Woodwind Quintet; No. 2 (1956); No. 3 (1958); No. 4 (1959). For Bernard Garfield; No. 5 (1959); No. 6 (1960); No. 7 (1964); No. 8 (1966) [also known as *Suite For Non-Voting Quintet*]; No. 9 (1969); No. 10 (ca. 1968); No. 11 (1971). For John Barrows; No. 12 (1975). For the Wingra Quintet; No. 13 (1977). [Margun]

World's Most Beautiful Girls (1955). Arranged for woodwind quintet from popular songs with girls' names in their titles, including Wilder's "Ellen" and "Sweet Lorena" and songs by other composers. [Margun]

Operas and Dramatic Works

An Axe, an Apple, and a Buckskin Jacket (1957). Story and lyrics by Arnold Sundgaard. Children's musical Christmas story. [Ludlow]

The Churkendoose (1946). Musical narrative. Text by Ben Ross Berenberg. [Ludlow: MCA]

Cumberland Fair (1953). One-act opera. Libretto by Arnold Sundgaard. [Ludlow]

Ellen (1964). Opera in two acts. [Originally titled *The Long Way*]. Libretto by William Engvick. [Margun]

Hermine Ermine in Rabbit Town (1946). Musical narrative. Text by Ben Ross Berenberg. [Ludlow]

The Impossible Forest (1958) Opera in two acts. Libretto by Marshall Barer. Produced by Rogers Brackett. [Ludlow]

The Lowland Sea (1952) One-act opera. Libretto by Arnold Sundgaard. [Schirmer]

Mountain Boy (1980) Church cantata. Libretto by Loonis McGlohon. [Margun]

The Opening (1972). Musical fable in one act. Libretto by Arnold Sundgaard. [Margun]

Sunday Excursion (1953). Wilder and Sundgaard. [Ludlow]

The Truth about Windmills (1975). One-act opera. Libretto by Arnold Sundgaard. [Margun]

Music Theater Productions

Haywire (1933). Musical revue. Book and lyrics by Wilder. [Unpublished]

Kittiwake Island (1953). Musical comedy in two acts. Book and lyrics by Arnold Sundgaard. [Ludlow: Schirmer]

Land of Oz (1968). Outdoor production of the classic children's story. Book and lyrics by Loonis McGlohon. [Navona]

Miss Chicken Little (1953). Musical fable in one act; based on the children's story. Libretto by William Engvick. [Hollis]

Nobody's Earnest (1978). Musical comedy in three acts. Based on the Oscar Wilde play *The Importance of Being Ernest*. Book by Arnold Sundgaard. Lyrics by Ethan Ayer. [Ludlow]

Pinocchio (1957). Television musical based on the children's story. Book and lyrics by William Engvick. [Ludlow]

Western Star (1975). Book and lyrics by Arnold Sundgaard. Originally titled *The Wind Blows Free*. Based on the play *Way Up Yonder* by Charlotte Perry, in turn based on the Book of Job. [Ludlow]

Film Scores

Albert Schweitzer (1957). Produced by Louis de Rochmont. Directed by Jerome Hill. [Ludlow]

The Sand Castle (1959) Produced and directed by Jerome Hill. [Ludlow]

Open the Door, See All the People (1963). Produced and directed by Jerome Hill. Originally titled *Peacock Feathers*. Includes Wilder songs "I See It Now," "Love Is When," "Mimosa and Me," "Remember, My Child," "Such a Lonely Girl Am I," "That's My Girl," "Unbelievable." [Ludlow]

Art Songs

Did You Ever Cross Over to Sneden's? (1947) Text by Wilder; introduced by Mabel Mercer. [Ludlow]

Five Vocalises (ca. 1971). For voice and piano or wind ensemble. For Eileen Farrell. [Margun]

Songs for Patricia (Undated). Text by Norman Rosten. [Ludlow]

Phyllis McGinley Song Cycle (1979) Mezzo-soprano with bassoon and harp. Set to poems of Phyllis McGinley. [Margun]

Popular Songs

"All the King's Horses" (1930). Music with Eddie Brandt. Lyric with Howard Dietz. From the Broadway revue *Three's A Crowd*. [Schirmer]

"Baggage Room Blues" (1954). Lyric by Arnold Sundgaard. [Ludlow]

"Be a Child" (1976). Lyric by Loonis McGlohon. Introduced by Cleo Laine. [Ludlow]

"Blackberry Winter" (1976). Lyric by Loonis McGlohon. [Ludlow]

"A Child Is Born" (1969). Music by Thad Jones. Lyric by Wilder. [D'Accord]

"Crazy in the Heart" (1956). Lyric by William Engvick. [Ludlow]

"Douglas Mountain" (1948). Lyric by Arnold Sundgaard. [Ludlow]

"Goodbye John" (1949). Lyric by Edward Eager. Written for Mabel Mercer. Introduced by Peggy Lee. [Ludlow]

"Homework" (1974). Instrumental. Written for Marian McPartland. [Ambrose]

"How Lovely Is Christmas" (1957). Lyric by Arnold Sundgaard. [Ludlow]

"I'll Be Around" (1942). Lyric by Wilder. Featured in the film *Joe Louis Story*. Introduced by Cab Calloway. [Ludlow]

"It's So Peaceful in the Country" (1941). Lyric by Wilder. [Ludlow]

"Jazz Waltz for a Friend" (1974). Instrumental. Written for Marian McPartland. [Ambrose]

"Mimosa and Me" (1964). Lyric by William Engvick. [Ludlow]

"Moon and Sand" (1941). Music with Morty Palitz. Lyric by William Engvick. Introduced by Xavier Cugat and his Orchestra. [Ludlow]

"Where Do You Go?" (1948). Lyric by Arnold Sundgaard. From the play *Western Star*. [Ludlow]

"While We're Young" (1943). Music with Morty Palitz. Lyric by William Engvick. Introduced by Mabel Mercer. [Ludlow]

Selected Discography

Recordings

Bacon, Thomas. *Nighthawks: The Music of Alec Wilder*. CD: Summit DCD 170. Contains: First, Second, Third Sonatas for Horn and Piano; Suite for Horn and Piano; Four Easy Pieces.

Baker, Chet. *Let's Get Lost*. CD: BMG/Novus 3054-4-N. Includes "Moon and Sand."

Barrows, John. *John Barrows and Milton Kaye*. LP: Golden Crest RE 7002. Includes Sonata No. 2 for Horn and Piano; Suite for Horn and Piano. John Barrows and Tait Barrows also recorded Sonata No. 3 for Horn and Piano (Golden Crest RE 7034).

Bennett, Tony. *Because of You*. LP: Columbia CL 6221. Includes "While We're Young." Tony Bennett also recorded "It's So Peaceful in the Country" and "While We're Young" (*Blue Velvet*, Columbia CL 1292); "I'll Be Around" (*Many Moods*, LP: Col. CL2141).

Burrell, Kenny. *Guitar Forms*, arr. by Gil Evans. Original release LP: Verve V6–8612; CD: Verve 314 521 403–2. Includes "Moon and Sand."

Clarion Wind Quintet. *See* Stout, Gordon; Crosby, Bing [with orchestra conducted by Mitch Miller]. *How Lovely Is Christmas*. LP: Golden LP 121. Includes "How Lovely Is Christmas"; *An Axe, An Apple and A Buckskin Jacket*. Bing Crosby also recorded "Lullaby Land" (Decca 24618).

DeGaetani, Jan. *Lullabies and Night Songs*. With arrangements by, and orch. conducted by Rayburn Wright. LP: Caedmon TCI 1777. Includes *Phyllis McGinley Song Cycle*; song selections from the book *Lullabies and Night Songs*.

Demsey, David. *Demsey Plays Wilder*. LP: Golden Crest RE 7109. Includes Air for Saxophone; Sonata for Alto Saxophone and Piano; Suite No. 1 for Tenor Saxophone and Piano; "If Someday Comes Ever Again"; "I'll Be Around"; "It's So Peaceful in the Country"; "A Long Night"; "Summer Is A-Comin' In."

Errante, Valerie, and Robert Wason. *Songs of Alec Wilder*. CD: Albany–Troy 404. Includes "The Lake and the Innisfree"; "The

Colleen"; "The Rose on the Wind"; "River Run"; "Spring"; "Margaret"; "Easter"; "When I Am Dead, My Dearest"; "In the Morning"; "Definition"; "If You Are Happy"; "Where Do You Go?"; "The Olive Tree"; "The Plowman"; "Listen to Your Heart"; "Blackberry Winter"; "The Echoes of My Life"; "It's a Fine Day for Walkin' Country Style"; "Don't Deny"; "The Winter of My Discontent"; "Remember My Child"; "A Child Is Born"; "The Wrong Blues"; "The Lady Sings the Blues"; "Moon and Sand"; "While We're Young"; "I'll Be Around."

Farrell, Eileen. *Eileen Farrell Sings Alec Wilder*. With Loonis McGlohon Trio. CD: Reference RR36. Includes "Blackberry Winter"; "If Someday Comes Ever Again"; "I'll Be Around"; "It's a Fine Day for Walkin' Country Style"; "'S Gonna Be a Cold, Cold Day"; "It's So Peaceful in the Country"; "Lovers and Losers"; "Moon and Sand"; "Where Do You Go?"; "Where's That Heartache?" "Who Can I Turn To?"; "The Worm Has Turned."

Getz, Stan, with Boston Pops Orchestra/Arthur Fiedler. *Song after Sundown*. LP: RCA Bluebird 6284–4-RB. Includes *Three Ballads for Stan* (also titled Suite No. 1 for Tenor Saxophone in Wilder's piano transcription version), "Where Do You Go?" (arr. Manny Albam).

Child's Introduction to the Orchestra, Golden Sympony Orchestra and the Sandpiper Chorus, conducted by Mitch Miller. LP: Golden Records GLP1.

Hammond, Don. *Don Hammond with Piano Accompaniment by Milton Kaye*. LP: Golden Crest RE 7005. Includes Air for Flute; Sonata No. 1 for Flute and Piano.

Hanna, Roland. *Roland Hanna Plays the Music of Alec Wilder*. LP: Inner City IC1072. Includes "I'll Be Around"; "It's So Peaceful in the Country"; "Ellen"; "Mimosa and Me"; "Moon and Sand"; "Remember, My Child"; "The Sounds around the House"; "Star Wish"; "The Starlighter"; "That's My Girl"; "While We're Young"; "You're Free."

Holiday, Billie. *Billie Holiday with Orchestra Conducted by Ray Ellis*. LP: Columbia CL 1157. Includes "I'll Be Around."

Jackie and Roy [Jackie Cain and Roy Kral]. *An Alec Wilder Collection*. CD: Audiophile AP-257. Includes "Don't Stop"; "The Echoes of My Life"; "I See It Now"; "I'll Be Around"; "It's So Peaceful in the Country"; "The Lady Sings the Blues"; "Love Is When"; "Mimosa and Me"; "Moon and Sand"; "Remember, My Child"; "That's My Girl"; "Unbelievable"; "Walk Pretty"; "While We're Young."

Jarrett, Keith Trio. *Standards, Volume 2*. CD: ECM 1289. Includes "Moon and Sand."

———. *Standards Live*. CD: ECM 1317. Includes "The Wrong Blues."

Jolley, David. *Alec Wilder: Music for Horn and Piano.* CD: Arabesque Z6665. Includes Sonatas No. 1, 2, 3 for Horn and Piano; Suite for Clarinet, Horn, and Piano; arrangement of *Three Ballads for Stan Getz* (Suite for Tenor Saxophone No. 1).

Juris, Vic. *Music of Alec Wilder.* CD: Double Time DTRCD 118. Includes "Where Is the One?"; "Goodbye John"; "Winter of My Discontent"; "Moon and Sand"; "Blackberry Winter"; "A Long Night"; "Lady Sings the Blues"; "That's My Girl"; "While We're Young"; "Homework"; "Such a Lonely Girl Am I"; "Little Circles."

Karr, Gary. *Gary Karr with Frederic Hand.* LP: Golden Crest RE 7031. Includes Suite for String Bass and Guitar; *Small Suite* for Bass and Piano; Sonata for Bass and Piano.

King, Teddi. *Lovers and Losers* [with the Loonis McGlohon Trio]. CD: Audiophile ACD-117. Includes "Lovers and Losers"; "Blackberry Winter"; "Be A Child."

Laine, Cleo. *Smilin' Through.* With Dudley Moore, piano. LP: Finesse FW3809. Includes "Be a Child"; "I'll Be Around." Cleo Laine recorded "Be a Child" again (LP: RCA APL 1–2407); and "Lady Sings the Blues" (LP: DRG MRS-502).

Lea, Barbara. *Barbara Lee.* CD: Audiophile AP-125. Includes "Who Can I Turn To?" Barbara Lea also recorded "Love Is When" (CD: Audiophile AP-175).

Levy, Robert. *Songs by Alec Wilder.* CD: Mark MCD 1641. Includes "Blackberry Winter"; "Moon and Sand"; "Where Do You Go?"; "Baggage Room Blues"; "I'll Be Around"; "It's So Peaceful in the Country"; "While We're Young"; "The Sounds around the House"; Mimosa and Me."

Lowe, Mundell and His Orchestra. *New Music of Alec Wilder.* LP: Riverside RLP 12–219. [Arrangements by Wilder; Liner notes by Frank Sinatra; also released as *Tacet for Neurotics* Offbeat OLP 3010]. Includes "Suggestion for Bored Dancers"; "She Never Wore Makeup"; "What Happened Last Night?"; "Walk Softly"; "Let's Get Together and Cry"; "Mama Never Dug This Scene"; "Pop, What's a Passacaglia?"; "No Plans"; "The Endless Quest"; "Around the World in 2:34"; "An Unrelenting Memory"; "Tacet for Neurotics."

Lucarelli, Humbert, oboe. *Corigliano/Wilder.* CD: Koch Classics 3–7187–2 H1. Includes Concerto for Oboe, Orchestra, and Percussion; Piece for Oboe and Improvisatory Percussion (Oboe and Bongos).

Manhattan Chamber Orchestra/Richard Auldon Clark. *For the Friends of Alec Wilder.* CD: Newport Classic NPD 85570. Includes *Carl Sandburg Suite*; Air for Flute; *Slow Dance*; Suite No. 2 for Tenor Saxophone and Strings; Air for Oboe; *Theme and Variations*; Air for Bassoon; Serenade for Winds.

Manhattan Chamber Orchestra/Richard Auldon Clark. *Neurotic Goldfish*. CD: Kleos Classic KL 5113. Includes Air for Saxophone; Andante for String Quartet; Scherzo for String Quartet; Andante; Invention; Air for Violin; Octets: *Kindergarten Flower Pageant*; *She'll Be Seven in May*; *It's Silk, Feel It!*; *Jack, This Is My Husband*; *Dance Man Buys a Farm*; *Seldom the Sun*; Untitled Octet No. 17; Untitled Octet No. 27; *A Little Girl Grows Up*; *Neurotic Goldfish*; *Please Do Not Disturb*.

McPartland, Marian. *Marian McPartland Plays the Music of Alec Wilder*. LP: Jazz Alliance TJA10016. Includes "Jazz Waltz for a Friend"; "Why?"; "While We're Young"; "Lullaby for a Lady"; "Inner Circle"; "I'll Be Around"; "Trouble Is a Man"; "Homework"; "Where Are the Good Companions?"; "It's So Peaceful in the Country."

Nanzetta, Virginia, and Milton Kaye. *Virginia Nanzetta and Milton Kaye*. LP: Golden Crest RE 7065. Includes *Small Suite* for Flute and Piano; Sonata No. 2 for Flute and Piano; Suite for Unaccompanied Flute.

New York Brass Quintet. *New York Brass Quintet*. LP: Golden Crest CR-4017. Includes Brass Quintet No. 1.

New York Woodwind Quintet. *New York Woodwind Quintet*. LP: Golden Crest CRS-4208. Includes "The World's Most Beautiful Girls"; "Ellen"; "Sweet Lorena." The New York Woodwind Quintet also recorded Solo Suite for Woodwind Quintet and Woodwind Quintet No. 2 (LP: Golden Crest CRS-4028); Woodwind Quintet No. 1 (LP: Philharmonia PH110); Woodwind Quintets Nos. 1 and 3 (LP: Concert Disc CS223).

Parker, Charlie. *Bird with Strings*. [With Mitch Miller, oboe; arrangements by Jimmy Carroll]. LP: Clef MGC 501; CD: Verve 314 523 984–2.

Phillips, Harvey. *Harvey Phillips Plays Alec Wilder's Tribute to the Phillips Family*. LP: Golden Crest RE 7054. Includes Suites Nos. 1, 2, 3, 4, 5 for Tuba and Piano. Harvey Phillips and Milton Kaye also recorded Sonata No. 1 for Tuba and Piano (LP: Golden Crest RE-7006).

Rockwell, Bob. *Bob's Wilder*. CD: Stunt STUCD 03072. Includes "I Like It Here"; "Mimosa and Me"; "If Love Is Like a Lark"; "Listen to Your Heart"; "I Like It Here"; "Moon and Sand"; "Lovers and Losers"; "Rain, Rain"; "Lady Sings the Blues"; "Don't Deny"; "The Wrong Blues"; "Where Do You Go?"

Russell, George. *Octet*. LP: MGM E3321. Includes 13 Octets: *The Children Met the Train*; *Dance Man Buys a Farm*; *House Detective Registers*; *The Amorous Poltergeist*; *Little Girl Grows Up*; *Little White Samba*; *Neurotic Goldfish*; *Pieces of Eight*; *Remember Me to Youth*; *Seldom the Sun*; *She'll Be Seven in May*; *Such a Tender Night*; *Walking Home in Spring*.

Sinatra. Frank. *Frank Sinatra Conducts the Music of Alec Wilder*. LP: Columbia CL 884; Odyssey 32 16 0262; CD: Sony Special Products A 4271. Includes Air for Oboe; Air for Bassoon; Air for Flute; Air for English Horn; Slow Dance; *Theme and Variations*; Octets: *Such a Tender Night*; *She'll Be Seven In May*; *It's Silk, Feel It!*; *Seldom the Sun*; *Her Old Man Was Suspicious*; *His First Long Pants*; *Pieces of Eight*.

Smithsonian Collection of Recordings/American Songbook Series: Alec Wilder. CD: Smithsonian RD 048–24 A 24574. Includes twenty-two Wilder songs, including hard-to-find recordings such as the Mills' Brothers "I'll Be Around"; Mildred Bailey's "It's So Peaceful in the Country"; plus performances by Lena Horne, Sarah Vaughan, Frank Sinatra, Dinah Washington Peggy Lee, Helen Merrill, Jackie and Roy, Eileen Farrell, Marlene VerPlanck, and others.

Stout, Gordon. *Gordon Stout with the Clarion Wind Quintet*. Golden Crest CRS-4190. Includes Suite for Flute and Marimba; Suite for Trumpet and Marimba

Sullivan, Maxine. *Maxine Sullivan with the Alec Wilder Octet*. LP: RCA Victor 26344. [Featuring "Turtle Dove" and "Ill Wind"].

Tidewater Brass Quintet. *Tidewater Brass Quintet*. LP: Golden Crest CRS-4156. Includes Brass Quintets Nos. 4, 5; *Brassininity*. The Tidewater Brass Quintet also recorded Brass Quintet No. 6 (LP: Golden Crest CRS-4174); Brass Quintet No. 7 (LP: Golden Crest CRS-4179); Brass Quintet No. 8 (LP: Golden Crest CRS-4205);

VerPlanck, Marlene. *Marlene VerPlanck Sings Alec Wilder*. With Loonis McGlohon Trio. CD: Audiophile AP-218. Includes "Blackberry Winter"; "Give Me Time"; "I Like It Here"; "I Like It Here (And This Is Where I'll Stay)"; "I Wish I Had The Blues Again"; "I'll Be Around"; "The Lady Sings the Blues"; "Love among the Young"; "Lovers and Losers"; "Remember My Child"; "That's My Guy [Girl]"; "Where Is the One?" CD re-release contains additional selections: "(So You've Had a) Change of Heart"; "Crazy in the Heart"; "I'm Alone Again"; "No One Ever Told Me"; "Please Stay with Me"; "The Wrong Blues."

Wilder, Alec. *Octet*. LP: Mercury MG-25008. Includes Eight Octets: *The Children Met the Train*; *Footnote to a Summer Love*; *Jack, This Is My Husband*; *A Little Girl Grows Up*; *Little White Samba*; *Remember Me to Youth*; *They Needed No Words*.

Wilder, Joe, and Milton Kaye. *Joe Wilder and Milton Kaye*. LP: Golden Crest RE 7007. Includes Sonata for Trumpet and Piano.

Zucker, Laurel. *Take a Walk on the Wilder Side*. CD: Cantilena 66014–2. Includes complete Wilder solo works for flute with piano, harpsichord, bongos, marimba.

Broadcasts

American Popular Song with Alec Wilder and Friends. Thirty-eight-program series on National Public Radio, 1976–78. (Complete set of recorded programs in the Alec Wilder Archive, Sibley Music Library, Eastman School of Music.) Features tributes to popular song composers, also including one Wilder selection in each program; with such singers as Tony Bennett, Johnny Hartman, Mabel Mercer, Dick Haymes, Bobby Short, Margaret Whiting, George Shearing, Woody Herman, and younger artists like Barbara Lea, Marlene VerPlanck, Mary Mayo, and Mark Murphy.

Selected Bibliography

Music by Alec Wilder

Lullabies and Night Songs. Songs composed or arranged by Alec Wilder. Edited by William Engvick. Illustrated by Maurice Sendak. New York: Harper and Row, 1965.

Songs by Alec Wilder Were Made to Sing. Edited by Judy Bell. New York: TRO; Ludlow Music, 1976. (28 Wilder songs, photographs by Louis Ouzer, Wilder biographical essay by William Engvick, a selected Wilder discography, and notes on each song written by Wilder for this collection. Three different edition each have slightly different contents.)

American Popular Song. New York: TRO; Ludlow Music, 1987. (33 Wilder songs, discography, introduction by William Engvick).

Songs from Alice in Wonderland. New York: TRO; Ludlow Music, 1998.

25 Songs for Solo Voice. New York: TRO; Ludlow music, 2002. (Collection of Wilder artsongs and popular songs, introduction by Robert Wason.)

Hal Leonard distributes the TRO printed works *Jazz Suite* for 4 Horns and the Sonata for Tuba and Piano.

TRO/The Richmond Organization distributes as print on demand the earlier chamber works such as the octets, the first three woodwind quintets, *Alice in Wonderland Suite*, and the various Airs.

Wilder solo works and chamber music are published by Margun Music, now a division of Music Sales Corp., which also owns G. Schirmer and Shawnee Press. Shawnee Press distributes Wilder's small works, and Schirmer is responsible for rentals and larger works.

Books and Articles by Alec Wilder:

"The Bird." Single-sheet newsletter created by Wilder and fellow Eastman School of Music students, ca. 1928. Unpublished. Alec Wilder Archive, Sibley Music Library, Eastman School of Music.

"The Search." Unpublished, 1970. Two handwritten notebooks, 176 pp. Alec Wilder Archive, Sibley Music Library, Eastman School of Music.

"Life Story." Unpublished, ca. 1971. Typescript, 189 pp. Alec Wilder Archive, Sibley Music Library, Eastman School of Music.

"The Emporer's New Clothes." *Allegro* (December 1974): 12.

American Popular Song: The Great Innovators, 1900–1950. Edited by James T. Maher. New York: Oxford Press, 1972; paperback ed., Oxford University Press, 1975).

Letters I Never Mailed: Clues to A Life. Boston: Little, Brown, 1975.

"The Elegant Refuge: A Memoir of a Life at the Algonquin Hotel." Unpublished, 1976. Typescript, 300 pp. Alec Wilder Archive, Sibley Music Library, Eastman School of Music.

Wilder, Alec, and Patrick Carr, "Rock—Mass Hysteria or Mass Art?" *New York Times*, November 5, 1972, Section 2, 17–18.

Books about Alec Wilder

Balliett, Whitney. *Alec Wilder and His Friends*. ———: Houghton Mifflin, 1974; Second unabridged ed., ———: Da Capo, 1983. Profiles of Bobby Hackett, Ruby Braff, Bob Elliott and Ray Goulding, Marie Marcs, Blossom Dearie, and Marian McPartland, with a final chapter which is a reprint of Balliett's *New Yorker* Wilder feature.

Demsey, David, and Ronald Prather. *Alec Wilder: A Bio-Bibliography*. Bio-Bibliographies in Music, No. 45. ———: Greenwood Press, 1993. A resource containing lists of Wilder's music, books, articles, and reviews by and about Wilder, and much other information about Wilder's life as an author and composer.

Stone, Desmond, *Alec Wilder In Spite of Himself: A Life of the Composer* (New York: Oxford University Press, 1996). The definitive Wilder biographical source.

Zeltsman, Nancy, ed., *Alec Wilder: An Introduction to the Man and His Music*. A list of works and collection of articles about Wilder, including short essays by Gunther Schuller, Loonis McGlohon, Robert Levy, and others; discography compiled by Judith Bell. (Newton, MA: Margun Music, 1991).

Articles and Other Sources about Alec Wilder

"Alec Wilder." *Newsweek*, July 28, 1941.

Balliett, Whitney. "Profiles: Alec Wilder: President of the Derrière-Garde," *New Yorker*, July 9, 1973, 36–40.

Bowen, Glenn H. "The Clarinet in the Chamber Music of Alec Wilder." DMA diss., Eastman School of Music, 1968.

McPartland, Marian. "Alec Wilder: The Compleat Composer." *Downbeat* 43 (October 21, 1976): 16–17.

Morgan, Edwin. "Long Hair, Short Hair—It's All Music." *Seventeen,* February 1947, 100–101, 235–37.

Ouzer, Louis. "Letters I Never Mailed." *Music Journal* 33 (1975): 20.

Prather, Ronald. "The Popular Songs of Alec Wilder." *Musical Quarterly* 74 (1990): 521–49.

Prather, Ronald, ed. *Newsletter of the Friends of Alec Wilder.* Contains updates on recent Wilder recordings, events, and performances, as well as information about the annual Wilder Celebration in New York City. Newsletter available free of charge: Ronald Prather, 78 Gleneden Avenue, Oakland, CA 94611. For information about The Friends of Alec Wilder, an organization dedicated to perpetuating the memory and life's work of Wilder, presenting annual Wilder Celebration concerts in New YorkCity, Rochester, and other cities, contact Tom Hampson, 83 Berkeley Street, Rochester, NY 14607.

———, moderator. Alec Wilder Mailing List. To join: awilder@brandxnet. com. This is an internet-based discussion group involving many well-known authors and musicians associated with Wilder and friends of the composer.

Ulanov, Barry. "Smart Alec." *Metronome* 16 (May 1947): 16.

"Wilder's Friends Don't Know the Fourth of It." *Downbeat* 22 (January 26, 1955): 6.

Index

See also the separate Index of Musical Works Cited, which follows this general one.

Index of Musical Works Cited

Eastman Studies in Music

Music and Musicians in the Escorial Liturgy under the Habsburgs, 1563–1700
Michael J. Noone

Berlioz: Past, Present, Future
Edited by Peter Bloom

The Musical Madhouse:
(Les Grotesques de la musique)
Hector Berlioz,
Translated and edited by
Alastair Bruce
Introduction by Hugh Macdonald

The Music of Luigi Dallapiccola
Raymond Fearn

Music's Modern Muse:
A Life of Winnaretta Singer,
Princesse de Polignac
Sylvia Kahan

The Sea on Fire: Jean Barraqué
Paul Griffiths

"Claude Debussy As I Knew Him" and Other Writings of Arthur Hartmann
Edited by Samuel Hsu,
Sidney Grolnic, and Mark Peters
Foreword by David Grayson

Schumann's Piano Cycles and the Novels of Jean Paul
Erika Reiman

Bach and the Pedal Clavichord:
An Organist's Guide
Joel Speerstra

Historical Musicology: Sources, Methods, Interpretations
Edited by Stephen A. Crist and
Roberta Montemorra Marvin

Portrait of Percy Grainger
Edited by Malcolm Gillies
and David Pear

The Pleasure of Modernist Music: Listening, Meaning, Intention, Ideology
Edited by Arved Ashby

Debussy's Letters to Inghelbrecht: The Story of a Musical Friendship
Annotated by Margaret G. Cobb

Explaining Tonality:
Schenkerian Theory and Beyond
Matthew Brown

The Substance of Things Heard: Writings about Music
Paul Griffiths

Musical Encounters at the 1889 Paris World's Fair
Annegret Fauser

Aspects of Unity in J. S. Bach's Partitas and Suites: An Analytical Study
David W. Beach

Letters I Never Mailed:
Clues to a Life
Alec Wilder
Annotated by David Demsey
Foreword by Marian McPartland

Letters I Never Mailed: Clues to a Life, by Alec Wilder, in a new, annotated edition with introduction and supplementary material by David Demsey, foreword by jazz pianist Marian McPartland, and photographs by Louis Ouzer.

Alec Wilder is a rare example of a composer who established a reputation both as a prolific composer of concertos, sonatas, and operas, and as a popular songwriter (including the hit "I'll Be Around"). He was fearsomely articulate, and had a wide and varied circle of friends, ranging from Graham Greene to Frank Sinatra and Stan Getz. *Letters I Never Mailed*, hailed at its first publication (in 1975, by Little, Brown), tells the story of Wilder's musical and personal life through "letters" addressed to various friends.

In it, he shares his insights—and sometimes salty opinions—on composing, musical life, and the tension between art and commercialism. This new, scholarly edition leaves Wilder's original text intact but decodes the mysteries of the original through an annotated index that identifies the letters' addressees, a biographical essay by David Demsey, and photographs by renowned photographer, and lifelong friend of Wilder, Louis Ouzer.

David Demsey is Professor of Music and Coordinator of Jazz Studies at William Paterson University and an active jazz and classical saxophonist. He is co-author of *Alec Wilder: A Bio-Bibliography* (Greenwood Press) and has contributed to *The Oxford Companion to Jazz*.

"Alec Wilder was one of the great composers of modern times. He wrote a suite for me with concert band. When I asked him about all the difficult notes in my part, he said, 'That's what you would have played if you had improvised!' In this new edition, David Demsey has been responsible for allowing people to understand some of Alec's equally mysterious letters, helping readers to better know one of my favorite people."

—Clark Terry, Jazz Trumpeter

"In *Letters I Never Mailed: Clues to a Life*, Alec Wilder wanted to reveal himself, but not entirely. And so he left unidentified the individuals to whom many of the letters were written. The detective work of David Demsey gives us a much better understanding of the enigma that was Alec Wilder."

—Marian McPartland, renowned jazz pianist,
recording artist, and host for over 25 years of
Marian McPartland's Piano Jazz (National Public Radio)